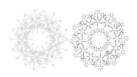

A SELECTION FROM
THE WAY FORWARD
HOLIDAY READING LIST

WITH BEST WISHES

John Bennett

J.P.Morgan

SPIRIT OF SERVICE

SPIRIT
★ of ★
SERVICE

Your Daily Stimulus for
Making a Difference

HarperOne
An Imprint of HarperCollinsPublishers

HarperOne

SPIRIT OF SERVICE: YOUR DAILY STIMULUS FOR MAKING A DIFFERENCE. Copyright © 2009 by HarperCollins Publishers. All rights reserved. Printed in the United States of America. No part of this book may be used or reproduced in any manner whatsoever without written permission except in the case of brief quotations embodied in critical articles and reviews. For information address HarperCollins Publishers, 10 East 53rd Street, New York, NY 10022.

HarperCollins books may be purchased for educational, business, or sales promotional use. For information please write: Special Markets Department, HarperCollins Publishers, 10 East 53rd Street, New York, NY 10022.

HarperCollins Web site: http://www.harpercollins.com

HarperCollins®, 📖®, and HarperOne™ are trademarks of HarperCollins Publishers

FIRST EDITION
Designed by Level C

Library of Congress Cataloging-in-Publication Data
Hancock, Nancy. Spirit of service : your daily stimulus for
making a difference / by Nancy Hancock. — 1st ed.
p. cm.
ISBN 978–0–06–192214–5
1. Voluntarism—United States. 2. National service—United States.
3. Communities—United States. 4. Social service—United States—
Citizen participation. I. Title.
HN49.V64.H364 2009
302'.14—dc22
2009026326

09 10 11 12 13   LP/RRDC   10 9 8 7 6 5 4 3 2 1

Acknowledgments

Thank you to all who participated in capturing the Spirit of Service. Special thanks to the many professionals and dedicated volunteers who are making a difference every day. Thank you also to the many who inspired these pages and shared their stories of hope and renewal.

CONTRIBUTING WRITERS
Money—Elsa Dixon
Energy—Sheila Buff
Focus—Penelope Franklin
Influence—Caroline Boch
Compassion—Christian Millman
Support—Susan K. Golant
Passage—Pam Liflander

CONTRIBUTING EXPERTS
Money—Ken Berger
Energy—Greg Baldwin
Focus—Kriss Deiglmeier
Influence—Joseph Grenny
Compassion—Sister Mary Scullion
Support—Peter Samuelson

Editor—Nancy Hancock
Research Support—Jim Oberman

Introduction

The idea for this book was born of President Obama's impassioned plea to Americans to step into the moment and take part in remaking America through service. While many of us are well intentioned, turning intention into action has become the aspiration of this daily guide.

This book is about cultivating the *spirit* of service, meaning you will be opening your heart, your mind, your resources, and your calendar to the needs of others. As you embark upon the 365 days, you may find that your own ego and needs melt away, making way for a new perspective and a more useful understanding of how you can truly contribute. While no reader is meant to follow the suggestions on every page, we encourage you to spend fifteen minutes a day fully giving yourself to the idea you're reading about and then imagining how you might become involved. To make it that much easier for you, we provide a way to get started by referring you to an organization, group, or resource related to the topic. Our suggestions for service range from the tiniest of actions to grand efforts to influence change. Our hope is that you will keep moving through the book daily, trying some suggestions immediately and bookmarking others to perhaps consider at a later time. Regardless of how you choose to use the information, we believe that each page can serve as a gateway for you to learn more. Some days may inspire a new interest for you, and some may spark discussion with others or simply increase your awareness. While some pages may not resonate with you, keep reading each day until you find your perfect fit. Along the way, we urge you to try new endeavors. And even if you don't see yourself picking up trash along a highway or learning to crochet a prayer shawl, we invite you to fully imagine the question, What if I did? We challenge you to just jump in with faith, knowing that every experience won't be ideal but that it may be worthwhile on your pathway to finding your best match for service.

Spirit of Service promotes the idea that individuals can make a difference and that at any moment you can influence an outcome. And guess what? That moment is *every* moment. Any time you want to heed the call, you can. You can become bigger than you are.

As you read, you may find that one day of the week resonates more than others and that one aspect of service compels you more than others. The hope is that you will find your unique connection to ways in which you want to be involved in the world.

Each week is presented with the following daily topics:

MONDAY / MONEY: Donating money is an immediate way to put a resource into action. It is always meaningful to organizations and individuals. Redirecting money that you would have spent on yourself can represent a sacrifice on your part or it can be an offering made in thanks for the abundance you enjoy. Regardless of the motivation, giving money makes a difference. If the demands of your life keep you from giving time and allowing you to participate in other ways, money is a great way to make sure the needs of others are met. Or, if money is just one of the ways that you choose to give, this book offers many suggestions of ways your money can contribute to the well-being of individuals, groups, and societies. Money always matters.

TUESDAY / ENERGY: Energy translates into action. This is especially evident when you show up to swing the hammer, to make the speech, to serve the soup, and to pick up the trash. Your presence says, "I care—let's get going." Energy in service is most often channeled through volunteering, and that is what we've focused on in our Energy entries, which you will read on Tuesdays. Volunteering is a proactive way that you can put intention into action. True, it takes time, but we offer ways in which you can meaningfully volunteer, from those that take just minutes all the way through to sabbaticals that are devoted to a cause. We urge you to try something you've never thought you would get involved in, for it's the experience of volunteering that puts you in direct contact with those you want to help.

WEDNESDAY / FOCUS: Focus is one of the primary ways that we bring about change. We're certain you've observed a local or national event that has shifted the world's focus to a problem or opportunity. But sometimes we need to better educate ourselves in order to decide what principles we want to support. Other times we want to bring attention to something that we're already passionate about and want to learn how we can draw others who might care into the discussion or movement toward change. Focus is also helpful when we have some of the pieces put together but lack critical members of a team or areas of expertise to further the cause.

Focus can create awareness and interest from others and can bring the right resources to you.

THURSDAY / INFLUENCE: Each of us has much more influence than we think we do. On the Thursdays of each week we will reveal myriad ways that you can tap into the resources you've built over a lifetime to influence what happens next. From your contacts and your authority to your skills and expertise, the personal equity of trust you've earned from others, and your enthusiasm, influence adds momentum to action. It also allows you to gather resources, attention, and heft to a cause or focus. Influence can help you make an impact by igniting the actions of one or some to become the actions of many. You already have influence—and our Thursday entries will teach you how to use it while inspiring you with stories of others who have already done so.

FRIDAY / COMPASSION: Compassion is the soil of service. It is the matter within which the seed grows to bear fruit as you explore the ideas offered in this book. Compassion can give you courage; it can cultivate traits that may have been lying dormant within you but that you fully possess. Compassion can be quiet in its way and as simple as the impulse that tells you to reach out and hold the hand of someone in pain. It can inspire you to become more than who you are. It can help you grow and develop into a totally different person. It can humble you and help you envision a world that might be. Most of all, it can lead you to love within yourself, to share with others, and to receive as part of the great circle of life.

SATURDAY / SUPPORT: Support is our rock. It's the phone call at 2 a.m. It is the person we know is in the waiting room praying for us as we're wheeled into surgery, and it is the connection we have to other humans, knowing that it may well be a stranger who will help us move the boulder that's crushing us. Support is humankind helping humankind—to survive, to exist, to rebalance our delicate ecosystems, to stand up for each other, and, when all else fails, to envelop someone with love. Support is the boost that gives us a leg up, and it is our wings when we're ready to soar. Support is the hand that reaches down and wipes the mud off our faces so we can see better. It shows up when those of us who have power in our legs stand up for those too weak to stand, and when those of us who are in full voice speak out for those without the courage or strength for words. We would die without support and so would our world. The Saturday entries inspire us to support other people, causes, ideas, and efforts through our own incredible resilience and strength.

SUNDAY / PASSAGE: Passage indicates movement, and our Passage entries focus on ways in which you can join another in their journey from one state of being to another—sometimes as a companion, sometimes as a guide, and sometimes as a fellow seeker. Passage requires commitment, trust in yourself and others, and faith to make the journey. Passage can open a pathway to sorrow and joy where you may not be able to see the destination, but the journey itself can become the catalyst to change. Even if you are retracing the steps you made into now familiar territory, each turn in the road will enable a fresh experience as you bring another through an important life passage.

Our goal is to inspire you to think each day: *What can I do today to help? How can my body, spirit, and soul be engaged in the practice of giving back? When I have been depleted, depressed, or down, what has helped me? How can I make life a little easier for someone or something else? Today I will open myself to the possibilities. Today I will do more than what is easiest. Today I will add my energy to that of the world in which I live.*

Today I will serve.

While the book spans an entire year, the hope is that once you experience the spirit of service, you'll live with that spirit for years to come! Some of these suggestions and stories will take you far beyond the book into a lifelong passion; some may serve as a temporary means to give back.

There are many reasons to serve—whichever one or combination of reasons drives you, dig into that and let it push you forward. You may have days at a time when work, family—life itself!—leave you gasping for air. But don't let a little setback snuff your spirit of service. Simply pick up where you left off and know that every moment you spend in an effort to better the world, no matter how brief, stirs the forces of positive change.

SPIRIT OF SERVICE

A Small Thing Makes a Big Difference

No one could make a greater mistake than he who did nothing because he could do only a little.
—Edmund Burke

To most of us, the mosquito is a pesky bug that might keep us awake at night with its buzzing. But in sub-Saharan Africa, the mosquito is a deadly menace that carries malaria. Malaria kills more children in Africa than any other disease—one child every thirty seconds. But it doesn't have to be this way. Malaria is both preventable and treatable, and there is a cheap and simple way to stop the spread of malaria—mosquito nets.

Providing nets and ensuring that they're used correctly can save the lives of nearly one million children who would otherwise fall victim to malaria each year. Ethiopia, Rwanda, and Eritrea have all reduced malaria deaths by more than 50 percent in just a few years by using mosquito nets and medicines; the islands of Zanzibar have nearly eliminated deaths. Ending malaria would make a huge difference in the lives of children, families, and entire countries.

Malaria No More is determined to help end malaria. A nonprofit, nongovernmental organization, Malaria No More has as a goal to cover every person at risk of contracting malaria in Africa with a mosquito net by the end of 2010 and to end malaria deaths by 2015. Thanks to a new generation of effective nets and medicines, this goal can be achieved.

Donations to Malaria No More go toward the purchase, transport, and distribution of insecticide-treated mosquito nets to African countries where they are needed most. Donations also help fund education and awareness programs about malaria and how to prevent infection.

Ten dollars buys one mosquito net that can cover a mother and child. "You really wouldn't believe the impact of a single ten-dollar bed net," says Emily Bergantino of Malaria No More. "For the price of a movie ticket you can make a huge impact on the future of a family in Africa. It's an incredible gift."

VISIT www.malarianomore.org or call (212) 792–7929.

Interview a Veteran

A soldier firm and stout of heart.
—William Shakespeare, *Henry V*

The men and women who have served their country in the armed forces have a great deal to tell us about the reality of war, if only we would ask. The Veterans History Project of the Library of Congress works with volunteer interviewers to collect, preserve, and make accessible the personal accounts of military veterans of all generations. Thousands of these oral histories and the documents and photos that often go with them have already been donated. Many more remain to be collected. In particular, the World War II veterans are dying away; volunteer interviewers are urgently needed to capture the memories of the Greatest Generation.

Volunteering to interview a veteran is easy. The Library of Congress has created a helpful field kit that gives you simple guidelines for conducting the interview. Record the veteran's story on audio or video or help write a memoir; follow the guidelines to gather photos, letters, diaries, and other documents to accompany the story. When you're done, submit the material to the Library of Congress, where it will become part of the permanent collections. The whole process usually takes only a couple of hours, and there is no charge for the interview kit.

Who can you interview? Many volunteers start with members of their own family—and many report being startled and moved by war stories they never heard before. Beyond your family, local veterans service groups, retirement communities, and other community groups are good places to start. You'll find that many veterans are very grateful for the chance to record their memories for their families and their friends, and for future generations.

TO LEARN more and get a free field kit for interviews, contact:

Veterans History Project / Library of Congress / 101 Independence Avenue SE / Washington, DC 20540–4615 / (888) 371–5848 / www.loc .gov/vets

The Meaning of "Enough"

If you focus on results, you will never change. If you focus on change, you will get results.
—John Dixon

Our culture depends on our buying into the idea that, amidst plenty, we don't have enough. This "scarcity myth"—the idea that we don't have enough money, time, energy, *stuff*—has weakened our nation. Sadly, we are blind to true hardship.

The truth is, we have more than we think, while others have less than we can imagine. Today, spearhead a group effort to remind others to give "enough" to those who rarely get their basic needs met.

ACTION STEPS

LOCAL: Choose a shelter in your area, such as a safe house for abused women and their children or the local Salvation Army shelter. Call and ask what they need for the people they help. Boxed or canned food? Soap, shampoo, deodorant, toothpaste? How about old reading glasses, shoelaces, toothbrushes? Write it all down. Show the list to your boss. Ask if you can start a monthly "bag day" at work.

In a brief meeting, describe the shelter to your co-workers. Ask if they'd each be willing to fill a bag with necessities once a month for six months, with the option of re-upping for another six months. Ask for a volunteer to help you drop off the bags each month too.

Set up a reminder on your computer's scheduling software for a few days before the bags are to be collected and delivered. Keep in touch with the shelter too. Ask which items are especially welcome and needed.

NATIONAL: Ask your workplace to become a member of the National Coalition of the Homeless, which provides homeless people with shelter, food, and opportunities to work and advocates on their behalf. Membership rates are tied to an organization's annual budget and can start as low as $65 a year. For more information, go to: www.nationalhomeless.org/want_to_help/index.html#c.

One Woman, One Book, a
Catalyst for a Movement

People say, "We wouldn't be allowed to use these things if they were dangerous." It just isn't so. Trusting so-called authority is not enough. A sense of personal responsibility is what we desperately need.
—Rachel Carson

She was accused of being an alarmist, a hysterical woman, going against common wisdom that widespread use of chemicals was good.

A soft-spoken marine biologist and acclaimed writer, Rachel Carson had no intention of being a crusader. She only envisioned a future where the sounds of spring are absent—and influenced our thinking about the natural world forever.

Her groundbreaking 1962 book, *Silent Spring,* provoked a heated controversy about unrestricted chemical use. *Silent Spring,* coupled with her 1963 congressional testimony, influenced the enactment of the Clean Air Act of 1963, the first federal legislation regarding air-pollution control, and the formation of the Environmental Protection Agency in 1970. DDT, a widely used pesticide, was banned in the United States in 1972.

Likening the effects of pesticides to those of atomic radiation, she said, "I wrote the book because I think there is a great danger that the next generation will have no chance to know nature as we do."

Carson died two years after the publication of *Silent Spring,* at age 56, of breast cancer. But her metaphor of a "silent spring," of a haunting silence, is still heard today.

ACTION STEPS
➤ Read *Silent Spring.*
➤ Visit the nonprofit Environmental Working Group (www.ewg.org) Web site. Make one commitment to act local and think global—stop using pesticides on your lawn and garden; explore organic options.

A Call to Action

You know, there's a lot of talk in this country about the federal deficit. But I think we should talk more about our empathy deficit—the ability to put ourselves in someone else's shoes; to see the world through the eyes of those who are different from us—the child who's hungry, the steelworker who's been laid off, the family who lost the entire life they built together when the storm came to town. When you think like this—when you choose to broaden your ambit of concern and empathize with the plight of others, whether they are close friends or distant strangers— it becomes harder not to act; harder not to help.
—President Barack Obama

Whatever your politics are, or even whether you espouse a political viewpoint at all, it's easy to see that the 2008 election of Barack Obama as president was a historic moment in United States history. Equally easy to see is that his call for an empathetic citizenry is a call to a good and just cause.

Answer this call in whatever fashion you see fit. But do answer it. When you allow compassion to broaden your circle of concern, you not only become a better person, you become a better person living in a better country that is part of a better world. And that's an outcome that transcends politics.

ACTION STEPS

➤ Scattered throughout this book, you'll find suggestions devoted to helping others. Let them help you choose a cause that is well suited to you.

➤ Let the main tenet of compassion—the alleviation of suffering—be the guiding principle for at least some of the time you spend as an empathetic citizen.

Painless Giving

**If you have much, give of your wealth,
if you have little, give of your heart.**
—Arab proverb

You may have the impulse to give, to share, or to support a favorite charity, but in a difficult economy even the best intentions may have to be abandoned to cope with painful realities. But what if you could give to your most cherished cause without having to spend a dime?

That's the idea behind GoodSearch, an Internet search engine powered by Yahoo that allows you to initiate a search but also specify a charity you wish to support. For every search you do, GoodSearch will donate about two pennies to the charity. And those pennies add up. For instance, a charity with one thousand supporters searching the Internet twice a day will receive $7,300 a year in donations. The American Society for the Prevention of Cruelty to Animals has raised $18,800 in this way. So far, users of this service have chosen sixty-eight thousand nonprofits and schools to receive donations. GoodSearch adds one hundred charities each day, all requested by users, and all vetted to confirm they are legitimate. Participation is free to the charities—a win-win all around.

How is all of this goodness possible? Like many other search engines, GoodSearch is financed by display ads that users can click on. GoodSearch splits these fees with Yahoo and then donates half of its revenue (about two cents for each click on an ad) to the charities specified.

ACTION STEPS

➤ Okay, you don't have the resources to support your favorite charities. How might you help in other ways? Can you volunteer? Use work-related skills such as writing or number crunching to add to their bottom line without hurting yours?

➤ Rather than turning to your usual search engine, next time you need to surf the Net, click on www.goodsearch.com, designate your favorite charity, and give painlessly.

Adopt a Premarin Foal

A horse is the projection of peoples' dreams about themselves—strong, powerful, beautiful.
—Pam Brown, poet

Anyone can adopt a dog, save a cat, or take care of someone's gerbils. But how many can truly save the life of a horse?

Premarin or PMU foals are the unfortunate by-products of the pharmaceutical industry. The drug Premarin (*PRE*gnant *MAR*e ur*IN*e) is a type of hormone replacement therapy used by women to alleviate the symptoms of menopause. It is synthesized from the urine of pregnant horses that are stabled both in Canada and in the United States. It takes over sixty thousand pregnant mares to supply nine million women around the world with this drug.

The story of the Premarin mare, and her foals, is typical of industrialized agriculture. The mares are treated badly throughout their lives, confined to small stalls, and hooked to urine extractors. As many as fifty thousand of their babies, or foals, are shipped each year to slaughterhouses for their meat, which is marketed to Europe and Asia. When the mares can no longer conceive, they are generally slaughtered as well.

Currently, the PMU mares and foals have no laws to protect them. Animal-rights activists have banded together in many forms of protest to stop this practice, and they need your help as well. By adopting a PMU foal or an older mare, you will literally be saving its life.

GETTING STARTED: For more information on how to adopt a horse or donate your time or money to their cause, visit the following two organizations: on the West Coast: www.PMURescue.org (916) 429–2457; East Coast: Spring Hill Horse Rescue, www.springhillrescue.com (802) 775–1098. Frequently updated Web sites like www.equineadvocates.org/index.html offer tons of information about how poorly these horses are treated. Then, put your passion to work by calling Wyeth-Ayerst, (800) 666–7248, the manufacturers of Premarin, to share your thoughts about how Premarin is produced.

For the Love of Literacy

I cannot live without books.
—Thomas Jefferson

For those of us who remember the joy of cuddling up with Mom or Dad to read a book, it's hard to believe that fewer than half of today's American children are read to daily and that 35 percent of children enter kindergarten lacking the basic language skills they need to learn to read.

Parents may not have money to buy books or may not have been read to as children; so millions of children are growing up without books. And children who start behind their classmates tend to stay behind, which can affect their performance throughout their school years and into adulthood. This is a tragedy not just for these kids, but for all of us—20 percent of workers in this country are functionally illiterate.

With this problem in mind, some pediatricians in the late eighties formed Reach Out and Read, a program in which doctors give children books during checkups. The program serves 3.5 million children and gives out over 5.7 million books each year. The books are culturally sensitive, and there are bilingual books in twelve different languages. By the time a child in the program is two, he or she can be as much as six months ahead of peers in reading and language skills.

Doctors get the pleasure of seeing how excited kids get when they are given their own books, but they can also use that moment to assess developmental milestones, such as how the children hold the books and how they interact with their parents about them. Doctors also talk to the parents about the importance of reading aloud.

Because the pediatricians volunteer the time they spend on early literacy, the cost of the program is low. The full five-year program costs just $40 per child, which means a child will own at least ten books by the time he or she starts kindergarten.

VISIT www.reachoutandread.org or call (617) 455–0600.

Be a National VIP

**The nation behaves well if it treats the natural
resources as assets which it must turn over to the next
generation increased, and not impaired, in value.**
—Theodore Roosevelt

The U.S. national park system has 390 units encompassing more than
84 million acres. With limited budgets and millions of acres to care
for, the National Park Service has been welcoming all the help it can get
since 1970 through the Volunteers-in-Parks (VIP) program.

Volunteers work on trail maintenance, plant trees, repair park buildings and other structures, document plants and wildlife, and perhaps
most important, assist visitors in the parks and help them have a positive
and enjoyable experience. By taking on these responsibilities, the volunteers free up the professional park rangers and other park personnel for
the bigger task of protecting and preserving the natural and cultural
heritage of our national parks.

Some VIP assignments, such a trail building, are fairly strenuous and
might require camping out in rugged terrain. Other volunteer assignments, such as staffing the information office, are much less physically
demanding. VIP management tries hard to match volunteer abilities
with park needs, and opportunities vary depending on the season and
the needs of individual parks. You can volunteer for as little as a week or
as long as a whole summer. The park service can sometimes provide accommodations in cabins or dormitories, but most volunteers camp at the
site. So popular is the VIP program that more than 150,000 volunteers
participate each year, including people who come from overseas.

Each unit of the National Park Service manages its own volunteers,
which means you have to apply directly to the site that interests you.
Slots fill up fast, so apply early and be flexible about where you'll go.

TO FIND out where the opportunities are, contact the NPS:

National Park Service Headquarters / 1849 C Street NW / Washington,
DC 20240 / (202) 208–6843 / www.nps.gov

Start a World News Readers' Circle

**Knowledge is happiness, because to have
knowledge—broad, deep knowledge—is to know
true ends from false, and lofty things from low.**
—Helen Keller

Globalization, the economic crisis, climate change, terrorism, and wars
have brought the world into our living rooms. Americans are learning
that all parts of the planet are interdependent. Knowledge is power, and
a neighborhood World News Reader's Circle is a way to empower a small
group by combining the interests of individuals. Each Circle member
focuses on one region, gathering news articles, books, Internet sources,
even films to present to the others. As the group discusses its findings, all
learn about how these issues are interconnected, and what can be done.

ACTION STEPS

LOCAL: What area of the world interests you most? Pose the same
question to your friends; ask them to join your Circle. Each of you can
begin by learning more about world news in general and your chosen
region in particular. Find additional members through librarians, bookstore owners, and by posting notices on community bulletin boards.

Go to www.readerscircle.org, an Internet resource that helps people
organize and sustain reader's circles. The site has a wealth of information;
you can also post a listing on the site to attract potential members and
connect with authors who will speak with your group by phone.

NATIONAL/INTERNATIONAL: Your studies may lead to action in
the form of letters to Congress, formation of advocacy groups, support for
international charities, even travel.

World news resources: BBC World News: Check local radio listings,
or listen and read at the www.bbcworldnews.com interactive news site.

Cable News Network International: Check local TV listings, or watch
and read at www.edition.cnn.com • Global Information Network: www
.globalinfo.org • United Nations: www.un.org

The Influence of Being the First

If we focus our energies on sharing ideas, finding solutions and using what is right with America to remedy what is wrong with it, we can make a difference. Our nation needs bridges, and bridges are built by those who look to the future and dedicate themselves to helping others.
—Sandra Day O'Connor

She grew up on the Lazy B Ranch in Arizona. In the 1930s the ranch didn't have electricity or running water, and Sandra Day O'Connor branded cattle and learned to fix what needed to be fixed.

Yet she traveled far, to graduate from Stanford University with a law degree, one of five women in a law class of 102 students, graduating with high honors. In spite of her accomplishments, no law firm in California in 1952 was willing to hire a female associate. She was offered a legal secretary job. So she turned to public service and ultimately became an Arizona legislator and state judge. And in 1981, she made history. Then-president Ronald Reagan broke over two hundred years of tradition and nominated her for the United States Supreme Court.

As in our own lives, we see with each first how what was once unimaginable is now commonplace. With each breakthrough, we can look to the future and see another bridge being built.

ACTION STEPS

➤ There is still one branch of government to which women have not built a bridge—if you wish to influence your daughters to be first in the executive branch, investigate www.ourcourts.org, launched by Justice O'Connor to inspire students to participate in democracy.

➤ Organize a "day in court" for a group of school kids. Arrange for a tour of the local courthouse, see a trial in action, and meet a local lawyer or judge. Local bar associations are great places to start, and many have community outreach programs for all young people.

The Hunger

**He who is dying of hunger must be
fed rather than taught.**
—St. Thomas Aquinas

Ramadan is the ninth month of the Islamic calendar and also the
month in which devout Muslims fast from sunup to sundown. They
must stop eating, according to the Koran, as soon as "you can plainly dis-
tinguish a white thread from a black thread by the daylight."

The daily fast is a very real reminder of the pangs of poverty and the
desperation of destitution. At such times, nothing else is important, only
the desire to stop the hunger.

With a vending machine on every floor and a burger joint on every
corner, it's understandably easy to forget that so many of our fellow
humans live under starvation conditions. In fact, when was the last time
you were truly hungry? Not just the "empty stomach" that comes with a
delayed dinner, but deep-down, all-consuming hungry? Can you imagine
what that must feel like and how everything else ceases to matter until
your belly and the bellies of those you love have been filled?

ACTION STEPS

➤ Plan a time when you can embark on a sunrise-to-sunset fast. If it's a
winter day, make the fast a minimum of twelve hours.

➤ At the end of your fast, go to a supermarket and shop while your
hunger is at a peak. Shop, not for yourself, but for a food bank. Let
your choices be guided by what would satisfy your hunger and, by
extension, the hunger of those who must seek out the help of food
banks. You may be surprised how few boxes of macaroni and cheese
you pick up and how, instead, you find yourself choosing nutrient-
dense items.

➤ Go home and prepare a meal. Savor it thoroughly, not only because
it's sating your hunger, but because you are among the lucky. The
next day, drop off the items you purchased at a food bank.

Enveloped in Love

Shawls . . . wrap, enfold, comfort, cover, give solace, mother, hug, shelter and beautify. Those who have received these shawls have been uplifted and affirmed, as if given wings to fly above their troubles.
—Janet Bristow, cofounder, the Prayer Shawl Ministry

What would it mean to surround someone who is ill, grieving, or in need with love and caring? What about sharing with a loved one in the joy of marriage or the birth of a child? We often think of sending loving and supportive energy, but do you know that this can be accomplished in a very tangible way, using a shawl you have created with your own hands that is imbued with your prayers?

The Prayer Shawl Ministry teaches you how to fold compassion and love of knitting into a spiritual practice that touches people needing comfort as well as those engaged in joyful celebration. The recipient may be a stranger or someone you love. You pray blessings for this person into every stitch throughout the shawl's creation. Upon completion, you may offer a final blessing before sending it to its recipient. Some who receive a prayer shawl continue the kindness by knitting shawls for others.

The Prayer Shawl Ministry encourages anyone from any faith or belief system to reach out to others as a gesture of love by embracing the spiritual practice of making and giving away shawls. This can be done in a group or individually. Each person or group decides how the shawls are to be distributed and how the ministry will fit their lives.

ACTION STEPS

➤ You'll find inspiration and instructions to start knitting or crocheting shawls at www.shawlministry.com. You can also e-mail the ministry at shawlministry@yahoo.com.

➤ If knitting isn't your thing—how else can you be supportive? Do you bake? Can you write a poem or song? Maybe you just need to be present and listen.

Reuniting Orphans in Nepal

The child must know that he is a miracle, that since the beginning of the world there hasn't been, and until the end of the world there will not be, another child like him.
—Pablo Casals

Since 1996, there have been more than thirty thousand "lost children" in Nepal. While a brutal civil war was raging, many well-intentioned parents gave their life savings to protect their children, sending them out of the countryside to schools in the capital city of Kathmandu. These parents were duped: traffickers took the money and dumped the children on the streets of the capital to fend for themselves. Or worse, they forced them into unpaid work or sold them into slavery. Girls were smuggled across the border to be sold as sex slaves in India. The luckiest ones found their way to orphanages, but they had little hope of ever being reunited with their parents.

Volunteers like Connor Grennan have been helping these Nepalese orphans find their families. Grennan has set up a new orphanage in Nepal and has raised money in the United States to fund it. He has also been able to personally reunite 125 lost children with their families.

But there is much more work to be done. Organizations such as Developing Hands, a U.S. nonprofit, have connected with orphanages in Nepal. They are looking for donations as well as volunteers to go to Nepal to teach these children English and help reconnect them with their families.

GETTING STARTED: One way to get involved is to take a volunteer holiday or vacation. The fees for these types of trips cover your expenses, and a portion goes to help the particular charity involved. Visit www .saga.co.uk/travel/General3/volunteer_intro.asp to find out more about travel volunteer holidays in general and about their ongoing program with the orphans of Nepal. Or contact www.developinghands.org, (720) 352–7716, to find out how you can volunteer in the United States to help these children.

The Planet Gets a Lawyer

**My profession is always to be alert, to find God
in nature, to know God's lurking places, to attend
to all the oratorios and the operas in nature.**
—Henry David Thoreau

In the pristine mountains near Yellowstone National Park, an old gold mine sat unused for decades while leaking contaminated water into the nearby Yellowstone River. Then, in the 1990s, a large Canadian mining company bought the claims to the mine. It was planning to reopen the mine and extract the remaining gold through a process where the ore is sprayed with cyanide, which leaves behind a terrible toxic mess.

The Park Service was opposed to this plan, as were many environmental groups. But because of the General Mining Law of 1872, there was nothing that could be done—the company had every right to reopen the mine. So the lawyers at Earthjustice decided to sue the company under the Clean Water Act and hold them accountable for the pollution that had been going on at the mine for years. They took the case to court, and it was ruled that the company would have to pay several million dollars in penalties. Subsequently, the company decided that using the mine was not worth the cost and gave its claims back to the government.

Earthjustice was founded by volunteer lawyers and began as a law firm for the Sierra Club. It now represents about eight hundred groups, most of them other nonprofit environmental groups. Most of the litigation it instigates is against the federal government for not enforcing or even following its own environmental laws. Other litigation is against private companies who threaten the environment.

Earthjustice is dedicated to protecting the magnificent places of this planet. A donation helps Earthjustice to continue to fight on behalf of public lands, national forests, parks, and wilderness areas, and to defend the right of all people to a healthy environment. As their tagline says, "The Earth needs a good lawyer."

VISIT www.earthjustice.org or call (510) 550–6700.

The Fifteen-Minute Volunteer

Until you value yourself, you won't value your time. Until you value your time, you will not do anything with it.
—M. Scott Peck

How long does it take to make a difference? Not long at all. You could volunteer for fifteen minutes or even less and still have an impact.

Making a check-in phone call to an elderly or homebound person takes only a few minutes a day. Your brief chat provides companionship and a way to make sure all's well. If the person doesn't respond or sounds like he or she is having trouble, you call in designated friends or relatives (or the police, if necessary). To find a telephone reassurance program near you, check with your local area agencies on aging—you can find them in the phone book or at www.eldercare.gov.

Another good way to help in just a short time is as a volunteer phone-banker. During fund drives, issue campaigns, and elections, volunteers are needed to make short, scripted calls from their own phones, usually in the evening. It's surprising how many calls you can make for a cause in just fifteen minutes.

But maybe volunteering for a daily commitment of ten or fifteen minute is still too much for you. What can you do just now and then, or even just once, that takes only fifteen minutes? How about sending a letter on an issue that's important to you? Many advocacy groups send action alerts to members when an issue arises, asking them to contact their elected representatives. Often all you have to do is provide your name and click on the button to send the letter by e-mail—a process that takes only a minute or two. If you have a bit more time, you can express yourself personally by writing a short letter or calling.

TO FIND the address and phone number of your senators, go to www .senate.gov; for your representative, go to www.house.gov. For state government and local officials, check state and municipal home pages or your phone book.

Calculate Your Family's Carbon Footprint, Then Set Goals to Reduce It

Nothing could be worse than the fear that one had given up too soon, and left one unexpended effort that might have saved the world.
—Jane Addams

Most of us have no idea how the simple choices we make daily impact the environment.

Everyone has a "carbon footprint." That's a measure of the carbon dioxide and other greenhouse gasses that you emit, directly and indirectly, through your daily actions and choices. The good news is, you can do something about it. In the process, your family will learn more about our planet's ecosystem and how individual choices matter.

ACTION STEPS

LOCAL: Use the Nature Conservancy's online carbon footprint calculator at www.natureconservancy.org. Then read their tips for reducing your family's carbon footprint. Once you have a clearer picture of the resources you consume, you will be in a better position to cut back on waste. Set goals for every member of the family, then present your research and plan to a school, church, or community organization. Set monthly targets for reducing the numbers, and encourage other families to do the same. You might form a group in which each member will make a commitment, then report back to others on their progress.

NATIONAL/INTERNATIONAL: Learn about international climate change treaties and U.S. policy at www.epa.gov/climatechange/policy/index.html. Reducing your carbon footprint, from ABC News: http://abcnews.go.com/Technology/Story?id=2049304&page=1. Reducing carbon emissions with cleaner energy: www.wecansolveit.org. Offsetting your carbon emissions: www.nativeentery.com/pages/why_carbon_offsets/12.php.

Influence, Tested

**Let it be said by our children's children that when
we were tested, we refused to let this journey end,
that we did not turn back, nor did we falter; and
with eyes fixed on the horizon and God's grace
upon us, we carried forth that great gift of freedom
and delivered it safely to future generations.**
—President Barack Obama, inauguration address

We often feel like others have more influence over the course of events than we do. We especially feel this way when we are faced with big, intractable, really hard problems: hunger, poverty, disease, genocide, and environment sustainability to name a few. We think that as long as these problems are not in our backyards, we refuse the test. It's for others, the government, to be graded on anyway.

In his inaugural address, on January 20, 1961, another president challenged this stance by declaring: "Ask not what your country can do for you—ask what you can do for your country." A lesser-known line follows, which widens this vision: "My fellow citizens of the world: ask not what America will do for you, but what together we can do for the freedom of man."

We have dithered too long over the idea that others will do what we can and must do as citizens of the world. The United Nations has outlined eight millennium goals to raise up the people of the world. Together, we must not turn back or falter. We must influence the world and pass the test.

ACTION STEPS

➤ If you are ready to stand as a citizen of the world, research the United Nations worldwide millennium goals at www.un.org.

➤ Write to your congressman or other elected officials challenging them to extend greater funding for support of the Millennium Development Goals.

Where Do We All Come From?

Living on Earth may be expensive, but it includes an annual free trip around the sun.
—Author unknown

This annual free trip around the sun is done in the company of about 7 billion people. Often we find ourselves surrounded by too many of them; we tend to withdraw into ourselves when we're swallowed up in crowds of people we don't know. We avoid eye contact. We put our earphones in. We bury our noses in books, newspapers, and laptops.

When we part from the crowd, we are unchanged from the moment we entered it, usually with no memory of anyone whose path we crossed. And we leave behind a missed opportunity to connect with our fellow travelers on a powerfully empathetic level.

ACTION STEPS

➤ Let your gaze wander over the multitudes, and then single out one person. Try to imagine that person's life in great detail, everything she has done, everywhere she has been, everyone she has loved or hated, all those countless things that have brought her to this exact point where your lives have intersected. Recognize in your heart the hard battle that has brought her here. Send her a kind thought or a short prayer.

➤ Once you've practiced this a few times on a single person in a crowd, broaden your perspective. Do the same thing with two or three people. Try to hold visions of their lives in your mind simultaneously. Again, finish by sending them blessings.

➤ And if that doesn't bog down your brain, back up even further and hold the whole crowd in your compassionate gaze. All those people, all those lives, all those incredible complexities that had to take place to gather you all in the same place. You will soon see your own life as it truly is—an inextricable part of something much bigger than you ever imagined. This time when you send out blessings, they will travel through that lovely web right back to you.

Stand Up for What You Believe In

When I marched in Selma, my feet were praying.
—Abraham Joshua Heschel, Jewish theologian

Sometimes, you have to put your money where your mouth is. Perhaps you're gripped by a political ideal or a moral one. Perhaps you feel impassioned or outraged. Perhaps you feel compassion. Perhaps you want to stand up for someone who has no voice. No matter what your motivation, supporting a cause helps the beneficiary and has the added benefit of making you feel empowered.

You can be one piece of a larger political movement. You don't have to organize a rally, but you can march in one. You can add your name to a petition, write or e-mail your congressperson, initiate an emergency telephone tree, send a letter to the editor, start a blog.

All of these small acts, when multiplied by millions of people, do make a difference. Think of the peaceful monks living a contemplative life in Tibet. At some point they reached a critical mass and rose up against their Chinese overlords. What journey did they make to act so incongruously to their belief system? All of us have to support the causes we believe in or we'll feel forever diminished by our inaction. Our involvement may feel like a spiritual as well as a moral imperative.

ACTION STEPS

➤ Think about two causes that get your blood flowing. What can you do to support their goals? You don't have to lead the fight, but you can participate in ways that make sense to you.

➤ How can you "pray with your feet"? What supportive actions can you take that have moral and spiritual value to you? Challenge yourself to define values that are important, and then get marching!

Supermarket Shopping for Homebound Seniors

If you want to lift yourself up, lift up someone else.
—Booker T. Washington

Today's senior citizens are living longer, and better, and are remaining in their own homes. As baby boomers age, social-service agencies across the country are preparing themselves to better serve the massive glut of new seniors who will not qualify for placement in assisted-living facilities. Many neighborhood programs are providing grocery shopping and case-management care that is designed to meet the physical, emotional, and social needs of our aging population. Typically, seniors will require shopping services when they can no longer drive.

While online services such as Peapod will bring groceries right to your door, many of today's elderly are not computer proficient. Instead, they rely on personal grocery shoppers to shop for them and bring the groceries to their homes. These services not only allow homebound seniors to remain independent, they also offer the opportunity to form compassionate relationships between the shoppers and the shoppees.

Whether you are shopping for a family friend or volunteering through a local social-services organization, you will not only be providing them with the food they need, but you'll be giving them the opportunity to age gracefully and with dignity. At the same time, you are acting as an extra set of eyes that can monitor any changes in health, mental status, or lifestyle.

GETTING STARTED: A few social-service organizations across the country have established shopping programs. Check out Jewish Family Services of Greenwich, Connecticut, at www.jfsgreenwich.org, or the Sudbury Fairbank Senior Center in Massachusetts at www.sudbury.ma.us/services/seniorcenter for ideas on how you can start a shopping service in your community. You can also volunteer your services through your place of worship or at the local hospital.

Saving the Sea Cow

**Animals are such agreeable friends—they ask
no questions, they pass no criticisms.**
—George Eliot

A face only a mother could love? Perhaps. But with the manatee's gentle, shy, keep-to-itself nature, many see it as cute and endearing. "I have heard a lot of people compare them to their family pet. They are just loveable," says Judith Vallee of Save the Manatee Club.

In 1973, when the Endangered Species Act became law, the manatee was immediately put on the list. A peaceful herbivore with no natural enemies, the manatee population was being decimated by high-powered motorboats. In Florida, about 3,800 manatees try to share the water with more than a million boats. Unfortunately, manatees often rest near the surface of the water and are very slow moving, so when a powerboat is speeding toward them, they simply cannot get out of the way fast enough. In 2008, a near-record ninety manatees were killed while many more were injured and maimed.

Save the Manatee Club was established in 1981 by former Florida governor Bob Graham and singer Jimmy Buffett. The club raises public awareness; sponsors research, rescues, and rehabilitation; and advocates at all levels of government for manatees.

Now you—and your kids!—can help these gentle creatures. By joining the Save the Manatee Club, children can learn about Florida ecology, the geography of the manatees' migrational area, and marine life in general. Most important, your child can "adopt" a manatee. When children adopt a manatee, they receive a photo of him or her, an adoption certificate, a membership handbook, and updates about their animal.

For $25, your child can adopt a manatee. For another $10, he or she will receive an adorable manatee plush toy.

VISIT www.savethemanatee.org or call (800) 432–5646.

Dig for Your Vacation

**An archaeologist is the best husband a woman can have.
The older she gets the more interested he is in her.**
—Agatha Christie

Every archaeological discovery means countless hours of hard work, often done by volunteers. And even though their work rarely gets any notice outside scholarly journals, they love doing it. They put up with the painstaking digging, the basic accommodations, the sunburn, and more, because they know that many crucial archaeological sites are in danger of being destroyed by uncontrolled development, looting, and vandalism. Their volunteer labor helps excavate or restore these sites before it's too late. If you're interested in preserving the culture of the past, consider taking a volunteer vacation on an archaeological dig. A number of programs seek volunteers to work on digs in Italy, Turkey, Israel, and Latin America. In addition to travel expenses, you may be charged fees to cover housing and food.

Closer to home, the USDA Forest Service offers the Passports in Time (PIT) program, volunteer archaeology and restoration opportunities that last anywhere from a few days to a few weeks. The projects take place at historic sites on the public lands of the extensive national forests.

The activities are diverse and include excavating sites, restoring rock art, gathering oral histories, curating artifacts, and stabilizing and restoring ancient structures. There's no fee for participating. Most PIT programs are on the rugged side—you'll probably be camping out in the backcountry, where you'll be responsible for your own food and gear. The professional historians and archaeologists of the Forest Service are your hosts, guides, and co-workers during your stay. This might not be the most restful vacation you ever take—you'll work hard—but you'll learn a lot and be part of saving our universal cultural heritage.

FOR DETAILS, contact the volunteer coordinator at:

Passport in Time Clearinghouse / Box 15728 / Rio Rancho, NM 87174–5728 / (800) 281–9176 / www.passportintime.com

Help Your Neighbors Barbecue
with Less Pollution

**We must be steady enough in ourselves, to be
open and to let the winds of life blow through
us, to be our breath, our inspiration.**
—Mary Caroline Richards, poet-potter

Did you know that charcoal lighter fluid contains volatile organic compounds (VOCs) that contribute to ground-level ozone? An estimated 46,200 tons of lighter fluid are used in the United States every year, which results in about 14,500 tons of VOCs being emitted into our air.

A program in the Kansas City, Kansas, area gave residents charcoal chimneys in exchange for bottles of lighter fluid. In four years of that program, 924 chimneys replaced 116 gallons of the fluid.

ACTION STEPS

LOCAL: Check locally or on the Internet to find a dealer that will give you a discount on a bulk purchase of chimney starters. Buy a starter for yourself; after you've practiced a few times, invite your neighbors over for a demonstration barbecue. Families can bring their own meat or veggies to grill. While your guests are enjoying drinks and appetizers, show how easy it is to start your charcoal; then cook your meal in your usual way. After dinner and a delicious dessert, you can take orders for the starters; if you've arranged a bulk discount, people will be more likely to buy on the spot. If possible, get a few close friends to agree, in advance, to order from you at this point; this will get the ball rolling.

NATIONAL: For more information about the Kansas chimney exchange program, see: www.wycokck.org/airquality.

For instructions on using a chimney starter, see: www.virtualweberbullet.com/chimney.html.

There are also demonstration videos on www.youtube.com.

The Dare

**It's not because things are difficult that we do not dare;
it is because we do not dare that they are difficult.**
—Seneca, Roman philosopher and statesman

Imagine for a moment a life without your sisters and brothers, or your children without each other, without shared memories to nurture them for the rest of their lives. For thousands of children separated from siblings while in foster care, this situation is an accepted reality.

Lynn Price knew the loneliness of such a childhood. When Lynn was eight, she discovered that her parents were really foster parents and that she had a birth sister who lived across town. As an adult, she became a court-appointed special advocate for children in foster care, volunteered at a local shelter, and became a licensed foster parent. Yet, when one little girl came to her in despair about being separated from her brother, Lynn boldly thought she must do more.

In 1995, Lynn founded the nonprofit Camp To Belong to reunite siblings separated by the foster-care system for a week each summer. Even more so, with her daily advocacy, she is daring to change the foster-care policies that tear apart siblings. She envisions the day when her camps are no longer needed because all siblings in foster care are living together.

Dare to do the difficult—to negate the influences of your childhood and all its accepted wisdoms and realities—and shape a future that serves all brothers and sisters of this world.

ACTION STEPS

➤ Is there a childhood experience that has dared you to act boldly on behalf of others? If you undertook the issue you thought most difficult in the world, what would you do?

➤ Use your influence to set up a local affiliate of Camp To Belong to reunite foster siblings in your area for a week they will never forget. More at www.camptobelong.org.

How Far a Pair of Shoes Can Go

I've got big shoes to fill. This is my chance to do something. I have to seize the moment.
—Andrew Jackson, seventh U.S. president

There's a wonderful story about Mohandas Gandhi, the great states- man and spiritual leader who rose to international prominence during India's struggle for independence from Great Britain. As the tale goes, he was boarding a train one day when one of his sandals slid off his foot and fell into the gap between the train and the platform. Seeing that he couldn't retrieve it, he took off the other sandal and threw it after the first.

The people with him were baffled. This is how Ghandi explained his seemingly bizarre actions to them: A poor person who finds one sandal is no better off than he was before. But a poor person who finds a pair of sandals is blessed by an incredible gift.

ACTION STEPS

➤ Find the most ill-fitting shoes you own. Spend just five minutes tramping around in them. Can you see how, with every step, those shoes are a reminder of just how hard life is for those who go barefoot or wear inadequate footwear?

➤ One charity, Soles4Souls, estimates that Americans have about 1.5 billion pairs of unused shoes lying in closets. Go through your shoes, and collect every single pair that hasn't been used in the last year, as well as any others you know you won't wear again (gently used shoes, please; remember how awful the old ones felt?). Donate them to the nearest thrift store.

➤ Curious to see just how much a pair of used shoes can change a life? Go to www.soles4souls.org to read how your sneakers can impact the world for the better.

Build a Support Circle

Promise me you'll always remember: You're braver than you believe, and stronger than you seem, and smarter than you think. But the most important thing is, even if we're apart, I'll always be with you.
—Christopher Robin to Pooh

There are so many stressors when someone becomes ill. Medical decisions to be researched and made; comfort to be rendered; childcare arrangements and meals to be organized; friends and family to be updated. Often caregivers are driven to distraction juggling it all. Making or returning all those phone calls can add to the distress. Sadly, those outside the immediate family want to participate but end up feeling helpless and out of the loop.

But there is an easier way for the family to share their story and build a support circle that includes everyone. The CarePages Web site provides free, customized, secure Web pages to facilitate communication among family and friends during a health event such as pregnancy and delivery, a medical crisis, or when long-term care is required. The patient or a loved one creates and manages the Web site and blog and uses it to update friends and family on the patient's condition. A message board allows visitors to post supportive comments. Photos can also be added along with details loved ones may need: hospital location and visiting hours, and news about the medical condition and treatments.

Although illness can be an isolating experience, a Web site such as CarePages helps those coping with it feel surrounded by loving friends.

ACTION STEPS

➤ Think about how you can create a support circle for a friend who is ill. You might organize a telephone tree, a childcare co-op, or a home-cooked dinner delivery service. What else might you do?

➤ Visit the CarePages Web site, www.carepages.com to find out how to create a supportive Web site and blog for a loved one with medical challenges.

Lay Religious Leaders

**Prayer is exhaling the spirit of man
and inhaling the spirit of God.**
—Edwin Keith

A church, synagogue, or mosque will only be as successful as its leadership is respected and its community participates. For the majority of world religions, congregants or the laity serve vital roles within their spiritual homes. Laypeople often hire the professional religious leaders and their staff, maintain the buildings, manage the congregation's finances, determine the congregation's position on difficult issues, and more. They also contribute to religious instruction or participate in rituals during services, special occasions, and on specific holidays.

All of these opportunities are important and valued not only by the organization but by the other members. By becoming involved in your place of worship, you are not only creating community, but you're providing the means for various life passages. You are making sure that religious needs are met for individuals and families, in good times and in bad. You are also an active participant in handing down the customs and traditions of your faith from one generation to the next.

Various titles are used for the participation of lay leaders during specific religious services. Christians often use the terms lay preacher, lay reader, lay speaker, or deacon interchangeably, although the last title can also refer to an ordained ministry. A gabbai or shamash is the person who assists in the running of a Jewish synagogue or temple and ensures that services run smoothly. In the Muslim tradition, the muezzin is a chosen person who leads the call to Friday service and the five daily prayers.

GETTING STARTED: Talk with your congregation's ritual committee or spiritual leader, and find out how you can get more involved. You might need some special training, or have to master the liturgy in a new way. You can also help others within your faith during times of loss by simply attending a funeral or prayer service. Some religions have specific roles for men, women, or children, and while different, all are valued and appreciated.

Finding the Lost

Most of the important things in the world have been accomplished by people who have kept on trying when there seemed to be no hope at all.
—Dale Carnegie

A frantic mother and father of a missing seventeen-year-old were trying to find their daughter. They suspected that she had been lured away by the father of one of her friends, but they did not know where he was or how to find him. The police were unable to help.

Having tried on their own for seven months to find their child, the parents contacted Child Find. The caseworker found out that the father of the daughter's friend had rented an apartment in Chicago, and she convinced Chicago police to go to the property. They did and found the girl in the company of two strangers. The girl, who had been trying to figure out a way to escape, was very grateful to be found and was soon reunited with her ecstatic parents.

Every day in America, 2,300 children are reported missing. A few are the victims of stranger abduction, but the majority are victims of abduction by the noncustodial parent. Others are runaways. Parents desperate for their return in many cases cannot afford a private detective to help find their child. In the meantime, the children (who have often been told the custodial parent no longer loves them or is even dead) suffer great psychological damage and may one day not even remember the parent.

Child Find offers investigation and location services, kidnapping prevention programs, and referral and support services—all for free. On average, Child Find spends 90 cents of every dollar donated directly on providing program services. Each year Child Find receives between fifteen and twenty thousand calls for help finding a missing child. A donation of $75 will pay for one day for Child Find to receive calls from parents desperate to find their missing children.

VISIT www.childfindofamerica.org or call (800) I–AM–LOST (426–5678).

Sustainable Agriculture

**I have great faith in a seed. Convince me that you have
a seed there, and I am prepared to expect wonders.**
—Henry David Thoreau

Sustainable agriculture means organic farming without the use of synthetic pesticides or conventional fertilizer. Helping to promote sustainable agriculture in your region benefits not only you but the whole planet. There's a problem, though: organic farming is more labor intensive than conventional farming. To make an organic farm successful, volunteers are needed.

One way to volunteer on an organic farm is by taking a share in your local community-supported agriculture (CSA) program. The innovative CSA concept allows individuals to buy a share of a farmer's crop in advance. A few hundred dollars a share provides an entire family with fresh, organically grown produce straight from the farm almost all year round. In exchange, the farmer gets a predictable income—crucial for helping to keep family farms in operation. CSA farms rely heavily on volunteers, including apprentice farmers, to make the system work. Some volunteers work in exchange for their share; others help out just because they enjoy getting their hands dirty and knowing exactly where their food comes from.

If you really want to get your hands dirty on an organic farm, volunteer as a short-term farm worker through WWOOF, or World Wide Opportunities on Organic Farms. This international organization connects farmers and workers around the world. As a worker, you help out on the farm for an agreed number of days; in exchange, you learn about organic methods firsthand; get free, if somewhat basic, accommodations; and get plenty of farm-fresh food. You're responsible for your own travel, but your time on the farm costs nothing. More than a thousand farms in the United States alone welcome WWOOFers; you can also travel abroad to farms all over the world.

FOR INFORMATION:

WWOOF-USA / Box 1098 / Philmont, NY 12565 / (831) 425–FARM (3276) / www.wwoofusa.org

Save an Endangered Historic Building

**My interest is in the future because I am
going to spend the rest of my life there.**
—Charles Kettering, engineer/inventor

Every day, buildings of historic value are torn down or allowed to de-
teriorate because no one cared to save them. Such a building might
be the former home of a famous man or woman, a good example of a
particular style of architecture, or the place where an important event
took place. Or it may simply be loved by the community because of the
memories it evokes.

ACTION STEPS

LOCAL: Research the building's history at your library or historic
museum and by talking to older people in the area. Pull together a group
of local people who appreciate the building, and begin to discuss possible
approaches to saving it. Find out who owns the building by checking
public records; then approach that person. Could it be for sale? Might it
be donated to your group for a tax write-off? Are there back taxes owed?
All these could provide openings for negotiation.

Get in touch with local lawmakers, historic preservation commissions,
architects, town planners, land-use groups, and zoning boards. Learn
about applicable regulations and codes. Identify interest groups that
might support your efforts; for instance, if the building was once the
home of a well-known doctor, contact the local medical society. Preservation projects, if done privately, take substantial financial commitments,
but you may be able to secure public funding or get a grant.

NATIONAL: Go to www.preservationdirectory.com for information.

Join the National Trust for Historic Preservation (www.preservation
nation.org) for up-to-date information on national and regional issues.
Check the American Institute of Architects Web site (www.aia.org) for
the closest chapter.

Influence, Hung Out to Dry

**Oh , let there be nothing on earth but laundry, /
Nothing but rosy hands in the rising steam / And
clear dances done in the sight of heaven.**
—Richard Wilbur, "Love Calls Us to the Things of This World"

When we think of using our influence to save energy, we usually think of turning off the lights or buying energy-saving lightbulbs or rechargeable batteries, all good things. Do we think of the clothes dryer?

After the refrigerator, the clothes dryer is the largest consumer of home power. We can turn from a high-energy to a cutting-edge, no-energy clothes-drying device and harness the power of the sun and wind along the way. We can hang our clothes out to dry. (Indoor drying racks accomplish the same energy-free job).

We can reduce greenhouse gases by 6.6 tons, the estimate of what every person in America emits, according to the Environmental Protection Agency, by making small but high-impact changes in everyday activities. We can influence the world with our laundry.

ACTION STEPS

➤ Wash your clothes (for less of a carbon print, use cool water and only one rinse cycle). String a clothesline. Purchase clothespins if you've never used a clothesline before. Carry the clean, wet clothes outside, hang them side by side on the line. Now go recycle, walk the dog, play catch. In a couple of hours the clothes will be dry.

➤ Look for Energy Star and EnergyGuide labels on appliances. These washers and dryers use 50 percent less energy. Many newly purchased energy-saving devices now have tax-saving options attached to them on the federal and/or state level. More at www.energystar.gov. Social network the saving details, and virally pass on the green.

➤ Talk to a friend shopping for appliances or building a new home. Encourage them to make their choices with environmental impact in mind. Mention your environmentally conscious purchase on your Facebook or MySpace pages.

Be Good for Goodness' Sake

**If you want others to be happy, practice compassion.
If you want to be happy, practice compassion.**
—Dalai Lama

This quote brings up two essential points: First, the connection between our happiness and the happiness of others is inextricable. It is as difficult to be happy in a vacuum as it is to breathe in one. Second, compassion is spiritual muscle that can be strengthened with use.

A man named Eric Weiner wrote a remarkable book called *The Geography of Bliss: One Grump's Search for the Happiest Places in the World*. He found that the principal commonality among the happiest places—countries as varied as Iceland, Bahamas, Canada, and the tiny South Asian kingdom of Bhutan—was a sense of community and togetherness that included friends and family, but also stretched beyond those boundaries to include strangers. A sense of community and togetherness, you may have guessed, is impossible without a highly developed sense of compassion.

ACTION STEPS

➤ Practicing compassion is no different than any other activity—just a whole lot more important (no disrespect intended to your piccolo lessons). Each morning when you rise, make it a practice—there's that word again—to incorporate compassion into your day whenever possible. Remind yourself of this frequently.

➤ To understand the real meaning of community, try this interesting exercise: Find a patch of earth (a warm, sunny one is nice, but not essential) and lie down on it. Feel your body in full contact with the ground, and try to get a sense of just how large this magnificent object you're lying against really is. Now send your awareness outward in an ever-widening circle and as it grows larger, imagine all the people who are sharing the surface of this earth with you. When you stand back up, you'll have a deepened appreciation of the fellowship of humanity.

Accept the Possibilities

**In the beginner's mind there are many possibilities,
but in the expert's mind there are few.**
—Shunrya Suzuki, Japanese Zen priest

You may be called upon to have faith in another without knowing the outcome, to support him in his endeavors without attachment to the result. Your son wants to strike out as an actor, a friend is divorcing her spouse, your brother has begun to remodel his house. The outcome is truly important to them, but can you stand by their side without judgment or expectations? Can you support them no matter what happens?

This may ask you to engage in the concept of *beginner's mind*, a Zen Buddhist practice. The beginner's mind is innocent of preconceptions and prejudices. It's just present to explore and observe what is. It is the mind that faces life like a small child, full of curiosity and wonder without a fixed point of view or a prior judgment. Once you decide you "know" something about someone, once you determine how you would like a situation to develop, you close yourself to new possibilities, new ways of appreciation. But a person who adopts a beginner's mind-set supports without expectation or grasping. You are there observing what occurs. You are ready for whatever experience arises in this moment. You offer your help and support no matter what. The end result—the content—is unimportant. What's of value is the process, your relationship, the support you offer. What counts is your loving heart.

ACTION STEPS

➤ Think about something difficult for you or about which you are self-critical. Then reframe it from the point of view of a young child who is open and curious. What would he or she see that you don't right now?

➤ Apply that curiosity and openness to a loved one struggling with a decision or embarking on a risky endeavor. Envision the possibilities, and support that person with love.

The Box Project

Poverty is like punishment for a crime you didn't commit.
—Eli Khamarov

The Box Project is a national nonprofit organization that matches volunteer sponsors with specific recipient families living in rural poverty throughout the United States, primarily in the Mississippi Delta, rural Maine, Appalachia (West Virginia and Kentucky), and Native American reservations in South Dakota and Florida. Since 1962, the Box Project has helped more than 15,000 American families. The goal of the organization is to change lives, one family at a time, right here in our country.

As a sponsor, you can choose when you volunteer according to your own schedule and your own means. About once a month, sponsors send boxes of food, clothing, or other supplies to their match family. But what makes the Box Project so unique is that you will develop a personal relationship with your match family. Part of your obligation is not only to find out what your match family needs in their box each month, but to get to know them through ongoing letter writing. Sponsors use the letters that accompany the boxes as an opportunity to mentor these families, and provide friendship.

As a mentor, you can guide your match family to a wide array of social services that are available in their region. You can also share elements of your life, and stress the importance of staying in school as a means to get out of the cycle of poverty. In return, you will receive letters from your match family, who will share their joys and challenges.

GETTING STARTED: To learn more, visit www.boxproject.org or call (800) 268–9928. Or, start your own "box project" right in your community. Check with local agencies to see if you can create a winter holiday "match" with a family in need. Start as early as October to make sure there is plenty of time to plan well ahead of the holidays!

Caring for Victims of Sexual Assault

The ax forgets, the tree remembers.
—African proverb

The statistics around rape and sexual assault in this country are staggering. Consider the following:

➤ One in six American women is a victim of sexual assault.

➤ Seventy-three percent of sexual assaults are perpetrated by someone known to the victim.

➤ About 80 percent of rape victims are under age thirty.

➤ Sixty percent of all sexual assaults go unreported.

The act of rape may be brief but the effects of the crime are long-lasting. Victims of sexual assault are three times more likely to suffer from depression, six times more likely to suffer from post-traumatic stress disorder, thirteen times more likely to abuse alcohol, twenty-six times more likely to abuse drugs, and four times more likely to contemplate suicide.

In response to this crisis, the Rape, Abuse & Incest National Network (RAINN), referring calls 24/7, has helped over 1.2 million people through the National Sexual Assault Hotlines in conjunction with over 1,100 local rape crisis centers around the country. RAINN also has created the National Sexual Assault *Online* Hotline. This first program of its kind allows victims (often young women who feel most comfortable communicating via the Internet) to seek help via instant-messaging where they can safely and anonymously communicate directly with trained crisis support volunteers.

Donating $28 to RAINN pays for four hours of training for a hotline volunteer; $30 pays to provide sexual-assault prevention tips to 1,500 college students; $42 pays for twelve hotline calls; and $71 lets RAINN print and distribute posters that will be viewed by 10,000 students in college dorms.

VISIT www.rainn.org or call (800) 656–HOPE (4673).

Help Monarch Butterflies

We delight in the beauty of the butterfly, but rarely admit the changes it has gone through to achieve that beauty.
—Maya Angelou

The monarch butterfly migration is one of the most remarkable natural wonders in the world. Every fall, hundreds of millions of monarch butterflies migrate from the United States and Canada to their overwintering areas thousands of miles away. Monarchs west of the Rocky Mountains travel to small groves of trees along the California coast; those east of the Rockies fly even further south, to small patches of forest high in the mountains of central Mexico. There they gather by the millions to wait out the winter and then return to their spring and summer breeding range.

This amazing life cycle is threatened by habitat loss not only at the roosting sites but throughout the breeding range. Development, the use of pesticides and genetically modified agriculture, and frequent mowing of roadsides all destroy the habitat for milkweed and the other host plants monarchs rely upon for nectar and for breeding. To help the monarchs, you can participate in the waystation program sponsored by Monarch Watch, a national organization devoted to monarch research and conservation. To create a waystation in your yard—or in a community garden, local park, schoolyard, vacant lot, or even a roadside—all you need is a seed kit from Monarch Watch. The kit contains seeds of about a dozen favorite monarch plants. The seeds are easy to plant, and once they're in the ground, all you have to do is make sure they don't get mowed down or sprayed with pesticides. You can register your waystation with Project Monarch Watch and get a Monarch Waystation sign to mark it.

FOR MORE INFORMATION and to get a waystation seed kit (there's a small fee), contact:

Monarch Watch / University of Kansas / 1200 Sunnyside Avenue / Lawrence, KS 66045 / (888) TAGGING (824–4464) / www.monarch watch.org

Rethink Your Need for Flowers

Where flowers bloom, so does hope.
—Lady Bird Johnson

Once upon a time, people grew their own flowers; more recently gigantic flower-producing farms have sprung up in many Third World countries. And we have become accustomed to gigantic bouquets at weddings and funerals, in stores and restaurants, and in our homes. Although they may seem inexpensive, the actual cost of such flowers is high; a tremendous amount of fuel is used to transport them thousands of miles, on refrigerated airplanes, to you. Not only that; many of these farms use pesticides that are harmful to local land and people—including the farmworkers. And they often use a disproportionate amount of scarce water resources.

Flowers confirm our connection to the life cycle and are a celebration of our love of nature. Why, then, would we want to buy blooms that have a negative impact on the environment?

ACTION STEPS

LOCAL: Grow your own! With a small plot of land or a sunny window, it's not hard to grow your own flowers in season. Seeds can be started indoors in late winter, then moved outside in spring. Encourage others to do so by giving away young plants or seeds through your local garden club, school, or place of worship. Many schools now have gardens or greenhouses; approach your kids' schools about starting such an initiative.

Buy flowers from local farms; most communities have greenmarkets. Encourage local flower shops to buy local.

If someone you know has a greenhouse, approach him or her about a cooperative flower-growing project during the cold months. Use organic methods; you can even heat the greenhouse with solar power!

NATIONAL: Support organizations that encourage local and organic farming. For more information: www.localharvest.org • www.rodale institute.org

Along the Spectrum

**I stood at one of the windows and watched the moon
rise up behind the mountain range to meet the stars.
A feeling of relief flooded me. For the first time in
months I felt safe in the present and hope in the
future. . . . That night I wrote in my diary: "I must
conquer my fears and not let them block my way."**
—Dr. Temple Grandin, *Emergence: Labeled Autistic*

She didn't speak until she was three and a half years old, instead letting the world know her frustration by screaming, peeping, and hum-
ming. In 1950, she was labeled "autistic," and her parents were told she
should be institutionalized.

Today, she is one of the most accomplished adults with autism. Dr.
Grandin received her PhD in animal science from the University of Illinois in 1989 and is one of the foremost authorities on livestock handling
equipment. She has designed the facilities in which half the cattle in the
United States are handled. She has changed the way we think about the
possibilities for people with autism.

The famous neurologist Oliver Sacks notes that Dr. Grandin is extraordinary, first of all, because before her, "it had been medical dogma for forty
years or more that there was no 'inside,' no inner life in the autistic."

By sharing her unique inner life, Dr. Grandin transformed our understanding of animals.

ACTION STEPS

➤ Dr. Grandin believes her success comes from her unique visual thinking skills. How does your thinking influence the story of your inner
life?

➤ World Autism Awareness Day is April 2. Find out more about local
chapters of the Autism Society of America (www.autism-society.org)
or of Autism Speaks at www.autismspeaks.org.

Closely Related to Tragedy

Love your enemies, do good to those who hate you.
—Luke 6:27

In 2006 a lone gunman walked into a one-room Amish schoolhouse in Pennsylvania. Less than an hour later, ten girls were shot, five of whom died, and the gunman had killed himself.

In 2007 a twenty-three-year-old English major at Virginia Tech went on a morning rampage with two pistols. By 10 a.m., he had killed twenty-seven of his fellow students, five faculty members, then himself. Twenty-three others were wounded as a result of the attack.

These stories, and many others like them, do not end with the death of the killers. In fact, this is where the truest forms of compassion often begin. The Amish community immediately offered forgiveness to the shooter and his family, even setting up a charitable fund for them. One report tells of how an Amish man held the shooter's father for an hour as the father sobbed uncontrollably. After the Virginia Tech killings, a group of women began sending cards of condolence to the family of the man responsible, trying to ease their grief and horror at what he had done.

Can you imagine the level of compassion in people who realize that the victims of tragedy also include the relatives of those responsible?

ACTION STEPS

➤ When a terrible wrong is committed, it is almost natural to assume that the perpetrator came from a family as evil as he. The first step is to understand that this is likely not true.

➤ The families of wrongdoers are blamed, shunned, and alone in their anguish. Help these families. It's incredibly important, as a letter to the Amish from the wife of the shooter so eloquently put it. In part, it read: "Your compassion has reached beyond our family, beyond our community, and is changing our world, and for this we sincerely thank you."

A Bond in Hunger

**And above all these things put on charity,
which is the bond of perfectness.**
—Colossians 3:14

The Irish Potato Famine (1845–1852), caused by blight, ravaged Ireland's principle food crop and led to starvation, disease, and mass emigration. Ireland's population was reduced by 25 percent. A million people died and a million more fled.

During this tragedy, a surprising group of people provided support. Upon learning of the famine, the Choctaw Indians sent $710 (a fortune by today's standards) to support relief in Ireland. The Choctaws had experienced their own privations and identified with the plight of the Irish. Sixteen years earlier, the Indian Removal Act allowed our government to resettle about 12,500 members of the tribe in Oklahoma and Kansas. They were the first Native Americans to travel the Trail of Tears. Many suffered exposure, disease, and starvation, and thousands died en route.

To mark the 150th anniversary of the Potato Famine, twenty-five Irish people retraced the five-hundred-mile Trail of Tears in reverse, from Oklahoma to Mississippi, to repay their debt to the Choctaw tribe. The charity walk was staged by Action From Ireland, a Dublin-based human-rights group that was raising money for the famine relief effort in Somalia. In 1995, Mary Robinson, the president of Ireland, visited the Choctaw Nation to convey her nation's thanks for their generosity.

ACTION STEPS

➤ Homelessness and hunger are present around you. What acts of kindness and assistance can you perform to help neighbors in need? Work at a soup kitchen. Deliver Meals on Wheels to elderly shut-ins. Teach your children to share your family's bounty.

➤ To honor the millions who suffered during the Potato Famine and the generosity of the Choctaw tribe, organize a food drive to collect root vegetables (potatoes, yams, carrots, etc.) for your local food bank.

Share Your Home with Puppies Training to Help the Blind

**Dogs are not our whole life, but
they make our lives whole.**
—Roger Caras, host of the Westminster Kennel Club Dog Show

Seeing-eye dogs come from very select stock: they need to have the right genes, the right disposition, and, more important, the right preparation. Seeing-eye dogs have to pass a series of rigorous tests before they are paired with a blind person, yet the schools that train these dogs are often underfunded or understaffed, and many rely on volunteers to help raise and train them. The love and time you can share with these dogs provides them with a wonderful beginning before they are taught to assist human companions.

For example, Guiding Eyes for the Blind, an internationally accredited, nonprofit guide dog school, has devised a network of volunteer opportunities for individuals and families to help raise seeing-eye dogs that are then sent all over the world.

The first set of volunteers offer Home Litter Care, taking care of the youngest puppies and the mother dog. Within one week of birth, the mother dog and her litter will come to your home, where you will provide grooming, feeding, exercise, and socialization for roughly six weeks.

Home Litter Care volunteers pass off the pups to Home Socializers, who care for two puppies each. Home Socializers work with the dogs to introduce them to new sights, sounds, and people, as well as beginning their training for typical dog activities: leash walking, riding in cars, sitting for meals, crate time, and such.

Next, the third level of volunteers, called Raisers, provide a home as well as patient teaching over a twelve- to sixteen-month period, before the dogs are ready for the school's professional training staff.

GETTING STARTED: The American Foundation for the Blind offers a complete list of guide dog schools in the United States: www.afb.org; (800) AFB–LINE (232–5463). Check out the schools closest to you.

A Simple Helping Hand

It is not wealth one asks for, but just enough to preserve one's dignity, to work unhampered, to be generous, frank and independent.
—W. Somerset Maugham

Angel is a thirty-year-old man in Bulgaria, a gypsy living with his mother and younger brother in a concrete house without running water. He dreamed of starting a bicycle shop but could not get a loan from a bank. Then he obtained a loan through Kiva, bought the repair tools and inventory he needed to get started, and worked hard to develop his business. Angel was so successful that he fully repaid his loan within twelve months, hired his brother to help in his shop, performed renovations on the family home, and invested in a supplemental metalworking business.

Kiva lets you lend to entrepreneurs like Angel, helping them to lift themselves out of poverty. You choose whom to lend to—whether a farmer in Afghanistan, a goatherder in Uganda, or a tailor in Iraq—and you can see their photos and stories online, their journal entries about their progress, and how quickly they are repaying the loan. You also get to see who else lent money to your entrepreneur and what other entrepreneurs those lenders are supporting, thereby creating an online community of people helping people that spans the globe.

Kiva does not give handouts. Many people like Angel in developing countries have both the dream of having a business and the work ethic to see it through, but they just need a helping hand to get them started. As the entrepreneur repays his or her loan, you get your money back. Then if, for example, you had lent $100, when it is paid back, you can relend it over and over, in essence giving the benefit of that $100 to several others at no additional cost to you.

Kiva has a repayment rate of more than 98 percent. They have made more than $69 million in loans, but even a loan as small as $25 can make an enormous difference in the life of someone in another part of the world.

VISIT www.kiva.org.

Join AmeriCorps

**I will get things done for America—to make
our people safer, smarter, and healthier.**
—AmeriCorps pledge

In 1993 then-president Bill Clinton signed the legislation that formally launched AmeriCorps. This new program incorporated two existing national service programs: VISTA and the National Civilian Community Corps. In 1994 the first class of AmeriCorps volunteers—twenty-thousand strong—began their service in a thousand communities. In 2003 then-president George W. Bush signed legislation that nearly doubled the size of AmeriCorps, and in 2009 President Obama signed the Edward M. Kennedy Serve America Act, which expanded AmeriCorps volunteer opportunities even further for both older and younger Americans. Over the coming years AmeriCorps will grow from 75,000 to 250,000 dedicated individuals serving their country.

As a volunteer, you help meet the critical needs of communities across America. Part-time or full-time, you can tutor and mentor disadvantaged youth, fight illiteracy, improve health services, build affordable housing, clean parks and streams, or manage after-school programs. The real reward comes when your efforts pay off in creating a better place to live. More tangibly, AmeriCorps volunteers of all ages are now eligible for significant educational awards.

The volunteer experience in AmeriCorps sticks with the participants. A long-term study of more than two thousand volunteers shows AmeriCorps is a pipeline to careers in public service. It creates leaders who continue to serve their communities long after their service has been completed.

AmeriCorps programs will soon fall into four new service areas: health care, clean energy, fighting poverty, and veteran support. These will incorporate the existing structure of AmeriCorps, including VISTA and NCCC.

TO LEARN which program is right for you, contact:

AmeriCorps / 1201 New York Avenue NW / Washington, DC 20525 / (202) 606–5000 / www.americorps.gov

Inform Your Neighbors About Nonpolluting Paint Alternatives

Do not wait for leaders; do it alone, person to person.
—Mother Teresa

Many people don't realize that toxic substances seep into the air from common petroleum-based paints, polluting our homes, our offices, and our bodies. These chemicals, which are bad for our health, are called volatile organic compounds (VOCs). Even after such paints dry, they can still emit VOCs for years.

The U.S. Environmental Protection Agency has ratings for:

➤ Low-VOC and zero-VOC paints. These ratings should be listed on paint cans; if you don't see them on a particular brand, contact the manufacturer for a "material safety data sheet."

➤ Natural paints, made from such substances as plant dyes and minerals, have no VOCs.

➤ "Reclaimed" paint is old paint that has been filtered (removing toxins and debris), mixed with new paint, and repackaged.

ACTION STEPS

LOCAL: Produce a flyer with basic information on ecofriendly paint. For help, see "How to Choose Eco-Friendly Paint" at www.ehow.com/how_2156671_choose-eco-friendly-paint.html. Also visit Green Seal, an organization that certifies eco-friendly products and services: www.greenseal.org. Get promotional material from makers of eco-friendly products. Ask local hardware/paint stores to set up tables on Saturday afternoons; pass out your literature.

NATIONAL: Did you know that the U.S. Environmental Protection Agency does not set any limits to the VOCs allowed in household paints? (see www.epa.gov/iaq/voc.html). Contact your representatives in Washington and demand that standards be set to protect the air we breathe!

Matchmaker

Nothing we do, however virtuous, can be accomplished alone; therefore, we are saved by love.
—Reinhold Niebuhr

On Monday morning, you can use your influence to move your company and impact the lives of many. You will need to start people talking. With your influence, you want to get people excited and with you on your idea.

The idea? Suggest your company start an employee matching-gift program, a charitable effort that aligns your colleagues' beliefs with what you hope are the company's beliefs. You all want to give back to the community, to the world at large, and you all can if your company matches your charitable giving, thereby doubling the donation.

You, your colleagues, and your company's leaders, want to give back more—and this is an easy way to do it. Important people in your company want to be seen as heroes. The company has strong roots in the community. It's a place with a conscience, a company that cares. This is why you work where you work. Start talking on Monday morning; the core of your influence today is about exciting others, letting them run with this idea, and doing more good than you could ever do alone.

ACTION STEPS

➤ The first step in suggesting a matching-gift program is to pull together a group of like-minded people in your company. Include employees from all levels of the company. Gather their input and create a unified presentation showing that it makes good business sense to do good.

➤ Arrange for a meeting with the most senior person available to you. Go into that meeting with more questions than answers. You want the senior executive to have a strong ownership stake in this project. Your ultimate goal is to dramatically increase your company's charitable giving, not get credit for the initiative.

Praying for Grace

Preach the Gospel at all times and
when necessary use words.
—St. Francis Assisi

In the annals of unlikely saints, Francis of Assisi may well be among the unlikeliest. The person who became the founder of the Order of Friars Minor (you probably know them as the Franciscans) was born in the twelfth century to a wealthy merchant family and grew into a young man with a reputation for drinking, brawling, and what some biographers euphemistically called "a love of pleasure."

Somehow, that man underwent such a profound transformation that so filled him with compassion and love that he gave up a life of plenty and spent his days tending to the poorest, the sickest, the most wretched of humanity. His compassion also extended to animals; one legend has it that St. Francis thanked his donkey for shouldering the burden of him throughout his life. The animal was so moved it wept.

The answer to the question of how Francis changed from a bawdy youth to a beautiful, gentle, compassionate soul can be summed up in one deeply powerful word. That word is grace.

ACTION STEPS

➤ You must first realize that grace cannot enter unbidden. Like Francis, you must open yourself to it unreservedly. The way to do this is through prayer.

➤ No matter what else you pray for, always include in your prayers your wholehearted desire to be filled with grace, the indwelling presence of the divine that illuminates every aspect of your being. Hold this prayer wordlessly in your heart and feel for grace's presence.

➤ Grace enters softly. Stay with this practice every day and it will become a greater part of who you are, whether or not you always know it. One of grace's greatest gifts is when your actions are guided by it even though you are unaware of it.

Take Your Medicine

**Love is a medicine for the sickness of the world;
a prescription often given, too rarely taken.**
—Author unknown

With one sixth of our nation uninsured and another 24 percent underinsured, an illness can cause catastrophic hardship to a family. Did you know that more than half the adults surveyed in 2009 cut back on healthcare spending during the previous twelve months because of cost concerns? Of the people surveyed, 21 percent did not fill drug prescriptions and 15 percent skipped doses or cut their pills in half.

This is tragic, especially since many drug companies and nonprofit organizations offer assistance programs to help people who can't afford their prescriptions get the drugs they need at little or no cost. What's even more puzzling is that many of these charitable programs are begging for participants. For instance, one biotech company has found that only one third of those qualifying for its program of free medications actually participate. Unfortunately, navigating their way to free or inexpensive help is beyond the grasp of many dealing with infirmity, advancing age, or serious health challenges. Help and support are available if you know where to turn. It can save a life.

ACTION STEPS

➤ If you have a loved one, acquaintance, or community member who needs medication but can't afford it, support him or her in enrolling in one of these programs. RxAssist (www.rxassist.org), (401) 729–3284, provides information about patient-assistance programs. Partnership for Prescription Assistance (www.pparx.org), (888) 477–2669, gives general and specific information on drug programs. Together Rx Access (www.togetherrxaccess.com), (800) 444–4106, provides a discount drug card that many pharmacies accept. It is for legal U.S. residents without public or private prescription coverage. The card is free and provides 25–40 percent discounts on more than three hundred drugs.

Mitzvah Projects:
Mark a Rite of Passage

The greatest danger to our future is apathy.
—Jane Goodall

In some religions, acts of service often accompany a rite of passage. For example, when Jewish boys and girls reach the age of thirteen, they are considered adults and are held responsible for their moral and religious duties. As such, many synagogues require the bar mitzvah boys or bat mitzvah girls to complete a "mitzvah project," where they participate in charitable work of their choosing to commemorate this milestone in their lives. Some choose a charity close to their hearts, or one that matches their family's giving history. Others choose something that is child related. The point is not so much where you give, but that you begin to get personally involved with service.

You don't have to be Jewish to perform mitzvot, or good deeds. And you certainly don't have to be thirteen. One important lesson from this service suggestion is to instill the concept of charity to our youngest members of society. Now, more than ever, it is a lesson worth learning. A 2002 study from the Center on Philanthropy at Indiana University showed that people who do not give philanthropically as youngsters are less likely to do so as they mature and age.

The second lesson is to mark your next passage or life cycle event with a gift of your time, or a donation, to the charity of your choosing. By doing so, you will also be participating in another Jewish custom, *tikkun olam,* or repairing the world with acts of kindness.

GETTING STARTED: This book offers 365 excellent suggestions for charitable giving and service opportunities. After you choose the one most suited for you or your family, choose a life cycle event that you would like to commemorate. Then, get to work!

Giving a Sense of Purpose

**There is no psychiatrist in the world
like a puppy licking your face.**
—Bernard Williams

A tall, muscular man stands in a prison yard surrounded by barbed wire. A large dog is poised at his feet, ready to carry out any command.

A frightening scene? Not exactly. The biggest risk you run with that dog is being overcome by her doggie breath while she slobbers your face. And that man with all the tattoos isn't looking for trouble. Instead, Jerome is hoping to help both society and himself by taking part in Puppies Behind Bars, a program that trains prisoners to teach young dogs to detect bombs for law enforcement.

Being responsible for his dog, Molly, and training her to follow a series of commands such as sniffing out and finding an object in the trunk of a car, gives Jerome responsibility, self-esteem, and a sense of purpose—feelings that are hard to find in prison. And while he'll be sad when Molly graduates, he knows that she too will have a sense of purpose—such as keeping the rest of us safe from explosives when we are in airports and government buildings.

"I'm a clean player now," says Jerome. "The dog has helped me become compassionate."

"I'm human again," says another inmate in the Puppies Behind Bars program. "It gave me a second chance at life."

For $3,000 you can buy a puppy to participate in the program (and you get to name it!). For $1,100 you can send a prisoner to a veterinary assistant's course. For $100 you can buy puppy food to feed a dog for three months, or for $25 you can buy a collar and leash. And for $10, $5, or whatever amount you want, you can buy a "Puppy Kiss"—the good feeling of knowing you have helped an inmate to gain self-respect, prepare to re-enter the world a more responsible and caring person—and, perhaps most of all, to let that prisoner experience a dog's unconditional love.

VISIT www.puppiesbehindbars.com or call (212) 680–9562.

Rebuilding Together

The home should be the treasure chest of living.
—Le Corbusier

A home should be a safe and healthy place—but keeping a home that way can sometimes be beyond the means of the owner. Rebuilding Together is a nonprofit organization uniting a network of more than two hundred volunteer affiliates around the country that work to preserve affordable homeownership and revitalize communities. Rebuilding Together provides free home modifications and repairs—help that can keep a family in its home or help an elderly or disabled person live independently.

Every year on the last Saturday in April, Rebuilding Together holds its signature event: National Rebuilding Day. The result of a full year of planning, National Rebuilding Day mobilizes hundreds of thousands of community volunteers for a single day of service. Volunteers repair and restore houses and nonprofit facilities, revitalize entire communities, and help their neighbors in need. They make homes safer, more accessible, and more energy efficient.

Volunteers with construction skills are at the heart of National Rebuilding Day, but just about anyone can pitch in and help. This is a great group opportunity for families with older kids and teens. Since 1988, with the help of 2.5 million volunteers, Rebuilding Together affiliates have rehabilitated more than 100,000 homes across the nation.

Rebuilding Together is busy the rest of the year too. A major ongoing initiative is the Safe at Home program, which provides free home modifications to seniors. Safe at Home volunteers make safety improvements such as wheelchair ramps, wider doorways, handrails, grab bars in the bathroom, and better lighting.

TO VOLUNTEER for National Rebuilding Day or the Safe at Home project, contact:

Rebuilding Together / 1899 L Street NW, Suite 1000 / Washington, DC 20036 / (800) 473–4229 / www.rebuildingtogether.org

Establish a Community Wildlife Habitat

**I have adopted the technique of
living life miracle to miracle.**
—Artur Rubinstein

A community Wildlife Habitat is a locality that has agreed, in cooperation with the National Wildlife Federation (NWF), to provide habitats
for wildlife in places like parks, backyards, school grounds, and businesses.
The residents agree to provide the basic things that wildlife needs: food,
water, cover, and safe areas to raise young. A project team teaches the community about gardening for wildlife and helps them clean and maintain
the habitats. Not only is this good for the earth, but it's a great way to get
young and old out of doors, exercising and learning about nature.

ACTION STEPS

LOCAL: A project like this needs widespread community support, so
spend time developing contacts with a wide variety of interested people.
Neighborhood associations, schools, farmers' organizations, garden clubs,
birding clubs, senior centers, conservation groups, and garden centers are
good places to start. Help choose a team leader who has a love of wildlife
and the outdoors, plus strong leadership skills. A habitat team of four to
ten people should then be formed to move the project forward.

The team will survey the local area, asking such questions as: What
wildlife and habitats are there? Are any habitats threatened? What wildlife should we preserve or attract? What areas (such as parks or trails) do
people enjoy and support? What community resources can we draw upon?
With NWF guidance, your team will develop goals, a vision statement,
and an action plan. Then, you will register your project with the NWF
and be listed on its Web site. As your habitat develops, the NWF will
answer your questions and help you keep community participation high.

NATIONAL: For more information, visit the National Wildlife Federation Web site: www.nwf.org/community/index/cfm or call (800)
822–9919.

A Drop of Water

**The thirst after happiness is never
extinguished in the heart of man.**
—Jean-Jacques Rousseau

The problem is mind-boggling to us. We turn on the faucet without even thinking twice. Yet according to the United Nations, 884 million people lack access to safe drinking water, almost all in developing countries. More than 3.5 million die each year from water-related disease. Some 43 percent of those deaths are due to diarrhea, mostly children. Every fifteen seconds, a child dies from a water-related disease. Yet an American taking a five-minute shower uses more water than the typical person in a developing country slum uses in a day.

In 2005, Tracy Hawkins from Atlanta, Georgia, took a three-week volunteer trip to teach pottery in Tanzania, saw the impact of unsafe drinking water, and has used her influence, her background in industrial engineering, and corporate America to change how this basic of human needs is met.

Filter Pure, Inc., a nonprofit company, which Hawkins started with Lisa Ballantine and with the technical support of Professor Manny Hernandez, was launched in 2008. They have combined centuries-old know-how with modern-day technology—and that is the genius of their influence, which is currently serving so many in the Dominican Republic and Tanzania.

Unglazed clay pots trap parasites and bacteria as clean water drips through the clay's pores. A life changed, all for about $30 per pot! One clay pot provides clean water for a family for five years.

ACTION STEPS

➤ Next time you take a shower, think of how you can serve others—cut short the shower, donate to www.filterpurefilters.org.

➤ Go to www.water.org, committed exclusively to providing safe drinking water and sanitation to people in developing countries, for more ideas on how to use your influence to serve clean water to the world today.

Laughing Wholeheartedly

**Never trust a man who, when left alone in a
room with a tea cozy, doesn't try it on.**
—Billy Connolly, Scottish comedian and actor

Many people think that being fully compassionate leads inevitably to a
stern demeanor and grim expression as the gravity of human suffering bears down on one's soul. Nothing could be further from the truth.

Think of the people past and present we associate most with compassion—people such as Nelson Mandela, the Dalai Lama, Mohandas Ghandi, Eleanor Roosevelt. All are known for a rich sense of humor and a propensity to break into laughter at a moment's notice. They are the sort of people you would find with a tea cozy on their heads should you re-enter a room unexpectedly.

This is because humor is the appropriate response to the absurdity of life. Humor is much more than joke-telling and prank-playing; it is the way the compassionate can live with the enormity of human grief. Without a well-developed sense of humor, we are just tragic characters in a cruel play.

ACTION STEPS

➤ If you need a reminder of how humor and compassion are such important complements to each other, rent the 1989 tearjerker *Steel Magnolias*. Pay particular attention to the way Olympia Dukakis's character, Clairee Belcher, deals with the overwhelming grief of Sally Field's character, M'Lynn Eatenton, after the death of her daughter.

➤ Go over your own life, and gently dwell on a few of the most emotionally painful moments. Examine those times for moments of lunacy, absurdity, and humor. See what you can find.

➤ Laughter is ultimately the balm that will break suffering's hold on someone. The delicate skill of helping someone remember how to laugh is the mark of someone who is truly compassionate.

Music Heals

**Music is the language of the spirit. It opens the
secret of life bringing peace, abolishing strife.**
—Kahlil Gibran

Poverty-stricken children in Venezuela suffer. Some are arrested for rob-
bery, violence, and drug offenses. Others are put to work long before
they should and heed the siren call of gangs and alcohol. However, even in
this poor nation, there is hope. The Fundación del Estado para el Sistema
de Orquesta Juvenil e Infantil de Venezuela (*el sistema*) offers youngsters the
opportunity to learn an instrument and join one of 125 youth orchestras
throughout the country. *El sistema*'s secretary, Xavier Moreno, explains, "Our
first goal is not to create professional musicians. Our goal is to rescue the
children." Four hundred thousand youngsters have been touched so far. One
gangster became a clarinetist in the Caracas Youth Orchestra and a tutor
at the Simon Bolivar Conservatory. Another, at seventeen, is the youngest
double bass player ever to perform with the Berlin Philharmonic.

Toddlers are given instruments as soon as they can hold them. Tuition,
outings, music, and social support are free in return for the child's agreement to play in one of *el sistema*'s ensembles. In this atmosphere of encouragement, support, and enjoyment, astonishing successes emerge, including
that of Gustavo Dudamel, the fiery new conductor of the Los Angeles
Philharmonic. He is now seeking to establish youth-orchestra programs
throughout Los Angeles.

ACTION STEPS

➤ Contribute to the success of a music program that supports disadvantaged youngsters with your time and energy. If no youth orchestra
exists, can you help organize one? Go to Gustavo Dudamel's Web site,
www.gustavodudamel.com, to find out more about *el sistema*.

➤ Arts programs are under budgetary attack nationwide. Can you help
lift up young lives? See this inspiring example! www.youtube.com/
watch?v=u_tcE4rWovI.

Artisan Mentoring

In every art beginners must start with models of those who have practiced the same art before them. . . . It is a matter of being drawn into the individual work of art, of realizing that it has been made by a real human being, and trying to discover the secret of its creation.
—Ruth Whitman

Maintaining the skills necessary to create traditional crafts is important for the fabric of our society. It not only allows for culturally specific clothing to be worn and crafts to be seen, but also continues the skills that had previously been passed down from one generation to the next. In earlier times, apprentices learned artisan skills from master craftspersons. Yet in our ever-changing world, these skills are beginning to vanish as our lives become more technologically focused. Metalwork, embroidery, jewelry-making, pottery, and leather crafts are practiced by few instead of many.

If you possess these talents, you would be doing a great service to pass them along to a new generation of artisans. By donating your time and sharing your proficiencies, your skills will continue to be appreciated. It's important that you share not only the how of what you do, but the why. Make sure to pass on the deeper meanings of symbolic artwork or the practical backstory as to why certain items were necessary or popular. This way, your traditions will live on, as well as your craft.

GETTING STARTED: Your local library, high school, or community center might be interested in hosting an ongoing class or even a onetime event. Advertise with flyers in local gathering spots, and you'll be surprised at just how many people would love to learn your art. You might also consider creating two types of educational programs: one for adults and one for younger learners. And bone up on your history so that you'll be prepared for the most inquisitive minds.

Saint Nick Helps Out

Christmas, my child, is love in action. Every time we love, every time we give, it's Christmas.
—Dale Evans Rogers

On all 365 days of the year, volunteer Santas from Santa-America visit children with serious or terminal illnesses such as cancer, children who have been through severe traumas, and children whose parents are dying.

Santas are required to first volunteer at a local hospice or pediatric hospital, where they get specialized training in death and bereavement.

The average hospital or hospice visit with a child is about an hour, as compared to the usual one-minute visit with Santa at a mall—and is not just a single visit, but the beginning of a relationship that can last for years as Santa comes back to visit the child again and again. Santa brings a small gift for the child (and gifts for his or her siblings, who often feel forgotten), but, more important, they bring the children "the greatest gifts of all—love, joy, and hope," says Santa-America founder and president Ernest Berger (a jovial man with a thick white beard).

On one occasion, Santa Ernest visited a young boy who had witnessed his best friend's death during Hurricane Katrina and had not uttered a single word since. When the boy sat on Berger's lap, Santa Ernest said, "I am just here to tell you that I love you, the reindeer love you, all of the elves love you, and that you are a very special boy." The boy threw himself into Santa Ernest's arms and said, "Oh, Santa, I thought you and the reindeer were dead—I thought Katrina killed you!" The dam was broken, and the child was then able to start counseling.

Santa Ernest believes that the love and support of a Santa is so profound that it affects children not just emotionally but also physiologically, and there is currently a pilot clinical trial taking place to test this theory in children with cystic fibrosis.

All Santas are volunteers and Santa-America is funded solely by private donations.

VISIT www.santa-america.org.

BioBlitzing

**The natural world offers myriad forms of value
in education, exploration, aesthetic experience,
and irreplaceable products and services.**
—E. O. Wilson

Bring together an eclectic group of botanists, mycologists, ornitholo-gists, lichenologists, bacteriologists, herpetologists, entomologists, and icthyologists, add in a lot of enthusiastic volunteers, put them all together in a large park, and tell them to count every living thing they see over the next twenty-four hours. That's a BioBlitz—a complete inven-tory of all living organisms in a defined area, completed in one intense twenty-four-hour period.

A BioBlitz is a scientific endeavor, an outdoor classroom, and a commu-nity event all in one. The excitement builds as the number of species mounts and the clock ticks down. Often there's at least one big surprise—a rare spe-cies or one never before recorded in the area, for instance. Throughout the twenty-four hours, volunteers get to do real fieldwork alongside working scientists in a hands-on environment. Volunteers who don't like touching creepy-crawly things will still find plenty to do, starting with providing the endless pots of coffee needed to fuel a round-the-clock undertaking.

Organizing a BioBlitz is a major project, so they're usually put to-gether by a local, regional, or state environmental research organization, often in conjunction with a state park. The National Geographic Society has been sponsoring BioBlitzes at a different national park every year since 2006. Community groups, such as local Audubon societies, pitch in to help plan the event and recruit the many volunteers needed to make a twenty-four-hour marathon effort run smoothly. No one organization coordinates BioBlitzes, but BioBlitz central for information is the E. O. Wilson Biodiversity Foundation, created to honor the scientist who is the founding father of biodiversity research.

CONTACT the Foundation at:

E. O. Wilson Biodiversity Foundation / Hillsborough, NC 27278 / (919) 933–1195 / www.eowilson.org

Start a Socially-Conscious Investment Club

To accomplish great things, we must dream as well as act.
—Anatole France

"**S**ocially-conscious" investors choose companies that have high ethical standards, care for the environment, and/or provide benefits to society. They don't produce harmful or addictive products or promote violence in any form; and they treat their workers well. Although it would be difficult for individuals to screen for all these criteria on their own, there is now a wealth of information available on the Internet. Joining with other investors to share knowledge and experience may help some individuals who would like to invest more consciously but aren't sure how to go it alone.

ACTION STEPS

LOCAL: A good place to start is the online Green Money Journal: www.greenmoneyjournal.com. At www.domini.com, you will find a detailed database of the 400 companies in the Domini 400 Social Index. Ask if like-minded others would be interested in pooling research efforts and discussing their investment results. Your group might meet personally or be conducted entirely by e-mail.

Members of your group might choose to invest in socially-conscious mutual funds. This is the simplest route but eliminates the possibility of screening for all the ethical criteria you may have in mind. If some members of your group are willing to do the required research, they might want to invest in individual companies that meet their criteria.

Conventional wisdom said, in the past, that socially-conscious investors sacrificed some small degree of profit. However, long-term returns of the Domini 400 companies have shown that this is not always the case.

NATIONAL: American Association of Individual Investors, a nonprofit educational organization: www.aaii.com.

"Socially Conscious Investing Gets Results," from *Financial Advisor* magazine: www.fa-mag.com/component/content/article/1193.html?maga zineID=1&issue=59&Itemid=73.

The Influence of a Short, Extraordinary Life

Think gently, speak gently, live gently.
—Mattie Stepanek's motto

He inspired Jimmy Carter, Oprah Winfrey, Dr. Maya Angelou, and millions of others with his poetry, his strength of character, and his fight to live life to the fullest in the face of daily adversity—he was Mattie Stepanek and he lived a short but wondrous life.

Mattie suffered from dysautomatic mitochondrial myopathy, a rare form of muscular dystrophy. He published several bestselling books of poetry. Yet, Mattie had even bigger dreams—specifically, the dream of global peace. He wanted to be remembered as a poet, peacemaker, and philosopher, who played.

The essence of Mattie's influence was to live his life with great optimism and great dreams—regardless of his physical challenges. His life philosophy was to "remember to play after every storm." His influence plays on.

ACTION STEPS

➤ Visit the Matt J. T. Stepanek Park, dedicated in 2008 in Rockville, Maryland. A twenty-six-acre recreational facility with an accessible playground and a Peace Garden dedicated to all children.

➤ Go to Three Dot Dash (www.threedotdash.org), an international initiative to spread the message of global peace through young people, directly influenced by Mattie's efforts for young people to spread global peace. The moniker of Three Dot Dash comes from the Morse telegraph signaling for peace. Young people across the globe know their universal hand signal for peace. It's simple—three center fingers on the left hand extended (for three dot) and the pointer finger on the right extended perpendicular to the left (for dash).

➤ Honor a young hero in your life. Encourage him or her to write a poem like Mattie did about the hope for global peace.

When in Rome

**Americans who travel abroad for the first time
are often shocked to discover that, despite all the
progress that has been made in the last 30 years,
many foreign people still speak in foreign languages.**
—Dave Barry

Americans have a terrible reputation in much of the world as being highly inconsiderate travelers. That's because many of us mutter ungraciously when we find that no one speaks English. We gripe that there is slow or no table service. The high prices in a strange currency make us think everyone is trying to rip us off. And we don't embrace differences, such as the fact that things are smaller (cars, hotel rooms, food portions). Instead, we make it known how much better things are in the United States.

Imagine how this comes across to residents of foreign lands—they see loud, rude, overweight people wearing funny shoes and baseball caps. However, someone who travels with the tenets of compassion in mind has a much better experience and leaves behind a much better impression.

ACTION STEPS

➤ Recognize that you are a guest in someone's home. Just because you've paid money to be there doesn't give you license to be disrespectful. Continually ask yourself how you would want guests in your home to act.

➤ Americans abroad often speak complaints loudly and praises softly. The order of this should be reversed.

➤ Compassionate travelers embrace cultural differences when they travel. It's important to observe and experience, rather than expect things to be as they are at home.

➤ Leave behind a little legacy. Find a way to contribute to the country you've been a guest in. Make a donation to a local effort. If you've brought clothes or gear for the trip that you won't use at home, find a needy place for them.

Support Our Troops

**The soldier above all others prays for peace,
for it is the soldier who must suffer and bear
the deepest wounds and scars of war.**
—General Douglas MacArthur

While some may disagree with the politics that have embroiled our country in wars, the fact remains that our men and women in the armed services are facing danger daily in alien lands far from home. Many are lonely and without contacts. They receive no letters or packages from loved ones. Perhaps you have thought about showing our troops some support but you didn't know how. AdoptaPlatoon can help you do so.

Founded in 1998 by a mother whose son was stationed in Bosnia, AdoptaPlatoon is a volunteer organization dedicated to ensuring that soldiers are not forgotten. The organization sends more than thirty thousand letters and cards to our troops every month. They also mail care packages with baby wipes, socks, hygiene items, toothpaste, toothbrushes, candy, cookies, beef jerky, sunscreen, and other comfort supplies that improve the morale of our troops serving far from home. You may not know that soldiers must purchase these items themselves at a PX, and that can be challenging when they're deployed in the Iraqi desert or the wilds of Afghanistan. In 2007, AdoptaPlatoon supported more than 175,000 service members. The organization also supports chaplains, field hospitals, and morale tents.

ACTION STEPS

➤ Contact AdoptaPlatoon at www.adoptaplatoon.org or P.O. Box 5038, Hagerstown, MD 21741–5038 to help show your support for our troops. You can adopt a troop by promising to send one letter and care package a month or get involved in bringing holiday cheer.

➤ Who in your life are fighting their own battles? What letter or "care" package might you give them that would help them feel supported and loved?

Host an Exchange Student

Our true nationality is mankind.
—H. G. Wells

Hosting an international exchange student is a wonderful experience. While you are hosting a student, you are exposing yourself, your family, and your social network to the culture and customs of a different country. At the same time, you are sharing not only your own set of morals and values, but the values we share as a nation. As a hosting family, you would be acting as a responsible representative, almost a goodwill ambassador. The individual interactions you have with your student can make a lasting impression when he or she returns home and shares with friends and family all the positive things that are happening in our country.

The Council on International Educational Exchange is one of many organizations approved by the United Nations that has been placing international students with American families for over sixty years. They service 1,300 exchange students a year. You will be providing a home for one of these students for either five or ten months while he or she attends your local high school.

While there are a variety of programs to choose from, the United Nations believes that the concept of exchange students has not been fully realized. Exchanges between countries in the Northern Hemisphere and Southern Hemisphere are limited. Few students from the developing world come to the United States. When choosing a program, think about how your family may be able to influence a young person who can impact the changing nature of the world.

GETTING STARTED: Contact the Council on International Educational Exchange: www.ciee.org, (800) 40–STUDY (407–8839), or the Center for Cultural Interchange: www.cci-exchange.com, (800) 634–4771. Then get the house ready: you'll need to provide a bedroom and study space for your exchange student. They are usually allowed to share a room with same-sex children if necessary.

Princess for a Day

No act of kindness, no matter how small, is ever wasted.
—Aesop

In early 2002 Laney Whitcanack and Kristen Smith Knutson were working at a nonprofit when a girl who had been part of their youth program dropped by say hello. Since the girl was a high-school senior, they started talking about the prom, and the girl, who was a recent immigrant to the United States, said, "I'd love to go, but I can't. The dresses are just too expensive."

Laney and Kristen knew they had friends who had closets filled with unwanted bridesmaid's dresses and formalwear, so they put out an e-mail to twenty people asking if anyone would be willing to donate a dress. That e-mail went viral and got forwarded from friend to friend. Within days, Laney and Kristen had five hundred responses from women willing to donate dresses! The Princess Project was born.

The Princess Project now gives prom dresses free of charge to thousands of young women a year who otherwise would be unable to attend. The girls get one dress and one accessory, such as a necklace, handbag, or wrap. They can bring one person (a mother or female friend) to help them choose a dress and do not have to prove financial need. "The girl that we originally wanted to help trusted us enough to confide that she couldn't afford a dress, so we in turn trust the girls," says Whitcanack.

The Princess Project has dresses available from size 2 to size 36. "The Princess Project is about giving girls the opportunity to feel really good about themselves and their bodies," says Whitcanack. "We want them to celebrate with confidence and style no matter what their shape or size."

Twenty-five dollars can make a girl feel like a princess and send her to the prom with a new or nearly new dress. One hundred dollars can send three friends along with her. The Princess Project also accepts dress donations.

VISIT www.princessproject.org.

Be a Docent

**In a completely rational society, the best
of us would be teachers and the rest of us
would have to settle for something else.**
—Lee Iacocca

A docent is a guide at a museum, gallery, or historical site—even a zoo. The word comes from the Latin *docere,* to instruct or tutor, and that's what a docent does—he or she helps you understand and learn from what you're seeing. Docents help bring art and history alive. At almost any cultural or historic site, these volunteers are on hand to lead tours, give gallery talks, and answer questions. And in an age of diminished budgets and hiring freezes, volunteer docents are crucial for helping cultural sites keep their doors open without cutting back on hours.

Docents are almost always local volunteers. Knowledge of the subject area isn't the primary requirement, though it certainly helps to be interested. Just as important are enthusiasm, the patience to answer the same questions over and over, being able to project your voice to a large tour group, and stamina—you're on your feet for a good part of the day. Being a bit of a ham also helps, especially if you're a docent at a historic site and need to dress in period costume and demonstrate crafts.

The education mission at museums, zoos, and historic sites is taken very seriously, and docents often lead educational programs on site, in local schools, and at community events.

THE FIRST STEP toward becoming a docent is finding an area, such as local history, that interests you. The next step is tracking down a relevant and nearby museum or historic site and asking to speak to the volunteer coordinator or the director. Once you're accepted as a docent, you'll need to spend time learning everything you can about your assignment before you can start leading tours. Don't want to be a docent but still love museums? There's plenty of other volunteer work available. You could collect entrance fees, staff the information booth, or work in conservation and archives—discuss the service possibilities with the volunteer coordinator.

Don't Waste Clothes Your Family No Longer Wants

Give what you have. To someone, it may be better than you dare to think.
—Henry Wadsworth Longfellow

Globalization has made clothing so cheap that many Americans now see it as disposable. But the price, in terms of pollution and harm to workers, is much higher than it seems. What do you do with clothes that are outgrown, no longer in fashion, or a bit faded?

The U.S. Environmental Protection Agency estimates that, on average, each American discards over sixty-eight pounds of clothing per year. These items clog landfills, and the constant demand for new products strains the earth's resources.

ACTION STEPS

LOCAL: Teach your family that newer is not necessarily better, and that your family's values do not include being "fashionable" at all times. Prove this by your own example: mend, restyle, share, or donate your used clothing. Dispose of items you no longer want at swap meets, garage sales, and flea markets. Better yet, start your own! Profits can be used to support the PTA or community organizations. Post notices on local bulletin boards. Ask your favorite charity to participate in exchange for a share of the profits.

NATIONAL/INTERNATIONAL: In addition to well-known national organizations like Goodwill Industries and the Salvation Army, there are other charities that will reuse your old clothing in unusual ways. For instance, you can donate old athletic shoes to Nike to be recycled into playing-field surfaces: www.nikereuseashoe.com. The Women's Alliance helps women who are looking for work by providing them with recycled business attire: www.thewomensalliance.org.

For tips on giving clothing to charities, go to the U.S. Better Business Bureau at www.bbb.org/us/donating-used-clothes-and-household-items.

I Recommend This Person: The Influence of a Personal Reference

Who shall set a limit to the influence of a human being?
—Ralph Waldo Emerson

When you agree or offer to write a reference, you serve the goals, dreams, and aspirations of another. You are contributing to a person's future, his success. You are using your experience with this person to acquaint another with his best qualities.

A heartfelt, extraordinary reference can change someone's life. A mediocre or rote one can ruin her chance to change her life by causing a potential employer to question the applicant's abilities or dedication. It is essential that you agree to give a reference only when you can enthusiastically describe the qualities of another.

You can serve another's future and honor the role you are playing in his life by understanding what the goals of the person asking for the referenced are—and by being specific in your reference about the qualities that speak to those goals. Take your time and ask the person requesting a reference to outline what he sees as his specific achievements in and out of work, and enrich your reference with details and anecdotes. Your recommendation should speak of his talent, drive, and outstanding abilities. Your enthusiasm in giving the reference will be one of the most generous influences you can give.

ACTION STEPS

➤ For practice, write a reference for yourself. Pay attention to the details and descriptions you provide that illustrate that you are the ideal candidate. A reference written for another person deserves even more care than the one you wrote for yourself.

➤ Pay it forward. Offer to give a reference for a first-time job seeker. Make a call to a colleague or to a former college roommate, and secure an interview for someone coming up the ladder.

Fools Rush In

You will do foolish things, but do them with enthusiasm.
—Colette, French novelist

Each year the Darwin Awards celebrate those who "do a service to humanity by removing themselves from the gene pool." These so-called awards are bestowed on people who, generally through remarkably stupid acts, end up dead or rendered sterile. You can well imagine that you don't want to be on the receiving end of one.

The awards are meant to be morbidly funny, and they often are. But they should not be read without also realizing one very important thing: there but for the grace of God go we.

We nonwinners are also frequently guilty of stupid acts, whether it's hitting on a supervisor at an office party or licking an ice-cold piece of metal (who among us hasn't tried this at least once?). Because of luck or grace or Kevlar underwear, we just didn't end up dead or neutered. Having compassion for the foolish and the reckless means that we recognize in ourselves the same tendency.

ACTION STEPS

➤ Be the first person to reach out to someone who has done something dumb and embarrassing. Others may be laughing at him or her but don't allow yourself to be one of them.

➤ Confide to him or her a time when you did something even more embarrassing. The aim is to get both of you laughing.

➤ Every once in a while, do something deliberately foolish (but safe) to get it out of your system. Strap on a parachute and jump out of a plane, meet an ex-boyfriend for lunch, tell your boss what you really think of an idea. This will give you the heady excitement that fuels so many unplanned foolish acts.

Paradoxical Support

**The most exquisite paradox . . . as soon as you give it
all up, you can have it all. As long as you want power,
you can't have it. The minute you don't want power,
you'll have more than you ever dreamed possible.**
—Ram Dass

The Buddha was teaching his followers and students. He held a bird
in his outstretched palm. Members of the assembled group tried to
mimic his feat, yet each time one of them tried to hold the bird, it flew
away. Intrigued, one of the students asked the sage how he had managed
when they had all failed. "Each of us needs a platform from which to
take off," the Buddha replied. "I drop my hand each time the bird makes
a move to fly away."

Sometimes you provide support by stepping aside. For a child to learn
to ride a bicycle, you must let go and allow her to struggle with balance
and motion. You must allow her to fall and recover, to fall again and finally get the hang of it. This is a paradoxical kind of support—support
characterized by its absence. Think of a basketball team rushing to the
hoop. One member provides an assist, then moves out of the way to give
his teammate a chance to tip in the ball and score. Sometimes support
means doing nothing, but allowing the other to come forward to fulfill
her own potential.

ACTION STEPS

➤ Think about whether there is someone at work whom you could pas-
sively mentor. How might you step aside to allow your co-worker to
shine in her own right? How might this add to the company's bottom
line and prestige?

➤ What might you do to support your child in becoming more independent? Do you keep dropping your hand so he has no platform from
which to fly or do you hold steady to give him a surface from which
to push away?

Help Interfaith Couples Prepare for Marriage

**The goal in marriage is not to think
alike, but to think together.**
—Robert C. Dodds

Many religious groups offer engaged couples their own version of marriage-preparation classes, which can include weekend retreats or the opportunity to speak frankly with a pastor, priest, or rabbi. However, interfaith couples cannot always participate in these types of conversations, especially if their faiths do not condone a marriage outside of their religion. Often, these couples have nowhere to turn for answers to their most pressing questions, which can include how to raise children to accept two religions, how to create a spiritual home, how to deal with questions from relatives, or how to continue to practice their individual faiths without offending their partner.

If you are currently in a positive, loving interfaith marriage or are the child of an interfaith marriage, you can lend your life-experience expertise to couples looking for guidance. Talking through the issues that an interfaith couple may face can lessen some of their anxiety, as well as the opportunity to provide real answers to some very tough questions. Simply knowing that there is an available resource is all that some couples may need. Most important, you will be showing others that they are not alone on their journey, that others have made the same decisions and have thrived.

GETTING STARTED: There are myriad resources on the Internet and in libraries that discuss the particular issues of different interfaith marriage combinations. You can add your experiences to this collection by creating a blog or personal Web site. Or, contact the most liberal denomination of your religious affiliation and offer your services through them.

Host an interfaith dinner party. Invite newly engaged interfaith couples to dine with your family, then share how you've made your marriage work within the context of religion. You can also invite local religious leaders or representatives from various places of worship, so that they can invite these new couples into their communities.

The Power of Education

**Wars against nations are fought to change maps;
wars against poverty are fought to map change.**
—Muhammad Ali

A woman in Africa gets up before dawn and walks for three miles to get water. She returns home with the water, then goes to work in the fields, all the while caring for her children. In the evening, she prepares, serves, and clears up dinner.

This is the daily reality for most women living in sub-Saharan Africa—sixteen-hour-plus days of backbreaking work. Women farm at least 80 percent of the food eaten by their families. And yet most have no voice in their communities. They often cannot own or inherit property or get loans to buy seeds to grow bigger crops, and agricultural workers provided by the government will not work with them to teach them better farming techniques—they will only work with men.

The Hunger Project is a global, nonprofit, strategic organization committed to the sustainable end of world hunger, with a focus on empowering and educating women. The Hunger Project does not give out food. Instead, it helps people—especially women—to get and keep all the tools they need to feed themselves and their families.

Commonly, when a woman in the developing world has extra money, she will spend it on her children, buying food and getting them healthcare. Education is the best way to help her earn this extra money. Even simply teaching a woman how to count can benefit her so she does not get shortchanged when she sells her food. For this reason, the Hunger Project supports literacy education, numeracy training, and training in animal husbandry, such as raising chickens.

The Hunger Project's programs have reached an estimated 35 million people. Every donation helps them teach women from around the world to become self-reliant and offers them perhaps their only hope of lifting themselves and their families out of abject poverty.

VISIT www.thp.org.

RSVP

**Sooner or later I'm going to die,
but I'm not going to retire.**
—Margaret Mead

RSVP stands for Retired Senior Volunteer Program, the largest volunteer network for people aged fifty-five and up. Sign up for RSVP, and you join forces with nearly half a million other active volunteers.

Just because RSVP volunteers are older doesn't mean they take it easy. Instead, they very deliberately choose to tackle some of the toughest issues in their communities. Some RSVP members in New York City, for instance, work through mentoring programs to help prisoners maintain meaningful ties with their families. Others help released prisoners reenter ordinary life through a criminal-record-repair counseling program, which helps them understand and manage their criminal histories as they seek employment and housing. The prisoner-aid programs that RSVP members created in New York have become models nationwide.

RSVP volunteer slots are meant to provide meaningful, invigorating opportunities for older adults while also helping nonprofit organizations reach more clients and provide more services. As an RSVP volunteer, you can opt for work that's as demanding as you want it to be. The program offers a full range of volunteer opportunities through partnerships with thousands of local and national organizations. You choose where you want to work, what you want to do, and how much time you want to give. You also have the option of drawing on the lifetime and professional skills you already have, or of learning entirely new ones. Not surprisingly, many RSVP volunteers do both—you could learn new cooking or baking skills at a soup kitchen, while also using your professional accounting skills to keep the organization's books. Your work in both areas will be greatly appreciated.

TO FIND an RSVP program that needs you, contact:

Senior Corps/RSVP / 1201 New York Avenue NW / Washington, DC 20525 / (202) 606–5000 / www.seniorcorps.org

Reduce Wasteful
Bottled-Water Consumption

Tomorrow is the most important thing in life. . . . It's perfect when it arrives and it puts itself in our hands. It hopes we've learned something from yesterday.
—John Wayne

Many people believe that bottled water is safer than tap water. Yet studies show that from 25 to 40 percent of all bottled water is simply processed from municipal sources. Just because water comes in a bottle does not mean it is healthier. In fact, bottled water is legally allowed to have more contaminants than tap water, which is more carefully monitored and regulated than the bottled kind. Over 90 percent of water systems in the United States meet EPA tap-water quality standards.

Manufacturing all those bottles is bad for the earth too. According to the Pacific Institute, making over 30 billion plastic water bottles in 2006 used over 17 million barrels of oil and produced more than 2.5 million tons of carbon dioxide.

ACTION STEPS

LOCAL: Tell everyone you know that you intend to stop using bottled water. Send others interested in making this choice to the Responsible Purchasing Network Web site's Guide to Bottled Water: www.responsible purchasing.org/purchasing_guides/bottled_water.

Ask your local government to stop wasting taxpayer resources on bottled water. Direct your mayor's office to the Corporate Accountability International's "Think Outside the Bottle" campaign: www.stopcorporate abuse.org/content/think-outside-bottle-campaign-overview.

NATIONAL: Check out the Center for the New American Dream Web site (www.newdream.org). They are campaigning for everyone in the United States to "Break the Bottled Water Habit" by utilizing reusable water bottles instead.

Housing Hope: One Bicyclist's Influence

Well into the twenty-first century, if the best our advanced society can do for the hundreds of thousands of homeless human beings . . . men, women and children . . . who live among us is the cast-off box our refrigerator came in, what exactly does that say about us?
—Peter Samuelson on www.edar.org

He was riding his bicycle from Westwood to Santa Monica. There was something different. More homeless. He counted. Sixty-two homeless people, including many women and several children.

This bicyclist, Peter Samuelson, a Hollywood producer and philanthropist, began talking with these men and women, interviewing them about one of the basic needs of every human being: shelter.

The genius of his influence is how he responded to their homelessness. He worked with a local college, the Pasadena Art Center College of Design, to sponsor a design competition to invent a low-cost minimal sleeping space, an alternative to the cardboard box. His passion and creativity invested the college students in devising a new temporary shelter.

The winning design is the EDAR unit, which stands for Everyone Deserves a Roof, a seven-foot-long tent suspended inches off the ground, which converts to a covered shopping cart where one can keep belongings.

Peter Samuelson's influence has started a revolution in hope for the homeless, and the genius of his creative influence has inspired us all.

ACTION STEPS

➤ EDAR is a nonprofit organization that works nationally with shelter organizations dedicated to the homeless to distribute the units free of charge. All involved understand that this is not an alternative to permanent housing. To learn more, visit: www.edar.org.

➤ Is there a problem in your community to which you can apply the ingenuity of college students? Go to your local college, outline the issue, and draw on their can-do spirit to help solve the problem. Create a contest and offer a prize.

Animals Other Than Human

**All the arguments to prove man's superiority
cannot shatter this hard fact: in suffering
the animals are our equals.**
—Peter Singer

One of the oldest religions in the world, yet one that few outside of India have heard about, is called Jainism. One of its central beliefs is that all life is sacred, not just the life that happens to find itself in human form. It's not uncommon to find animal hospitals and shelters run by Jains across India. Jains, not surprisingly, are vegetarians. Some of the most devout go to extreme lengths to avoid harming animals, even to the point of stepping carefully to avoid ground-dwelling insects and wearing cloths over their mouths to avoid killing flies by inadvertently inhaling them.

While it may be hard to accept that all tenets of Jainism are necessary or realistic, it's obvious that we humans could do a better job of extending compassion beyond our own species. On this earth, animals eat animals, and nature's food chain can seem to be cruel. But we have a choice. We have the ability to reduce suffering where we can, simply because nothing deserves to feel unnecessary pain or fear.

ACTION STEPS

➤ Most of us eat too much meat. But most of us would eat less if we truly took into consideration the suffering caused by our desire for yet another burger. You don't have to become a vegetarian, but consider going meatless one day to bring awareness to how much meat you are consuming. Think compassionately about the animals connected to the meat choices that you've given up for the day.

➤ When you do eat meat, try to buy from local markets, and avoid large factory-farmed meats where the living conditions for the animals can be horrific.

➤ Always give recognition that something died so that you may live when you eat animal products. It should not go unnoticed.

No Baby in the House

**A new baby is like the beginning of all things—
wonder, hope, a dream of possibilities.**
—Eda J. LeShan, psychologist

The arrival of an infant represents anticipation for the future and the joys it may bring. But what if that child is stillborn or dies during its first year? Dreams, hopes, and expectations die too. The sorrow experienced by the family is immeasurable. The loss unimaginable. The hurt inconsolable.

Often, friends and loved ones, not knowing what to say, avoid the grieving family, leaving them to their lonely suffering. Others blurt homilies they think will help—"It wasn't in God's plan." "You'll have another baby." "This was for the best."—but these hurt more. More than 70 percent of women report suicidal thoughts after the death of their baby. Often families don't know where to turn for help with coping.

The MISS Foundation is a volunteer-based organization committed to providing crisis support and long-term aid to families after the death of a child. Among other services, it provides immediate, ongoing support groups to grieving families. "A community of sorrow is the strongest community of all," says MISS Foundation founder Joanne Cacciatore. The organization helps keep grieving families connected, not only to one another, but also to a larger community. This safeguards against negative coping. Eventually, members not only return to a prior level of functioning, but many transcend grief to create a legacy to their lost child.

ACTION STEPS

➤ Have you ever lost a child or experienced a miscarriage? What kind of support did you need? What kind did you receive? Think back to a situation in which a friend or relative lost a child. How did you respond? How could you have been more supportive?

➤ If you know someone who could benefit from being in touch with the MISS Foundation, share the Web site: www.missfoundation.org. E-mail address: info@missfoundation.org. Phone: (623) 979–1000.

Inner-City Outings

**In every walk with nature one receives
far more than he seeks.**
—John Muir

The plights of inner-city kids remain constant: their concrete jungle cannot provide the respite from the cruelness of the world that nature can. Organizations like the Fresh Air Fund can take kids out of the city for weeks at a time. But what can you do for just one day to make a difference?

Inner City Outings (ICO) is part of the Sierra Club, an organization whose mission is to create environmental conscientiousness. This particular program focuses on educating youth from urban communities who have limited access to nature. It's hard to imagine that even today many of the kids this organization services have never been outside their neighborhoods. In fifty different cities in the United States, ICO volunteers lead more than twelve thousand young people a year on day trips into the wilderness.

These outings positively impact the kids on many levels. They instill a love of nature as well as greater self-esteem. Many ICO participants credit the program with helping them to succeed in school long after their day in the wilderness is over, as they face new challenges and learn to see the world in a different light.

As an ICO volunteer, you will accompany a group of kids on a day hike to local wilderness areas. Depending on your location, you might bicycle, backpack, camp, canoe, kayak, cross-country ski, river raft, or perform environmental service projects. ICO volunteers also work with schools, community agencies, youth groups, and rehabilitation centers to recruit participants from their local neighborhoods. By participating in the program, you will be opening the hearts and minds of today's young people to the beauty and wonder of nature.

GETTING STARTED: Visit the Sierra Club Web site, www.sierraclub .org/ico, to find the ICO program closest to you. The Web site is organized by U.S. regions. You can also contact youth groups in your area to see if they would be interested in participating in an ICO program.

Go Green by Living Blue

We cannot command nature except by obeying her.
—Francis Bacon

The vast majority of the surface of our planet is a beautiful and wild landscape of unchartered terrain, with underwater mountains higher than the Alps and canyons deeper than the Grand Canyon. Covering more than 70 percent of our planet, the oceans are connected to all that keeps us alive: the food we eat, the water we drink, and the air we breathe.

The ocean is the lifeblood of our planet, and we cannot be healthy if it is not healthy. Ocean Conservancy is committed to restoring and maintaining the health of both the ocean and the creatures within it. Among many other things, Ocean Conservancy:

➤ **ADVOCATES FOR MARINE WILDLIFE**

Ocean Conservancy works with fishermen to save hundreds of sea turtles, whales, sharks, and other vulnerable marine animals.

➤ **CLEANS UP THE BEACHES**

This year Ocean Conservancy led 400,000 volunteers in 104 countries to remove 6.8 million pounds of trash from beaches.

➤ **IMPROVES FISHING POLICIES**

One million tons of seafood feed the world each year, and species like tuna and swordfish have been depleted in the wild by 90 percent. Ocean Conservatory works with fishery-management councils to combat overfishing.

➤ **PROTECTS OUR NATURAL TREASURES**

While 12 percent of the land on Earth has been set aside as parks, wildlife refuges, and wilderness areas, less than 1 percent of the ocean has been similarly protected. Ocean Conservancy lobbies for lasting protection of our most precious underwater treasures.

The ocean belongs to all of us—and is the responsibility of us all.

VISIT www.oceanconservancy.org to help fight on behalf of the ocean.

Plant a Row for the Hungry

I used to visit and revisit it a dozen times a day, and stand in deep contemplation over my vegetable progeny with a love that nobody could share or conceive of who had never taken part in the process of creation.
—Nathaniel Hawthorne

As you're standing knee-deep in tomatoes and zucchini in your vegetable garden, wondering how you can possibly use all that abundance, remember that one in ten households in America experiences hunger or the risk of hunger daily.

The simplest way is to donate your harvest directly to a local food bank, soup kitchen, or service organization. That's fine if there happens to be a good cause close by, if you happen to have the time to get your produce there on a regular basis, and if you have enough to make a dent in the needs of the local food organization. If not, there's a good solution: participate in your local Plant a Row for the Hungry program.

This grassroots program, founded and sponsored by the Garden Writers Association Foundation, counts on the fact that there are more than 70 million enthusiastic home gardeners in the United States. If every one of those gardeners volunteered to plant just one extra row of vegetables and get it to a local food organization, the impact on reducing hunger would be huge. Agencies could take the money they budget for fresh produce and spend it elsewhere—and hungry people would get delicious fresh vegetables to add to their diets.

Plant a Row for the Hungry provides direction and support to volunteers growing food at the local level. Members coordinate collecting and delivering the produce. In fifteen years of service, volunteers and gardeners grew, gathered, and delivered over 14 million pounds of produce. That's a lot of tomatoes for a lot of hungry people.

TO LEARN how you can grow a row, contact:

Garden Writers Association Foundation / 10210 Leatherleaf Court / Manassas, VA 20111 / (877) 492–2727 / www.gardenwriters.org

Adopt a Road

**Every single life becomes great when the individual
sets upon a goal or goals which they really believe in,
which they can really commit themselves to, which
they can put their whole heart and soul into.**
—Brian Tracy, author/motivational speaker

Nothing can spoil a beautiful drive like piles of litter. Messy roadways are bad for tourism and local business. Knowing this, many states now sponsor Adopt-A-Road (or Adopt-A-Highway) programs in urban and rural areas. Thousands of people volunteer through community groups to keep stretches of roads free of trash. Sometimes they also maintain vegetation, mow roadsides, even plant flowers. It's a great way to get outdoor exercise, make friends, and help your community.

ACTION STEPS

LOCAL: Find out who sponsors Adopt-A-Road programs in your area by contacting your state's Department of Transportation. Talk to the volunteer coordinator, if there is one. Ask if teenagers can participate with adult supervision. The local government generally holds safety training sessions for the crew and picks up bagged debris, but get the details. Find out what skills are needed and whether protective clothing will be supplied. Ask what insurance coverage, if any, is provided. Then approach people at your workplace or community group and explain that your business or organization will benefit from free publicity: a sign by the roadside with their name, visible to a large number of people. Often, the volunteers get to keep any recyclables found, which can be a source of revenue to the group.

NATIONAL: To learn how some states operate Adopt a Highway programs, visit: **TEXAS**: www.dot.state.tx.us/trv/aah/history.htm • **PENNSYLVANIA**: www.dot.state.pa.us/Internet/Bureaus/pdHwyBeau. nsf/infoAdoptHighway?readform • **MICHIGAN**: www.michigan.gov/ mdot/0,1607,7–151–9621_11041_14408——,00.html

Never Too Old

You're never too old to grow young.
—Mae West

"**A**nyone can get old. All you have to do is live long enough," remarked Groucho Marx. But to grow old and still see each day in all its wonder is to live a life that influences others in its sense of possibility.

You're never too old to experience the new. And you're never too old to start giving of yourself. The Mayo Clinic reports that older people who serve others have lower rates of heart disease and live longer than their peers who do not.

"For the ignorant, old age is winter; for the learned, it is the harvest," is a classic Jewish saying. For all of us to look ahead and think growing older is a beginning, a time to start reaping what we have sown all our life, to share our bounty of knowledge and experience, to plant new ideas in ourselves and the next generation—that is bountiful joy, that is the influence of life well-served.

And as you are imagining an influential future, remember Yogi Berra's saying, "The future ain't what it used to be," and live an influential life in service to others right now. The future is now.

ACTION STEPS

➤ Draft your own eulogy. Make it poignant and funny and real. Use it as a roadmap for how you want to act, serve others, and so be remembered from here on.

➤ Plan a roast for yourself. Let others share in the joy of your life. Let them expound on your foibles and your milestones. Make it fun. Outlandish even. Use your roast to share with others what it means to live a full and joyful and meaningful life.

➤ Write letters. Age carries authority, and letters from older, wiser people exert timeless influence. A thoughtful letter from you to a much younger person showing appreciation or affirming positive qualities in them will help them value even more deeply the good they are capable of.

81

A Welcoming Table

Be not forgetful to entertain strangers, for thereby some have entertained angels unawares.
—Hebrews 13:2

In Judaism, there is a lovely practice called setting a place for Elijah. Traditionally, an extra table setting is laid out at Passover for Elijah, the prophet whose return is supposed to precede that of the Messiah. It began as a way to welcome Elijah into people's homes. Mischievous fathers have been known to rattle the empty plates a little from under the table to create a little drama for their children that Elijah might be appearing.

Less traditionally, the practice of setting a place for Elijah has been modified by some Jews and non-Jews alike to symbolize that their family homes are always open to unseen guests. And making a place for others serves as a reminder to the whole family that there is always something to share for those in need.

Other families set a place in honor of those relatives and friends who have moved far away. For them, the place setting symbolizes that those people are never really far away and that a meal is waiting for them any time they walk through the door. For still others, it's a way of marking the anniversary of a loved one's death and of showing that that person will always be a part of their lives.

It's easy to use this powerful ritual at your table so that it reminds your family of the importance of compassion.

ACTION STEPS

➤ Designate one night a week as Elijah's night. Set an extra place setting. When everyone is seated, give thanks for the plenty you have and for the ability to share it with others.

➤ Designate one night a month to invite someone to share a meal with your family. Perhaps it's a single co-worker. Or someone new to town. Or a lonely neighbor. Elijah himself would smile at his place being used in such a kind way.

Help a Child Feel Normal Again

**They sat and combed their beautiful hair
Their long, bright tresses, one by one.**
—Nora Perry, American poet, "After the Ball"

Imagine the pain and embarrassment of a young girl who is permanently bald due to the medical condition alopecia areata, which has no known cause or cure, or for other medical reasons. Imagine that her family is too poor to afford a wig of human hair made to fit her small head. She withdraws from childhood activities such as swimming, going to the mall, or playing with friends, fearing someone will discover her secret.

Now, imagine supporting this young girl in feeling whole again.

Locks of Love is a nonprofit organization that provides hairpieces to financially disadvantaged children suffering from long-term medical hair loss. It meets a unique need by using donated ponytails (6–10 per hairpiece) to create the highest-quality, custom-made hair prosthetics. Due to a vacuum seal, these hairpieces stay put, diminishing fears about classmates pulling them off. Kids can swim, shower, and do gymnastics. Each prosthetic arrives long, so recipients may style them to fit their faces.

The hairpieces help restore the children's self-esteem, sense of normalcy, and confidence, enabling them to face the world and their friends. They usually retail for between $3,500 and $6,000, but needy children receive them free or on a sliding scale, based on financial need.

ACTION STEPS

➤ You may donate a ponytail or nominate a child who needs a wig but can't afford one. For instructions, contact:

Locks of Love / 234 Southern Boulevard / West Palm Beach, FL 33405 / (561) 833–7332 / www.locksoflove.org / E-mail: info@locksoflove.org

➤ Start a fund-raiser for this organization. E-mail: volunteer@locksoflove.org. In addition to providing free hairpieces, Locks of Love has awarded $500,000 to the University of Miami Department of Dermatology to fund research into alopecia areata.

Be a Running Partner

There is no greater challenge than to have someone relying upon you; no greater satisfaction than to vindicate his expectation.
—Kingman Brewster, former president of Yale University

First-time marathon runners know that they can't do it alone. These races require months of physical and mental training. If you are a runner who has completed this ultimate goal, you can help others looking to achieve it for themselves.

Marathons are tremendous events that offer many different opportunities for you to volunteer your services, either for someone specific or for the larger running community. First-time marathon runners will have an easier time if they know there is someone at the race, supporting them. Marathon courses are lined with friends and family, or even complete strangers, who cheer on all the runners, literally encouraging them to run that extra mile. They hand out cups of water, small bits of easily digestible foods, or simply express their excitement and good wishes.

If you are a marathon runner, you can help train others as you prepare for your race. You can help local runners by sharing your training techniques and knowledge of the race. You will be teaching newbies how to prepare for the race, including creating an exercise routine and eating plan. More important, you can share your experiences so that they will better understand what to expect and how to handle adversity.

However you decide to volunteer your time, you will experience immense pride when those you've worked with cross the finish line. You will have the unique satisfaction of knowing that you helped someone during an extraordinary journey.

GETTING STARTED: Simply attend a marathon and cheer on the runners. If you are training for one, contact your local running club to see if they will allow you to offer your services as a running partner. Many running clubs across the United States will connect runners over the Internet by hosting bulletin boards.

Throwing a Lifeline to a Stranger

**Never be bullied into silence. Never allow
yourself to be made a victim. Accept no one's
definition of your life; define yourself.**
—Harvey Fierstein

A sixteen-year-old named Jamie stands on the edge of the roof of a parking garage. He knows what he came here to do, but looking down at the concrete below and imagining his broken body lying there next to the Dumpsters, he is having second thoughts. Getting out his cell phone, he dials a telephone number he once saw in a gay newspaper.

"This is the Trevor Project Helpline. How can I help?" At the sound of this caring voice on the other end of the line, Jamie starts to cry.

"I'm gay, and I come from a strict Mormon family," he says. "When I came out, I lost everyone and everything—my family, my friends, my church. My parents told me I'd be better off dead!"

The trained volunteer tries to calm Jamie down while getting him to reveal where he is. While Jamie spills out the heartbreak of being disowned by his family, police and an ambulance are dispatched. The volunteer keeps Jamie on the phone until they arrive and can bring him to safety.

A few weeks later, Jamie calls the Helpline again. He reports that he is now out of the hospital, in foster care, seeing a counselor, and—for the first time in years—feeling cautiously hopeful about the future.

"You saved my life," he says simply.

The despair Jamie felt is not unique. Lesbian, gay, bisexual, transgender, and questioning youth are up to four times more likely to attempt suicide than their heterosexual peers, and those who come from families who have rejected them are nine times more likely. Luckily there is the Trevor Helpline, the only nationwide, around-the-clock crisis and suicide-prevention helpline for LGBTQ youth. It is free, confidential, and, for the eighteen thousand young people who call it every year, it is sometimes the last beacon of hope before they do the unthinkable.

VISIT www.thetrevorproject.org or call (310) 271–8845 to help.

Friendly Visiting

Who knows what true loneliness is?
—Joseph Conrad

The simple act of calling or visiting an isolated senior—of making the human connection on a regular basis—can do wonders. With companionship comes improved health, a more positive outlook, and a sense of security from knowing someone cares.

You can break through a senior's isolation by becoming a friendly visitor. Matches between volunteers and seniors are often set up informally through churches and other community groups. Many local nonprofits and government agencies for the aging operate official friendly visitor programs that link you to a lonely older adult. After an interview to make sure you're suitable, and perhaps a brief training session, you'll be sent to meet your partner. Your goal is to use your companionship to help bring your elderly partner back into a more connected life. There aren't any rules on how to do this, but most often it involves just talking and listening. You might also take your partner out for something as simple as a trip to the supermarket or lunch at a coffee shop—a change of scenery can do wonders to brighten someone's day. Over time, many friendly visitors learn to appreciate the wisdom that age gives their partners and find that their volunteer job deepens into a caring friendship.

To find a friendly visiting program near you, check with your local, county, or state office of the aging. You can also get in touch with Friendly Visiting Worldwide, a nonprofit that promotes intergenerational friendly visiting throughout the United States and internationally. Visit their Web site at www.friendlyvisiting.org. Friendly Visiting Worldwide is a program of DOROT, a nonprofit, multiservice agency dedicated to enhancing the lives of homebound and homeless elders and fostering friendship and respect between the generations. It's pronounced doe-ROTE, the Hebrew word for "generations."

CONTACT THEM at:

DOROT / 171 West 85 Street / New York, NY 10024 / (212) 769–2850 / www.dorotusa.org

Collect Used Bicycles for People in Developing Countries

Too often we underestimate the power of a touch, a smile, a kind word, a listening ear, an honest compliment, or the smallest act of caring, all of which have the potential to turn a life around.
—Leo Buscaglia

Americans buy 22 million new bicycles every year; millions of discarded ones end up in landfills. Unused bikes rust away in sheds, basements, or garages. Meanwhile, they could change the lives of poor people in developing countries who have no means of transportation.

Several organizations collect, repair, and ship bicycles to dozens of countries, where they are used for transportation to work, school, markets, and healthcare—even to carry water or small livestock! These groups also provide parts and training and help people set up bicycle repair shops.

ACTION STEPS

LOCAL: Conduct an informal survey. How many bikes can you find unused in your neighborhood? Ask your department of sanitation how many are left on the street or taken to landfills each month. Then contact the organizations below to learn how to donate to them. Be sure to ask what condition bikes must be in.

Find secure storage space. Ask a friend with a truck to help pick up the bikes. Contact schools and organizations and ask them to announce your recycle-a-bicycle program. Give a contact phone number, and arrange pickup or delivery times. Arrange for a special drop-off area at the landfill. Your partner organization will help you arrange shipment to them.

NATIONAL/INTERNATIONAL: For information and to explore partnership: www.bicycles-for-humanity.org • Pedals for Progress: www.p4p .org. • www.bikesfortheworld.org • Visit the Web site of Bicycles for Africa, a British organization, to learn what they are doing: www.re-cycle.org

Fighting for Fairness

**In fact, I will never see a cent. But with the president's
signature today I have an even richer award.**
—Lilly Ledbetter

She didn't set out to be a trailblazer. She was employed for nineteen years at the Goodyear tire plant in Gadsden, Alabama, and was planning on taking an early retirement when an anonymous note let her know that for years she had been paid less than her male co-workers for the same job.

In 2008 her wage-discrimination case, having gone all the way to the U.S. Supreme Court, was met with a 5–4 decision against her. But she kept pursuing justice—equal pay for equal work—and when one avenue of justice closed to her, she set out for others. Lilly Ledbetter would not have other women suffer the injustice she did in her career.

As President Obama noted when he signed the first bill of his new presidency—the Lilly Ledbetter Fair Pay Restoration Act—"I sign this bill for my daughters, and all those who will come after us. . . . In the end, that's why Lilly stayed the course. She knew it was too late for her— that this bill wouldn't undo the years of injustice she faced or restore the earnings she was denied. But this grandmother from Alabama kept on fighting, because she was thinking about the next generation. It's what we've always done in America—set our sights high for ourselves, but even higher for our children and grandchildren."

ACTION STEPS

➤ Women still earn about 78 cents for every dollar that men earn; women of color, even less. Know your rights. The U.S. Equal Employment Opportunity Commission enforces federal discrimination laws. More at www.eeoc.gov.

➤ Fair pay is an issue that affects every family struggling to make ends meet, pay college tuitions, or save for retirement. Go to the nonprofit National Women's Law Center for ways to become involved in more fair pay issues: www.nwlc.org.

Who Says It's Work?

When the sun rises, I go to work.
When the sun goes down, I take my rest,
I dig the well from which I drink,
I farm the soil which yields my food,
I share creation. Kings can do no more.
—Chinese proverb

If you are a Zen monk, you know how to sweep a floor spotless, dust a room until nary a mote is left, polish a floor to a deep gloss, scrub a toilet with the same care as a shrine, and tend to a garden with a botanist's glee. If you are not a Zen monk, you may be tempted to ask: just *what* has all this got to do with compassion?

Everything.

To the compassionate, work is so much more than that thing you shuffle off to in the wee hours of the morning. As the great Lebanese poet and philosopher Kahlil Gibran said, work is love made visible. Work affords you—literally and figuratively—the most effective opportunity to extend the caring in your heart to others. It brings you into contact with more people than anything else you do. It is, to many saints, monks, and joyful janitors, the greatest spiritual practice on earth.

And you thought it was just a paycheck.

ACTION STEPS

➤ No matter your job, employ the Buddhist concept of right livelihood. Tomorrow morning, wake up, and approach your job with the same excitement you feel when you head out on vacation.

➤ As soon as you walk into your place of employment, greet everyone with a smile, even those who wear a permanent scowl. Just for the day, use all the creativity at your disposal to find ways to make your job be more of service to others.

➤ At the end of the day, take note of how you feel compared to a regular workday. Like it? Try it again the next day.

A Marriage Made in High Tech

Innovation distinguishes between a leader and a follower.
—Steve Jobs, cofounder of Apple

High tech and philanthropy seem worlds apart—one is all head, while the other is all heart. But these labels are arbitrary. Charities rely on computers to do their good works. The trick is to find a way to make these two worlds meet, especially today when nonprofits need increasing support as they struggle with funding challenges.

TechSoup Stock serves the nonprofit community by helping charities obtain donated technology tailored to their needs. The company relies on corporate partners (industry giants such as Adobe, Cisco, Microsoft, Symantec) to create a philanthropy service that helps nonprofits be more efficient. Some partners donate their products outright, while others lower their fees significantly. Partners have given more than $1.2 billion in high-tech products at a fraction of their cost. Free technology supports philanthropies by allowing them to redirect funds they would have otherwise spent on equipment to the people and causes they are dedicated to serve. They highlight that this means more beds can be purchased for homeless shelters, more tutors can be hired for after-school programs, and more meals can be prepared in soup kitchens.

ACTION STEPS

➤ If you have high-tech skills, think about how you can support a favorite cause by donating your time and energy. Perhaps you can be their go-to person when the computers crash. Maybe you can set up software or run a tutorial to increase efficiency.

➤ If you know of a charitable organization that could use the assistance of TechSoup Stock, help them make the connection at www.techsoup.org or (800) 659–3579, ext. 700.

➤ The Internal Revenue Code offers accelerated write-offs that strongly incentivize donations-in-kind by companies to charities that use the donated merchandise directly for child clients.

Teach an Adult How to Read

**Reading gives us someplace to go when
we have to stay where we are.**
—Professor Mason Cooley

Literacy is more than just the ability to read; it encompasses writing, computing, and using technology so that one can reach one's full potential. There are more than 774 million adults around the world who are illiterate in their native languages, two-thirds of whom are women. In the United States alone over 30 million people over age sixteen don't read well enough to understand a newspaper or fill out a job application.

The gift of literacy is the door that opens any and every possibility to adults. By tutoring others to learn to read, you will be providing a new hope for those likely to be in desperate situations. You will improve their chances of better jobs, better healthcare, and greater involvement in their communities. You are truly teaching others how to improve their own lives.

ACTION STEPS:

LOCAL: Contact your local library, public school system, or place of worship to see if they have a literacy program. When you locate one, ask how you can be trained to become a volunteer teacher. You won't need to know any language but English; however, if you are proficient in another tongue, your help will be even more appreciated by new arrivals in this country. You could also ask the program coordinator what else they need. Even if you don't want to teach, you may be able to help by coordinating classes, raising funds, or preparing written materials.

NATIONAL/INTERNATIONAL: These Web sites have a wealth of information about illiteracy and volunteer opportunities:

www.literacydirectory.org, for a searchable directory of U.S. literacy programs.

The National Center for Family Literacy: www.famlit.org.

A Rain-Forest Dream

We cannot hold a torch to light another's path without brightening our own.
—Ben Sweetland

Lynne Twist had worked as an executive for twenty-odd years when she had an experience in Guatemala that changed her life. Taking part in a shamanic ceremony, she had a vivid dream of becoming a large bird and flying over the rain forest and clearly saw men with orange face paint and feathered crowns looking up at her through the treetop canopy. The shaman told her, "You are being called by a people, and you must go to them."

Ms. Twist traveled to a remote part of the Ecuadorian Amazon, where she found the Achuar people, who had the orange face paint and colorful headdresses she had seen in her dream. Seeing how their way of life was under threat from outside forces, she became committed to helping them protect their rain forest.

The Achuar people told her, "It is vital that we save these beautiful forests, but you must also change your own modern world." Accepting this challenge, Ms. Twist and her husband, Bill, founded the Pachamama Alliance ("Pachamama" means Mother Earth in the Andes), which is committed to sustainable living in the Amazon, in the United States, and, increasingly, around the planet.

Ms. Twist and her organization challenge you to take $25 a month that you are unwittingly using to fund the destruction of Earth's resources and to instead donate that money to the Pachamama Alliance for the preservation of the rain forest. Simple ways to save money: use long-life, eco-friendly lightbulbs, use a metal canteen instead of purchasing bottled water, or ride a bicycle instead of driving a car.

Monthly e-mails from the Pachamama Alliance provide ideas on how to make simple changes to both save money and reduce your carbon footprint. The e-mails also offer tips on achieving the spiritual fulfillment that comes with living in accord with your most deeply held beliefs.

VISIT www.pachamama.org.

National Trails Day

He knew a path that wanted walking.
—Robert Frost

Millions of Americans enjoy the 200,000 miles of trails that crisscross our public lands. They hike, bike, run, backpack, cross-country ski, and snowmobile on them—often without realizing how much volunteer work goes into creating and maintaining them. National Trails Day, an annual event since 1993, is a chance to thank the volunteers, land agencies, and other trail partners for their hard work and support. Sponsored by the American Hiking Society (AHS), an organization dedicated to promoting and protecting foot trails and the hiking experience, this is the only nationwide celebration of trails. Well over a thousand National Trails Day events are registered with the AHS each year.

The official date for National Trails Day is the first Saturday in June, though that's loosely interpreted to mean a day or weekend around that time. Local trail groups around the country schedule their own events, all designed to showcase their own trails and invite people out to enjoy them. Many groups also schedule volunteer trail maintenance and cleanup days in advance or as part of the event.

National Trails Day raises local awareness and support of nearby trails, parks, and other outdoor recreation areas, but it depends heavily on volunteers. A lot of preparation work and trail maintenance needs to be done in advance of the day, and on the day a lot of extra volunteers are needed to do everything from directing traffic to leading nature walks. If you're not already in touch with your local outdoors groups, AHS can help you find events scheduled near you.

FIND INFORMATION at:

American Hiking Society / 1422 Fenwick Lane / Silver Spring, MD 20910 / (800) 972–8608 / www.americanhiking.org

Help Stem the Tide of Junk Mail

You must give some time to your fellow men. Even if it's a little thing, do something for others—something for which you get no pay but the privilege of doing it.
—Albert Schweitzer

About 104.7 billion pieces of junk mail arrive in U.S. mailboxes yearly—that's 30 percent of all the world's mail. Most of us think of it simply as a nuisance, but the facts show that junk mail is much more hazardous than that. It not only clogs our mailboxes; it wastes a massive amount of natural resources. The trees cut to produce all this paper—6.5 million tons—would equal clear-cutting of the entire Rocky Mountain National Park three times a year!

Incredibly, almost half of all junk mail is never opened, and only a small percentage is acted upon. State and local governments spend hundreds of millions of dollars per year to collect and dispose of bulk mail that isn't recycled. However, doing your part to stem this tide is a simple step that only takes a few minutes.

ACTION STEPS

LOCAL: Tell friends and neighbors the facts about junk mail, and then help them reduce the amount that they receive. To do this, go to the Direct Marketing Association (DMA) Web site, www.dmachoice.org. (This association represents many, but not all, of the direct-mail marketers in the United States.) There you can enter names and street addresses in a "Choice Mail Preference Service" form; this will notify all DMA members to remove them from their mailing lists. You can also print the form and give copies to everyone you know, along with stamped envelopes addressed to the Direct Marketing Association.

NATIONAL: Every year Americans receive about 848 pieces of junk mail per household. Learn more about the negative consequences of junk mail, and sign a petition to stop it at www.donotmail.org.

A Good Complaint

**Everybody talks about the weather, but
nobody does anything about it.**
—often attributed to Mark Twain

We do complain a lot. In 2008, the five industries we complained about most, according to the Better Business Bureau, were cell phone services and equipment, auto dealers and new cars, banks, Internet shopping, and cable and satellite television providers. The Better Business Bureau officially recorded over 862,280 complaints.

We can use our influence, our power as consumers, to change the way companies do business by offering a customer-service representative suggestions with clarity, specificity, and a little grace. Remember that you are complaining to a person, a customer-service representative who is like you, trying to do his job the best way he can. Empathy rather than anger may move the customer representative to act quicker.

But being calm and specific about the complaint and by ending with asking for a commitment such as, "what can I expect to be your next step?" will enable you, the customer-service representative, and the company to serve you better, and others as well.

ACTION STEPS

➤ Many companies have Web sites and 800 numbers for consumer feedback. The Better Business Bureau (BBB) encourages consumers to first attempt to resolve complaints with the company. However, the BBB accepts complaints whether or not the business is accredited with the BBB. Your complaint will be forwarded to the company within two business days and it will be asked for a response within fourteen days. More on BBB at www.bbb.org.

➤ Join Consumers Union, publisher of *Consumer Reports,* since 1936 an expert, independent, nonprofit organization. Enlist with other influential consumers to rate and evaluate products and support the interests of American consumers: www.consumereports.org.

The Hugging Saint

There's nothing like a mama-hug.
—Adabella Radici

For over thirty-five years, a devout Hindu woman from a fishing village in India has been doing something she hopes will ease humanity's suffering—she hugs people. Now known simply as Amma—for Mata Amritanandamayi (Mother of Immortal Bliss)—she has embraced over 25 million people in all corners of the world.

These are no ordinary hugs. People line up by the thousands to feel the extraordinary compassion in her embrace. They leave with a blissful smile on their faces, a lightness in their hearts, and a sense of ease in their minds. They often also receive a gift from her—advice, a rose petal, an apple, or simply her lingering perfumed scent on their clothes.

Many people are so moved by her embrace that they donate money to her charity, although she asks for none. The money funds food and clothing for the poor, helps charitable hospitals operate, educates children in impoverished areas, and many other such activities. One particularly notable example: Her organization contributed over $23 million to tsunami relief in 2006.

You don't need Amma's global charity or her lifelong sense of purpose to emulate her effect on those around you. All you need are your arms.

ACTION STEPS

➤ The next time you see a family member, take that person wholly in your arms. Think of nothing else except how much you love him or her. Let the hug last as long as it wants to.

➤ Touch is a touchy subject with people who aren't family or dear friends, even though human contact is exceptionally healing. Let your common sense guide you. If a hug isn't appropriate for someone who's having a bad day, a hand on the shoulder might be.

➤ If you want to experience one of Amma's hugs yourself, go to www.amma .org. She travels often enough that you might find her not far away.

Pitching In

**Everyone can be great because everyone can serve.
You don't have to have a college education to serve.
You don't even have to make your subjects and verbs
agree to serve. . . . You only need a heart full of grace.**
—Dr. Martin Luther King Jr.

When most of us think of Hollywood Boulevard, good works and social action usually don't spring to mind. But that's exactly where Big Sunday was born—at Temple Israel of Hollywood, a Reform synagogue on that famous boulevard.

Why there? One of the obligations of a Jew is to perform good deeds—mitzvahs. To fulfill this obligation, the congregation established a Mitzvah Day at the Temple in 1999. Three hundred congregants worked for a few hours on seventeen small cleanup and restoration projects. Today fifty thousand volunteers of all races and religions at 250 cosponsoring organizations fan out from San Diego to Santa Barbara to engage in four hundred community projects that include painting murals on classroom walls, planting trees, cleaning homeless and battered-women's shelters, giving blood, baking cookies for residents of Ronald McDonald House, and hundreds of other projects.

Executive director David Levinson organizes this massive undertaking. He says the purpose of Big Sunday is community building. "Everyone has some way they can help someone else," he explains. Today, in conjunction with the city of Los Angeles and with the involvement of its mayor, Big Sunday has become "the largest day of community service ever in America."

ACTION STEPS

➤ Create your own Big Sunday in your community. Read about who is being helped and how supported they feel at www.bigsunday.org. Phone (323) 549–9944 to talk about what it takes.

Translate a Letter

**Language is not an abstract construction of the
learned, or of dictionary-makers, but is something
arising out of the work, needs, ties, joys, affections,
tastes, of long generations of humanity, and has
its bases broad and low, close to the ground.**
—Walt Whitman

The United States was often referred to as "the great melting pot," because people from all over the world came here to create a better life. Along the way, these immigrants were supposed to become a new homogenous "American." But in many communities across the country, we are more like a salad bowl; instead of becoming a new culture, we are a proud accumulation of many.

While English is certainly our official language, many of our citizens and guests continue to cling to their native tongues, and have difficulty fitting into the more bureaucratic aspects of life here in the United States. New immigrants often require help translating a legal document, such as a contract, or even a parking ticket. They may also need assistance if they receive an invitation or an announcement, like to a wedding, or if a business opportunity presents itself.

If you are fluent in a particular language, you can help others navigate our complex world here in the United States. You would be providing an invaluable service at times of crisis or great joy. Best of all, you will be using your own innate talents to make a difference in the lives of others.

GETTING STARTED: Contact your local library, community center, or places of worship to offer your services. You can also create a Web site or blog that offers your skill. The Internet is teeming with requests for translations, and the "free software" available isn't as good, or easy to use, as it should be. One Web site, www.prospector.cz, lists lots of free translation software, in case you get stuck on a word.

Compassion for All Creatures

How wonderful it is that nobody need wait a single moment before starting to improve the world.
—Anne Frank

A fragile newborn baby goat, considered worthless by the farmer who owned him, was abandoned and left to die in a cold and filthy stockyard. Luckily, a Farm Sanctuary humane officer discovered the tiny three-pound kid, who was suffering from hypothermia and pneumonia, and rushed him to the vet, then brought him to the Farm Sanctuary's New York shelter. The little goat, now named Jack, is still tiny and in need of medical care, but he is sweet and loving and always looking for a cuddle. Best of all, he now actually stands a chance of growing to adulthood.

Farm Sanctuary is committed to rescuing abused farm animals and providing them with a safe place to live on either a 175-acre farm amidst rolling green hills in the Finger Lakes Region of upstate New York or on a 300-acre California farm.

Farm Sanctuary cares for cows, pigs, chickens, and other rescued farm animals that have been victims of cruel abuse. It is dedicated to promoting compassionate living and the humane treatment of animals through rescue, education, and advocacy. Their sanctuaries provide places where farm animals can seek refuge and where people can see the animals in their natural environment and have a chance to interact with them.

"Farm animals need love and protection just like cats and dogs do," says Tricia Barry of Farm Sanctuary. "There are so many organizations like the ASPCA protecting companion animals, but so little being done for farm animals."

A contribution of $20 or more gets you a Farm Sanctuary membership for one year. Members receive the organization's quarterly newsletter and discounted rates at the bed-and-breakfast at the sanctuary. You can visit the farm year-round. Or you can adopt your very own animal at the farm—annual adoption fees range from $120 for a chicken to $600 for a cow.

VISIT www.farmsanctuary.org or call (607) 583–2225.

Summer Volunteer Programs

In a lot of areas of my life, particularly in my teenage years, I began to think about the world, and to think about the universe as being a part of my conscious everyday life.
—Julius Erving

If your teenager is old enough to drive a car and have a job, he or she is old enough to do some serious summer volunteering. There are a lot of options available, which means it's easy to find a summer volunteer opportunity that's right for your teen—one where his or her contribution will be valuable, educational, and maybe even inspirational.

Looking locally, teenage summer volunteers are always needed in community recreation programs, tutoring programs, camps for physically challenged kids, educational programs at environmental centers, and so on. High-school students are actually in demand for these areas—there may be recruitment efforts through the school. If not, simply asking the possible volunteer venues if they need summer help will probably be productive.

Teens can also volunteer for any number of overseas programs that will put them to work on community-service projects in developing nations. These trips can be real eye-openers for teens as they experience a different culture firsthand. They usually involve transportation and program costs, but the return on the investment is worth the expense. Many teens gain a much more mature outlook and an enhanced sense of purpose.

One well-established summer program for teens is AMIGOS, which has been offering medical missions for students for more than forty years. Volunteers spend six to eight weeks working in a Latin American country helping to build health clinics and improve local infrastructure. The students live with local families in small communities in rural and semiurban areas and get a close-up look at the realities of daily life.

FOR INFORMATION:

Amigos de las Américas / 5618 Star Lane / Houston, TX 77057 / (800) 231–7796 / www.amigoslink.org

Start an Interfaith Discussion Group

**The universal brotherhood of man is
our most precious possession.**
—Mark Twain

It's no secret that disagreements between faith groups can escalate into violence, yet most people desperately want peaceful environments in which to live, work, and raise their families. Interfaith discussion groups are a small step that, if taken in every community, could increase the chances for peace in the world. Once people of different faiths get to know one another as individuals, they learn to listen to and respect opposing points of view. Such groups have been the basis for social action in many conflict-prone areas of the world.

ACTION STEPS

LOCAL: Move slowly at first, thinking carefully about the needs of your community: Is there a gulf between faith communities on some specific issue? Is a conflict elsewhere in the world leading members of different groups to take sides? Approach people you know and trust; ask them to reach out to colleagues from other faiths. Start with a small group (a dozen people or fewer), and gradually build membership.

Consider these principles from beliefnet: www.beliefnet.com/faiths/2001/10/principles-for-starting-an-interfaith-dialogue.aspx.

Don't make assumptions about others' values, worldviews, or priorities. Start by asking what issues are important to each. Don't deny points of contrast or conflict, but steer away from them at first. Explore areas of agreement—for instance, the importance of family life—and build on them. When there is rapport among group members, ease into points of difference. Understand that wisdom is not the province of any one faith.

NATIONAL/INTERNATIONAL: Learn more about interfaith groups at: www.interfaithforums.com • www.interfaith.org

Learn about the role of religions in conflict situations: www.beyond intractability.org/essay/religion_and_conflict/?nid=6725.

Experience a World Without

**We do not need magic to transform the world.
We carry all the power we need inside ourselves
already. We have power to imagine better.**
—J. K. Rowling, Harvard University commencement, 2008

On the last Saturday in March, lights in four thousand cities in eighty-eight countries, in venues including the Empire State Building, the United Nations, Times Square in New York City, the Las Vegas Strip, and San Francisco's Golden Gate Bridge, magically went dark. The lights on Big Ben in London, the Eiffel Tower in Paris, the opera house in Sydney, and lights from Europe to Latin America, Russia, and Asia shut down. This was not some mysterious blackout of epic proportions, but a vivid signal to the world about the urgent need to address global warming.

Earth Hour, spearheaded by the World Wildlife Fund, urged people, landmarks, towns, and cities to switch off their lights from 8:30 p.m. to 9:30 p.m. local time. A world with no man-made light became a star-filled one.

The essential quality Earth Hour and any campaign with an imperative to turn off rather than turn on, to stop rather than to continue, encourages us to imagine a radically different world, a more sustainable one, and perhaps even a more magical one.

ACTION STEPS

➤ Envision a world without _____ (fill in the blank—or join one of the many existing campaigns—Earth Hour, Turn Off TV, Great American Smoke Out). Set up one day in your community in which many, through the power of the Internet, pledge to join your world without _____, and learn how much you all gain.

➤ Any community, large or small, can take part in a future Earth Hour. A quick guide for how to run an Earth Hour in your city and town is available at www.earthhour.org.

Think Small

Sometimes when we are generous in small, barely detectable ways it can change someone's life forever.
—Margaret Cho

It's natural to get bogged down by all-or-nothing thinking. If we can't write a check for a hundred dollars to a charity, we don't write one at all. If we can't spend an hour in a hospital room with a sick friend, we don't go at all.

This is wholly understandable. "Go big or go home" is the term marketing types and snowboarders love to use. We want to feel as if our actions matter and that they're making a noticeable difference in the lives of others.

The difficulty with this type of thinking is that it denies the smallest comforts to those who need them most. Imagine a starving person— would he begrudge you for only giving him what little you could, or would he eat hungrily and gratefully whatever amount you offered?

ACTION STEPS

➤ Today, go out of your way to engage in the smallest acts of kindness possible. Think of it in the same way as compound interest—a little bit over a long time turns into great riches. Send a two-sentence post-card to a friend having a tough time ("Miss you. Thinking of you constantly."). Take one piece of trash out of your teenager's room. Drop a quarter in the charity jar at the cash register.

➤ Buy a little notebook and keep it handy at all times. Jot down thoughts for small, compassionate things to do at later dates, things you won't be able to do today: "Cindy's son is having an operation on the 18th. Send her an e-mail the day before." "Spend five minutes ironing Joe's shirt the morning of his big presentation." You'll be delighted how many genuinely thoughtful ideas come to mind that will only take moments to do.

Social Support

**No man is an island entire of itself; every man
is part of a continent, part of the main.**
—John Donne

We humans are social animals. We live in clans, villages, towns, cities. We work in teams. We need one another. Our habits hearken back to our primate ancestors who groomed and protected one another, raised one another's babies, and called out to warn the troop of an approaching lion. Although we diverge in customs, religion, race, and political affiliation, we all have common emotional responses to a baby's smile, a lover's kiss, a mother's tear. There is still more that unites than divides.

Support is woven into the fabric of human interactions. We listen to a friend's complaints about work or love; we kiss a child's skinned knee to make it better; we wait at the hospital with an aunt to hear about her husband's fate. We comfort the bereaved. We need to do these things, and we feel washed with love when others reciprocate.

Support brings hope when all seems hopeless, comfort when we are alone, empowerment when we feel helpless. And it also brings good mental and physical health by reducing stress, helping us cope, and enhancing self-esteem and self-efficacy.

ACTION STEPS

➤ Think back to situations in which you have felt supported. How did support lessen your distress? How did it help you move forward in your life?

➤ What lessons could you glean from having been supported by others? Who can you support? What would they need from you?

➤ Study the best volunteering organizations that provide service in your area of interest. Find out which ones do not yet serve your local community and ask if you can help them expand. Offer to create a support committee to explore the local possibilities.

Become a Scout Leader

**The unselfish effort to bring cheer to others
will be the beginning of a happier
life for ourselves.**
—Helen Keller

The concept of scouting began in England in 1907. It was based on the ideas of Sir Robert S. S. Baden-Powell that were documented in his book, *Scouting for Boys*. Since the beginning, Baden-Powell's ideas have had universal appeal for boys and girls, and scouting has spread to almost every country and exists on every continent.

The overall mission of scouting is to prepare young people to make ethical and moral choices over their lifetimes. It is a terrific opportunity to help shape our children's future while providing them—and yourself—with wholesome entertainment. All scouting organizations rely on volunteers to lead troops and participate in events, and you don't have to have a child in a troop to participate. As a troop leader, you will be responsible for a group of children for at least one school year. You will be creating engaging projects and field trips, teaching camping methods, as well as life lessons.

Boy Scouts, Girl Scouts, and Cub Scouts, are just some of the most familiar names in the United States, but scouting can include any youth group that follows a distinct set of rules that is based on morals, good conduct, teaching life lessons, and having fun. One of the less well known U.S. "scouting" groups are the Indian Princesses and the Indian Guides, which are sponsored through local YMCAs. Indian Guides and Indian Princesses are parent-child programs that are set up specifically to support the parent's family role as teacher, counselor, and friend. This program's membership is over a half million children and adults across the country.

GETTING STARTED: To find out about the different volunteer opportunities that are available in your community, contact your local Boy Scout or Girl Scout council, or YMCA. The national Web sites are Boy Scouts: www .scouting.org; Girl Scouts: www.girlscouts.org. There are also opportunities overseas to work with either American troops or international groups.

A Smile Mended

**Let us always meet each other with a smile,
for the smile is the beginning of love.**
—Mother Teresa

Six-year-old Ritka, a smart and playful little girl who loves to dance, lives in Bolpur, one of the most impoverished regions of India. Ritka had a cleft lip and a cleft palate, which made speaking difficult. She was shunned by the other villagers where she lives, and was so badly teased by her classmates that she stopped going to school. (Eighty-five percent of children worldwide with cleft lips do not attend school.)

Like so many children with cleft lips, Ritka had been hidden away out of sight as an embarrassment to the family. Without an education and without marriage prospects, Ritka's future looked bleak. But in some ways she was better off than other children with a cleft palate, who can have so much difficulty eating that they become malnourished.

The operation to correct a cleft lip and cleft palate is affordable in the United States, is routinely done after birth, and takes only as little as 45 minutes. But to hundreds of thousands of people in developing countries, it is an unattainable dream. Enter Operation Smile, which was founded by a plastic surgeon and his wife, a nurse and social worker. It started in 1982 with one mission, to offer free cleft lip and cleft palate surgeries to children in the Philippines, and now has a presence in 51 countries. Operation Smile has treated more than 130,000 children and young adults with cleft lips, cleft palates, and other facial deformities.

Ritka was one of the lucky children of Bolpur who was chosen to receive the operation. Surgery is frightening for any child, but Ritka's transformation has been extraordinary. She is now a luminously beautiful child who can talk normally, attend school, and participate in village life. Her future is now as bright as her smile.

A donation of $240 (or $20 a month for a year) pays for an operation to fix a cleft lip and cleft palate that will change a child's life forever.

VISIT www.operationsmile.org or call (888) 677–6453.

Volunteer for Your Town

Throughout my life, I've seen the difference that volunteering efforts can make in people's lives. I know the personal value of service as a local volunteer.
—Jimmy Carter

Voting for local officials and paying local taxes are usually about the extent of the average resident's involvement with the municipality. But without their large cadre of dedicated volunteers, most towns would grind to a halt very quickly.

Volunteers in local government are the unsung heroes. They're the people who sit on the zoning board, the planning board, the recreation committee, the water board, the economic development agency, the environmental advisory board, block committees, and all the other volunteer slots in town. Some jobs carry small stipends, but they don't begin to cover the hours the participants put in. And even the people who get elected, such as town board and school board members, usually receive so little in payment for their many hours of service that they're effectively volunteers too.

These people are your neighbors. They volunteer to spend hours each week reviewing documents and attending meetings. They rarely get much in the way of thanks as a return—they're much more likely to hear complaints, criticism, and outright abuse. Despite all the work and the lack of appreciation, they stick with it. Why?

Because they want to help make their town a better place to live. That's not usually a glamorous or particularly visible job. Sitting on the water board isn't very exciting, but it is necessary—a safe water supply is vital to your community's health.

IF YOU CARE about your community, consider volunteering for one of the many local boards and committees that undoubtedly need your help. Do politics play a role here? Sometimes yes, but often no. The reality is that volunteer slots are often open simply for lack of anyone willing to commit to them. If you want to help, a good starting point is your town clerk, who usually has a very accurate idea of where volunteers are needed.

Promote Organic Gardening to the Residents of Your Community

**To own a bit of ground, to scratch it with a hoe,
to plant seeds and watch their renewal of life—
this is the commonest delight of the race.**
—Charles Dudley Warner, newspaperman/author

More and more people are concerned about the dangers of synthetic pesticides and herbicides in our food and environment. The U.S. Department of Agriculture reports that the average American is exposed to residues from ten to thirteen pesticides every day. Home gardens are where children play, and kids are even more vulnerable than adults to the risks of these substances. At least 90 million pounds of pesticides are applied annually to home lawns and gardens in the United States. They are tracked indoors by pets and people's shoes.

Organic gardeners only use naturally occurring fertilizers such as compost and manure and natural pest control, without chemical insecticides. Studies show that organically grown produce is not only safer but more nutritious.

ACTION STEPS

LOCAL: Learn about the dangers of pesticides at www.chem-tox.com/pesticides. Read up on organic gardening, then begin the transition to organic in your own garden. There is a wealth of information available on the Internet:

www.organicgardening.com • www.organicgardeningguru.com • www.organiclawncare101.com • www.organicgardeninfo.com • www.instantorganicgarden.com

A good book for beginners: *No Green Thumb Required! Organic Family Gardening Made Easy* by Don Rosenberg.

NATIONAL: The National Coalition for Pesticide-Free Lawns: www.beyondpesticides.org/pesticidefreelawns.

Shouting from the Rooftops

**Each of us can work to change a small portion
of events, and in the total of all those will be
written the history of this generation.**
—Robert F. Kennedy

We are often involved with a cause or event that is doing remarkable things, changing lives, making a difference. We want to shout from the rooftops the incredible contribution of so many. But what we need to do is be ready to approach the media and publicize these efforts.

We all can be successful with our public-relations outreach. The surest way to be effective is to be as local as possible. Newspapers, television, and radio thrive on local stories. If you're involved in a national cause, work the community angle. Understand that there are different roles at any media outlet. Take time to know those roles. Who is covering stories like yours? For example, don't call the sports reporter with a story about a fund-raiser to fight domestic violence. They will be sympathetic but unable to help.

Or go to the top. Call an influential person such as an editor or the station manager. Start your conversation with a line such as: "A story on our event will make a difference because . . ." Your ability to communicate with conviction will ultimately help your cause.

ACTION STEPS

➤ Practice writing a media advisory, a one-page document that outlines the major details of any event for the press: What—When—Where—Media Contact Information. It should be concise and timely. A media advisory is the most influential press communication you can write.

➤ The Nonprofit Leadership Institute, and their Good Practice Guide, offers advice for the nonprofessional working with the media. Under the auspices of Grand Valley State University, this compendium of invaluable articles and resources is available online at www.npgood practice.org. In addition, via their Web site, you can submit specific questions on any nonprofit issue to their "experts in residence."

Strong Nations

**Human kindness has never weakened the stamina
or softened the fiber of a free people. A nation
does not have to be cruel to be tough.**
—Franklin D. Roosevelt

During World War II, a German POW was interned in a camp in the Midwest where he and fellow prisoners were put to work as replacement farmhands, given that so many American men were off fighting the war. He later talked about how, when he and his fellow POWs were served steak for dinner one night, he realized Germany would lose. The prison rations, even on the worst days, were better than anything he had been served as a soldier in the German forces.

This story illustrates not only the richness of this country, but also its heart. America was rich enough to serve POWs steak once in a while even though it was not required to do so. That it came from the values of common decency and compassion is a major part of the identity of this country. Take a position on this noble tradition by insisting that your government act compassionately to citizens and noncitizens alike, especially in periods of strife.

ACTION STEPS

➤ The actions of democratic governments are a reflection of the people who elected them. Never allow actions that aren't in keeping with compassionate values to go unchallenged. Your response can be as quick as writing a letter to the editor or to your congressperson.

➤ If you see a continuous lack of compassion at any level of government, do something about it. Lend your support to the campaign of someone who better exemplifies your values. Or run for office yourself. The best way to know whether your elected officials are acting compassionately is through their votes. Monitor that through Project Vote Smart at www.votesmart.org. This group of volunteers of all political stripes faithfully records voting records at the federal and state levels.

Nurture Creativity

**It is our light, not our darkness that most frightens
us. We ask ourselves, who am I to be brilliant,
gorgeous, talented, fabulous? Actually, who
are you not to be? You are a child of God. . . .
We are all meant to shine as children do.**

—Marianne Williamson

Every child deserves to shine . . . to express his or her creativity in
art, dance, or music. But so many are hampered by their circumstances. Foster children have few resources. Those living in the inner
city lack contacts, connections, and perhaps motivation. Children with
learning disabilities and discipline problems struggle in a typical school
environment. How do we reach these youngsters before their spirits are
crushed?

ArtSeed is an innovative visual-arts education program for children
with learning differences, financial obstacles, and/or discipline problems.
Based in San Francisco, ArtSeed's intergenerational projects connect students from the inner city with artists in a variety of fields. The program
touches four to five hundred schoolchildren yearly and also supports one-
on-one apprenticeships for budding young artists. They create their own
designs and documents, culminating in exhibitions of their individual
portfolios or larger collaborative pieces. Not only does this activity foster
self-expression and self-esteem, but it also allows these children and their
hidden talents to shine.

ACTION STEPS

➤ Everyone has the need for self-expression. Advocate for arts education
  in your local school or place of worship.

➤ Contact ArtSeed at www.artseed.org, info@artseed.org, or (415) 409–
  1761 to learn about their programs and see how you might collaborate
  with them or start a similar program in your community.

Volunteer Mediation

Act with kindness, but do not expect gratitude.
—Confucius

Mediation is a way for people to solve problems with the help of an impartial third party. A mediator assists the parties involved by having them talk through their problem until it is resolved. Depending upon which state you live in, the courts generally honor these agreements as binding contracts. Statistics have shown that at least 80 percent of disputes that go to mediation are resolved. As a volunteer mediator, you can serve your community by helping people resolve conflicts.

Communities across the country are developing volunteer mediation banks as part of their social-service offerings. Mediation can resolve different types of conflicts, including landlord-tenant disputes, neighborhood disputes, small-claims-court cases, contract disputes, school conflicts, family disputes, and elder care. Elder care raises some of the most complex issues in mediation; there can be a dozen or more interested parties involved, and all have to come to a consensus. However, this offers a perfect opportunity for volunteer mediators to make a difference during a critical time in people's lives.

Topics that are often discussed in elder-care mediation include parental living arrangements, health and personal care (such as driving), provisions for terminal illness, home upkeep and repair, financial concerns, trust and estate issues, guardianship, and power of attorney. During these conversations, the mediator acts as a facilitator and is not allowed to make any decisions for the family. Rather, the mediator keeps the family focused on priorities and points out opportunities for clarification.

GETTING STARTED: Volunteer mediators come from various backgrounds. They often have to complete a training course, followed by a set number of hours observing actual mediations. And they must mediate under the observation of an experienced mediator before they can do it on their own. Speak with your local social services agencies, such as United Way, to find out if there are volunteer opportunities in your area.

Providing Care for the Elderly

**Being deeply loved by someone gives you strength,
while loving someone deeply gives you courage.**
—Lao Tzu

Taking care of a loved one who is ill or elderly can be extremely stressful. People who have no medical training can suddenly find themselves nursing a person with cancer, Alzheimer's, or dementia. Some caregivers of aging parents are also raising children, working full-time jobs, and running homes and can quickly become exhausted and overwhelmed.

In Pennsylvania in the late seventies a group of neighbors who were taking care of their aging parents began meeting to share their feelings and to try to find solutions to their problems—and CAPS (Children with Aging Parents) was born. Then, in 1986, Ann Landers mentioned CAPS in her column, and the organization was deluged with an avalanche of mail from caregivers from around the country who were desperate for help.

Clearly, there was an overwhelming need for CAPS, and that need has only grown—caregiving is now the fastest-growing unpaid profession in America. CAPS receives thousands of calls a year from caregivers seeking assistance, and that number will doubtless continue to rise. What is not likely to change is the love and concern that caregivers feel for their elderly parents—as well as the unexpected anger, confusion, and guilt that can sometimes result from the stress of caregiving.

When that stress becomes overwhelming, CAPS is a place that caregivers can get relief. In addition to helping people start and run local support groups that can make a crucial difference in the lives of caregivers, CAPS publishes a quarterly newsletter and has a Web site full of information and helpful links. CAPS also assists by providing names and numbers of nursing homes, retirement communities, elder-law attorneys, and much more.

A donation of $50 would cover the cost of sending out a hundred informational letters to caregivers who have contacted CAPS seeking help and support.

VISIT www.caps4caregivers.org or call (800) 227–7294.

Make Your Neighborhood a Safer Place

**No matter how big and powerful government
gets, and the many services it provides, it
can never take the place of volunteers.**
—Ronald Reagan

When community members voluntarily come together in their neighborhoods and work with local law enforcement, crime rates drop, and the quality of life improves. That's the simple concept behind the many neighborhood watch programs that have arisen since the National Sheriffs' Association helped the first begin in 1972.

Neighborhood watches serve as the extra eyes and ears for local law enforcement. The programs teach citizens how to help themselves by identifying and reporting suspicious activity in their neighborhoods. The idea is a proactive, all-volunteer, community-oriented approach to crime prevention. Most watch programs are organized around a block or neighborhood and are started with the help of a local law enforcement agency. Volunteers who donate their time and resources are at the core of these programs, which rarely have a formal budget or a reliable source of funding. For extra effectiveness, they often link their watch program to other community groups such as tenants' associations and community-development offices. People volunteer and stick with neighborhood watches because they can see the difference their efforts make in their communities.

Citizen patrols are just one of the services a watch program provides. Even if you can't get around much, you can be a window watcher, looking out for the kids in the neighborhood and reporting any unusual activities. You can also be a block parent, someone whose home is designated as a safe place to go for kids facing a frightening situation or an emergency.

FOR A FREE MANUAL on how to start a neighborhood watch, contact:

National Sheriffs' Association / 1450 Duke Street / Alexandria, VA 22314 / (703) 836–7827 / www.usaonwatch.org

Keep Kids in Your Community Safe from Guns

There is nothing wrong with America that the faith, love of freedom, intelligence and energy of her citizens cannot cure.
—Dwight D. Eisenhower

About seventy-five children receive gunshot wounds every day in the United States; fifteen of them die. Most of these fatal incidents occur in the home. Schools are not necessarily safe either; more than a million American kids bring guns to class each year. Gun-rights advocates say safety training is the answer, but accidents happen, even when safety-trained adults are present. For instance, eight-year-old Christopher Bizilj was killed at a Massachusetts gun show in 2008 while test-firing an automatic weapon as his father and a trained instructor watched. Laws take time to change, but you can do something now to keep your community's kids safer.

ACTION STEPS

LOCAL: Learn what your state is doing to prevent gun violence at www.stategunlaws.org. Tell your elected representatives what you think.

Make sure that any guns in your home are secured, with keys hidden. Talk to your kids about the dangers of guns. Tell them never to touch a firearm, even if they think it's not loaded. Ask the parents of your children's friends if they have guns. Say that you will not let your children visit their homes unless the weapons are locked away.

Monitor the TV shows, news, and movies your kids watch. Limit their exposure to gun violence on the screen. Talk to them about the physical and emotional pain that gun injuries cause to victims and their families.

NATIONAL: Get the facts, and join national campaigns against gun violence: www.bradycampaign.org • www.stophandgunviolence.org

Go to www.familyeducation.com and type "guns" in the search box.

Carpe Diem! Influence Seized

**I'm asking you to believe. Not just in my ability
to bring about real change in Washington. . . .
I'm asking you to believe in yours.**
—President Barack Obama

As a major in the Illinois Army National Guard, Tammy Duckworth served in Iraq and flew combat missions as a Black Hawk helicopter pilot. During a mission in 2004, a rocket-propelled grenade struck Duckworth's helicopter. The result was the loss of both legs and the partial use of one arm.

"We serve because we believe in this great nation," said Duckworth from the podium at the 2008 Democratic National Convention.

As a double-amputee Asian-American female war veteran, she has used her influence to fight for better veteran healthcare, testifying before the Senate Committee on Veterans' Affairs. With the state of Illinois, she set up the nation's first-of-its-kind free screening program for every Illinois National Guard member, past and present, for post-traumatic brain injury.

No one would fault her if she retired, if she finished her PhD in political science and lived in a quiet way. *Carpe Diem,* seize the day, rings out from her Web site: www.tammyduckworth.com. Now with the U.S. Department of Veteran Affairs, she has seized on public service even after serving her country in a dramatic, life-changing way.

ACTION STEPS

➤ Do you have a cause with national implications? Arrange to visit the Washington, DC, offices of your senators or congressperson or key government agency by contacting their communications director.

➤ Consider a dramatic change—working within the system today to enact changes for all for tomorrow. Visit www.usajobs.com, the official job site of the U.S. federal government. Its headline: "You Can Change America."

Fighting Compassion Fatigue

Compassion literally means to feel with, to suffer with. Everyone is capable of compassion, and yet everyone tends to avoid it because it's uncomfortable. And the avoidance produces psychic numbing—resistance to experiencing our pain for the world and other beings.
—Joanna Macy

The term "bleeding heart" is often used in a derogatory manner these days, but its true meaning is both lovely and sorrowful. It describes those who are truly compassionate, whose hearts bleed for the grief of others.

Many bleeding hearts are drawn to professions that will help them alleviate the suffering of others and make the world a better place. You'll often find them in careers in healthcare, journalism, law, and education, to name just a few.

Because of their ability to feel so deeply, they are particularly prone to compassion fatigue, the self-protective numbness that can set in after years of seeing tragedy on a regular basis. The most unfortunate thing about compassion fatigue is that it affects those who are most compassionate to begin with, and it deprives the rest of us of their remarkable ability to care. To help people fight against it is a noble thing—it is to have compassion for the compassionate.

ACTION STEPS

➤ The next time you watch or read the news and see a story that involves a tragedy, don't only take note of the victims. Also pay close attention to those who have helped—the firefighters, the police, the volunteer aid workers, the people who see these sorts of events too often.

➤ If you can, jot down their names, where they work, or what organization they represent. Track down an address and handwrite a note, thanking them for what they do for all of us. Let them know how grateful you are. If you can't find an address, send your letter to the media outlet where you saw the story and ask that it be forwarded.

Widows of War

**Face your deficiencies and acknowledge them;
but do not let them master you. Let them teach
you patience, sweetness, insight. When we do
the best we can, we never know what miracle is
wrought in our life, or in the life of another.**
—Helen Keller

To love someone is to understand the inevitability of loss. One day, under painful circumstances, one of you will go on alone. We hope that day will come sometime far in the future, during old age and infirmity. But for the war widow or widower, that moment comes all too soon. The heartbreak of this loss leaves the spouse bereft with stunning suddenness. The "knock on the door." The uniformed officers delivering grim news. The return of the spouse's belongings in six black boxes. The distance, the violent circumstances, the tragedy of youth cut down in its prime, the absence of husband, wife, father, mother, lover, partner.

Taryn Davis was twenty-three when she experienced this loss. Her husband was killed by roadside bombs in Iraq. An emotional wreck, she surfed the Internet fourteen hours a day, looking for resources, but found none. So she began visiting other war widows around the country, interviewing them and filming their stories. From this grew a documentary (distributed free to war widows and widowers) as well as a support Web site for the bereaved where they can learn coping strategies and share stories, tears, and laughter. Taryn had hoped to learn about what her life would be like without her young husband. Instead, she learned that she was not alone.

ACTION STEPS

➤ If someone in your community has been widowed by war, support them in contacting www.americanwidowproject.org.

➤ Other widows or widowers may need your emotional support. Help them accept their new situation by being present with them as they express their sorrow. Make a point of spending time with them.

Mentor Former Prisoners

**The only real mistake is the one from
which we learn nothing.**
—John Powell

Every year, former prisoners are released back into our society. Most realize they have made terrible mistakes in their pasts and want to start their lives again. Yet even with active parole boards, many fall into the same traps that brought them to prison in the first place: associating with bad influences, taking drugs, or worse. If we could assist the passage from prison to our larger community, we could help thousands of men and women begin new lives that are self-respecting and self-supporting.

One organization that has taken on this challenge is VIP Mentors. Since 1972, they have been matching lawyers with parolees in California, helping them build better futures. Mentors serve as guides, advisors, friends, and role models, but they do not provide legal representation or money. Not only are they assisting these individuals one-on-one, they are also helping to create better and safer communities for all of us. On average, 41 percent of California parolees violate their parole and return to custody within a year, yet only 6 percent of parolees with VIP mentors are reincarcerated.

As a mentor, you are assigned a vetted parolee. Mentors check in with their parolees every week and spend a few hours a month on cultural, educational, or sports activities or just hanging out. These activities provide hope and a better chance for a successful return to society, as well as the nuts-and-bolts knowledge of how life works on the "outside."

GETTING STARTED: Former- and current-prisoner mentoring programs exist across the country. Some have a religious orientation, and others, like VIP Mentors, are purely secular. VIP Mentors are specifically looking for attorneys to be mentors, although many other programs do not have this qualification. There are even opportunities for formerly incarcerated individuals to be mentors. The Center for Faith-Based & Community Initiatives (CFBCI) at the U.S. Department of Labor is an excellent resource: their Web site is www.dol.gov/cfbci.

Healing the Whole Family

Praise youth and it will prosper.
—Irish proverb

In 1998 Melanie Goldish was caring for her five-year-old son, Travis, who had been diagnosed with a rare, high-risk cancer. When they returned home from the hospital after his bone-marrow transplant, there were numerous gifts waiting for him and, one day, also a gift for her four-year-old son, Spencer.

Spencer's face lit up as he saw his gift—a large trophy with his name on it. He proudly said, "Someone remembered ME!" In that instant, Goldish understood how invisible he had been feeling. She realized that there was support for children with cancer and their parents but none for their siblings. Goldish then founded SuperSibs!, a nonprofit organization serving nineteen thousand siblings of children facing cancer across North America. Siblings can access age-appropriate support on the Sib Spot at www.supersibs.org, and they receive ongoing Comfort and Care Packages that include personalized trophies, newsletters, feelings magnets, sibling books, journals, wristbands, and grief comfort for those who are bereaved.

"Every day in this country, forty-six children are diagnosed with cancer . . . and *everyone* in that family needs healing, including the siblings," Goldish says. Siblings often feel abandoned, forgotten, angry, and insignificant. "These brothers and sisters need to know that they are important and supported too."

"SuperSibs! helps siblings . . . emerge from the cancer journey with strength, and to build coping skills to face life's challenges in the future," says Goldish.

SuperSibs! also offers outreach and education for teachers, nurses, and social workers, as well as a college scholarship program. An $80 gift covers full Comfort and Care services for one child. A gift of $10 buys a personalized trophy. And $5 buys a sibling journal. All of these help these "shadow survivors" to heal.

VISIT www.supersibs.org or call (866) 444–SIBS (7427).

Lawyers Without Borders

No man is above the law and no man below it.
—Theodore Roosevelt

All lawyers are expected to do—even want to do—pro-bono work. There are plenty of worthy local opportunities to work for the public good, but for lawyers who really want a volunteer challenge, there's Lawyers Without Borders (LWOB). Founded in 2000, this international nonprofit organization brings together lawyers from around the world to support rule-of-law projects, economic development, peace-building, and sustainability throughout the world. LWOB holds special consultative status with the United Nations and works with other international non-profit organizations to promote the rule of law and address human-rights issues in developing nations.

Lawyers, paralegals, judges, and others with legal training can volunteer for LWOB and work in African nations such as Liberia, Mozambique, Kenya, Rwanda, and Uganda. Volunteers link with and mentor lawyers in these countries, act as trial and tribunal observers, help address threats to lawyers in conflict regions, provide counsel to nongovernmental organizations, and work on rule-of-law capacity-building projects.

At least a hundred volunteers travel overseas for LWOB every year as part of assessment or evaluation teams. This work is sometimes risky—intervening to protect a human-rights lawyer who is under threat in a developing nation takes a certain amount of fearlessness. Because of this, many innovative LWOB projects operate very quietly and from behind the scenes. For every volunteer who travels to a possibly dangerous place, however, there are many more, including nonlawyers, who do valuable work—research, writing, advising, mentoring, capacity-building, fundraising, and training—safely from home.

VOLUNTEERING for LWOB goes beyond the usual pro-bono work. If you're up to the challenge, contact:

Lawyers Without Borders, Inc. / 750 Main Street, Suite 1500 / Hartford, CT 06103 / (860) 541–2288 / www.lawyerswithoutborders.org

Take Action to Reverse Global Warming

I could not, at any age, be content to take my place by the fireside and simply look on. Life was meant to be lived and curiosity must be kept alive. One must never, for whatever reason, turn his back on life.
—Eleanor Roosevelt

Worldwide climate change is a massive event, and thinking about it may feel overwhelming. But the good news is, everyone can do something to help. You can take responsibility for learning about, and educating your neighbors about, global warming's potential impact on your small part of the world.

ACTION STEPS

LOCAL: First, read a short article about how local efforts matter: www .futurist.com/articles/future-trends/global-warming-local-solutions. Then, look at the National Geographic Society's interactive map of "Likely Scenarios if Climate Change Continues": http://environment.nationalgeo-graphic.com/environment/global-warming/gw-impacts-interactive.html. Click on your region to learn more, then click on "What You Can Do to Help." Remember, these scenarios only suggest what may happen if we *do nothing.* See "the top ten things you can do to reduce global warming": http://environment.about.com/od/globalwarming/tp/globalwarmtips.htm.

Spread the word at your neighborhood group, civic organization, or place of worship. Say exactly what you plan to do, and ask others to join you. Get your kids involved. See these Web sites especially for them:

http://epa.gov/climatechange/kids/index.html • http://tiki.oneworld. net/global_warming/climate_home.html • www.ecokids.ca/pub/ games_activities/climate_change/index.cfm

NATIONAL: Sign up for Campaign Earth's "Monthly Challenge": www.campaignearth.org/challenge/challenge.asp. Learn how to improve your personal "pollution inventory": www.edf.org/page.cfm?tagID=820.

Tell Me a Story:
The Influence of Your Life's Narrative

We tell ourselves stories in order to live.
—Joan Didion

We can give PowerPoint presentations and outline all the goals and objectives from now until the end of time. We can expound, expand, and elaborate on what we must do to change the world.

None of it will have the impact of a story to move another.

Our greatest politicians have known this for some time. Our life's narratives show the world who we are and what we believe in. We reveal ourselves, our influences, when we share our stories. "God made man because He loved stories," noted the writer Isak Dinesen.

The essence of the story, our life's narrative, lies in the questions that shape them. Envision the big questions. What makes this life one of service and love and meaning? Questions evolve into themes, into the stories that define us and help us serve others by helping them shape *their* questions and *their* stories.

ACTION STEPS

➤ Imagine you have a grandchild on your knee. The request is innocent: tell me a story. But the wish at the heart of the child really is: tell me, what do you value and what should I? What story do you now tell to answer the question?

➤ Shape your life's narrative as if you were giving a speech accepting the presidential nomination. Visit www.thisibelieve.org, an international forum to engage people in writing, sharing, and discussing their core values—the most compelling told in storytelling format.

➤ Check out the International Storytelling Center in Jonesborough, Tennessee, at www.storytellingcenter.net.

Nourishing Your Soul

Long before institutionalized religion came along with temples and churches, there was an unquestioned recognition that what goes on in the kitchen is holy.
—*The New Laurel's Kitchen*

In the Oscar-winning Danish film *Babette's Feast,* the main character shows up on the doorstep of two spinster sisters, seeking refuge from violence in Paris. For the next fourteen years, Babette works as their housekeeper and cook, preparing the bland Danish foods the elderly sisters request.

In secret, knowing the pious sisters wouldn't approve, she has a friend renew her lottery ticket in France each year. One day, she wins. She asks the sisters if she can prepare a feast for them and for a small number of guests. The sisters reluctantly agree under the condition she keep it a modest affair, befitting their strict sense of propriety.

So begins continuous deliveries of exotic ingredients, fine china, and expensive wines. The sisters look on disapprovingly. But then Babette begins to cook, with near-religious intensity. By the end of the movie, in a scene as delightful as the transition of Ebenezer Scrooge from misanthrope to philanthropist, the guests and sisters find themselves spiritually uplifted, old hurts and wrongs forgotten.

Only then do they discover that Babette was once one of Paris's most celebrated chefs, a high priestess of the culinary arts. The film may be fiction, but it accurately portrays the power of compassionate cooking.

ACTION STEPS

➤ Just for tonight, set aside any resentment about having to cook. Vow to put all your heart, soul, and love into it, no matter how simple the meal. Don't mention this—it's your secret gift.

➤ Set a beautiful table, even if a simple one: a flower in a bud vase, a votive candle by each place setting, a sprig of rosemary on each person's plate.

➤ Before the food is served, say a silent prayer that this food may ease each person's burdens.

Paying It Forward

Young people are more susceptible to change, and thus have a greater potential for rehabilitation.
—Mary Robinson, first female president of Ireland

Jeff Henderson spent ten years in prison, convicted of drug trafficking. While there, he humbled himself, took responsibility for his crimes, attended classes, and learned to read. Eventually, he found his way into the kitchen. His job? Washing pots and pans. But soon other inmates took a liking to him and gave him cooking jobs. He found his passion there and taught himself to cook.

After his release, he talked his way into several professional kitchens—usually proving himself by starting as a dishwasher or line cook. His talent was obvious. He began a catering business in which he employed ex-offenders and at-risk youths from the Job Corps. More than culinary skills, he taught these kids about taking responsibility, listening, and showing up. He became, he says, "their preacher, father, teacher."

Soon Chef Jeff, as he was now called, rose to the top of the kitchen in some of Los Angeles's best restaurants. He was the first African American Chef de Cuisine at two Las Vegas luxury hotels. And he became the star of his own television reality show on the Food Network—*The Chef Jeff Project*—in which he taught youngsters with convictions for drug addiction, petty crime, and gang activity to cook. "It's all about second chances," he says. "and it ties back to the community." Jeff, having been supported by his fellow inmates, pays it forward to support other at-risk youth in leading more fulfilling lives.

ACTION STEPS

➤ Everyone makes mistakes. Who do you know who has made a big mistake and now has no path back? Can you help them find it? How could you support them in turning their lives around and finding their passion?

➤ Go to Jeff Henderson's Web site, www.chefjeffcooked.com, to learn more about his transformation and the power of supporting potential.

Disaster Relief

**Real generosity is doing something nice
for someone who will never find out.**
—Frank A. Clark

Wildfires, hurricanes, tornadoes, tsunamis, and floods have become part of a constant conversation in our lives, when before they seemed like rare occurrences. Each year, victims of more than 70,000 disasters require aid in the restoration of their communities and, often, their lives. By lending a hand during these troubling times, you could be helping thousands of people in the United States or abroad get back on track after a war or natural disaster occurs.

Volunteers respond to dozens of disasters in various roles. They can be ditch diggers, sand baggers, snow removers, or debris managers. They race to the need of disaster victims directly on site, or work in make-shift back offices organizing the necessary arrangements for distribution of the most basic needs, like fresh water or food staples. They work with the Army Corps of Engineers or just respond to a neighborhood call. The Federal Emergency Management Agency (FEMA) has also started a brand-new initiative, called Citizen Corps, which aims to involve each of us in emergency preparedness and resilience. Citizen Corps asks volunteers to embrace the personal responsibility to be prepared; to get training in first aid and emergency skills; and to support local emergency responders, disaster relief, and community safety.

Each of these opportunities directly affects the lives of others during a critical passage. For many, this is the ultimate gift of service: to help another through a rough time.

GETTING STARTED: FEMA hosts two excellent Web sites. The first, www.citizencorps.gov, provides a way to register for voluntary disaster relief. The second, www.ready.gov, teaches that one of the best ways to help out during a natural disaster is to be prepared in the first place. This Web site can help get your home, your office, and your children prepared for any type of disaster.

A Voice for the Young

**If we don't stand up for children, then
we don't stand for much.**
—Marian Wright Edelman

Every year, approximately 800,000 abused and neglected children in the United States are caught up in the child-welfare system. When they are taken out of their homes, the world suddenly becomes a frightening place filled with police, therapists, social workers, judges, and lawyers.

With luck, one of the new strangers in their lives will be a Court Appointed Special Advocates (CASA) volunteer. The CASA program was started by a judge who felt he was not getting enough information to make the best decisions regarding the futures of the children in his court, so he decided to match each child with a private citizen who could both advocate for and watch over the child. CASA volunteers get thirty hours of specialized training in such subjects as cultural competency, writing reports, identifying markers of mental disability, understanding the court process, etc. In addition, they receive fifteen hours of follow-up training yearly and are under close and constant supervision with their local CASA chapter.

Social workers are typically overwhelmed, following forty or more children at a time, causing some to "fall through the cracks." But CASA volunteers (and there are 68,000 of them) advocate for just one child at a time. During a series of moves from one foster home to another, a child's one stable adult presence might be a CASA volunteer, and that advocacy may be the one thing that helps get a child what he or she wants and needs the most—a safe and permanent home.

It costs $79 a month, or $950 per year, to give a child a CASA volunteer. Eighty-seven percent of the money received goes to recruiting, training, and supervising volunteers. However, Jim Clune, chief communications officer with the National CASA Association, says no donation is too small. He explains that *all* donations are crucial in helping the organization provide trained advocates for abused and neglected children.

VISIT www.nationalcasa.org.

Best Buddies

The only way to have a friend is to be one.
—Ralph Waldo Emerson

Friends respect us, teach us, help us—they guide and encourage us on the path of life. Young people with intellectual disabilities want and need to have friends, but all too often they're isolated and lonesome, left out of social activities. Best Buddies, a national nonprofit service organization, recognizes this need and meets it by bringing together intellectually disabled young people with their peers in middle school, high school, and college. By matching a student with a buddy of the same age, the invisible line that separates those with disabilities from those without is crossed. When that barrier falls in the face of friendship, intellectually disabled people become better equipped to enter mainstream society and become as independent as possible. Those without disabilities learn compassion and tolerance. Both buddies learn self-esteem, confidence, and the true meaning of friendship.

Best Buddies was founded in 1989 by Anthony Kennedy Shriver as a way to honor his aunt, Rosemary Kennedy, who was mentally disabled. Best Buddies has grown to more than 1,400 chapters in colleges, high schools, and middle schools across America and in forty-two countries, making a difference for more than 400,000 people every year.

The primary goal of Best Buddies is friendship among young people of the same age, but volunteering here isn't just for kids. The Best Buddies Citizens program pairs people with intellectual disabilities with friends from the corporate and civic worlds. Best eBuddies creates e-mail friendships in an innovative and creative program that teaches people with intellectual disabilities how to use computers. Volunteers are always needed to help out at the many Best Buddies friendship events and fundraisers held around the country every year.

TO FIND a Best Buddies campus chapter near you, or to start one of your own, contact:

Best Buddies International / 100 Southeast Second Street, Suite 2200 / Miami, FL 33131 / (800) 892–8339 / www.bestbuddies.org

Help Kids Get Lost in Books

Those who educate children well are more to be honored than they who produce them; for these only gave them life, those the art of living well.
—Aristotle

On average, American kids spend almost four hours a day watching television, according to the Kaiser Family Foundation. Studies show that too much time in front of the screen reduces children's ability to learn, damages their school achievement, and even affects their chances of graduating from college. Be one of the concerned adults who helps turn this trend around—with a book club for kids.

ACTION STEPS

LOCAL: Talk to a friendly librarian first. Get a list of the most popular books for various ages. Decide what ages your program will serve. Children under seven or so enjoy being read to; learning to read will become more fun for them. For older kids, think about starting a book club for science fiction, detective stories, animal books, or another subject that will excite them. Approach people at the public library, PTA, or community association about donating time, books, funds, or space.

Find a cheerful place in which to meet after school or on weekends. From the first day, make it fun! Bring a variety of books, and let the kids choose. Don't make the group a chore; be positive, listen, and encourage everyone's efforts. Give kids reading goals for the next meeting.

NATIONAL: For ideas on how to motivate your children to read, try:

Reading to Kids, a Los Angeles grassroots organization: www.readingtokids.org/Home/main.php.

Tips from kids who don't watch TV: www.funfamilyeducation.com/television/family-time/32796.html.

Kaiser Family Foundation: www.kff.org/entmedia/1535index.cfm.

Fast Influence

**You say you want a revolution / Well you
know / we all want to change the world.**
—John Lennon and Paul McCartney, "Revolution"

You have an idea, a big idea, a great idea. You say you want a revolution? You want to use your influence and mobilize others fast?

One young women had a vision for her Brooklyn, New York, neighborhood. She planted it on her blog. "The goal is to sow wildflower seeds on every single patch of abandoned soil," the *New York Times* reported her saying. She thought she'd have to meet with neighbors and community leaders to enact it. Instead, the blog (www.21stcenturyplowshare.com) virtually planted the idea, and it quickly gained support. Donations poured in for seeds. Over one hundred volunteers gathered in the rain and planted eighteen different types of wildflower seeds including sunflowers, cornflowers, and black-eyed Susans.

Her influence flowered because of how she quickly mobilized her vision. New technologies—from blogs to vlogs to social networking sites and the power of 140 characters via Twitter to text messages—have revolutionized how fast we can use our influence to serve others.

ACTION STEPS

➤ Expand the reach of your effort by going high-tech. For example, learn how to set up a blog at www.wikihow.com, which outlines in eight steps, with video, how to do it. Also, Blogger is a free blog-publishing tool from Google with detailed instructions available at www.blogger.com.

➤ All of this technology relies on compelling content and links to other sites. Use your influence to enlist the most interesting voices you know to update your organization's blog or social-networking site, on at least a weekly basis. Use your newfound technological passion to set up a "linking" task force designed to identify and foster links to others via Web sites and within social-networking arenas.

Days Yet to Come

When I was young, my ambition was to be one of the people who made a difference in this world. My hope is to leave the world a little better for having been there.
—Jim Henson, creator of "The Muppets"

Perhaps you've heard of seven-generation thinking. It's the tradition by which many North American Indian tribes made important decisions—how it would affect the next seven generations of their descendants. Many people have heard of this tradition, but how many people have actually attempted something that would beneficially impact people they'll never meet, people who haven't even been born yet?

The ability to have compassion for future generations—to anticipate and try to prevent suffering and strife that doesn't yet exist—is more than an exercise in the theoretical. It is a deep and abiding understanding that the future cannot be stable without a strong foundation built in the present. And it also represents a recognition that the gifts of the present were laid down long ago by ancestors to whom we owe an enormous debt of gratitude.

Why don't you take a few moments to think about how you can leave the world a little better for having been here?

ACTION STEPS

➤ At least once in your life, tackle a big, long-lasting project such as raising funds to build a bike path between towns, complete a new fire station, or purchase a piece of public art.

➤ When possible, repair broken family relationships. Part of the ability to positively affect the future depends on continuity between generations.

➤ Be an engaged citizen. From corporations to bodies of government, you will see many attempts to pass off hardship to future generations. Do not let these attempts go unchallenged. Speak up in whatever way you can.

Lending Your Voice to the Voiceless

If you want to tell the untold stories, if you want to give voice to the voiceless, you've got to find a language.
—Salman Rushdie

How might you be able to impact the world? Your efforts could be particularly important when taking on the concerns of the voiceless among us—those individuals who have little or no clout: people with a mental illness who are homeless or incarcerated; battered women huddling in shelters with their children; the offspring of drug-addicted parents; abused children placed in foster care; the newly impoverished; the aged staring at futureless lives in nursing homes; the person institutionalized with schizophrenia; the abandoned and forsaken.

Without a constituency to argue their causes before legislative bodies, these people have little clout. Lending your voice and support can mean the difference between life and death for them. Take the example of Tanya Tull, a former social worker in Los Angeles. She couldn't stand the idea of homeless children playing with dead pigeons in the streets or being locked alone into skid-row hotel rooms. In 1980, with grit and determination, she created a social-service agency, Para Los Niños (For the Children) that now serves thousands of children and at-risk families each year, offering educational and support services to children as young as six weeks and as old as twenty-one. These are augmented with programs for parents: support groups, mental-health counseling, and parenting classes, among other services. One person can make a difference if he or she has the courage to speak out and support those who can't.

ACTION STEPS

➤ What constituency in your community is without a voice and can use your help? How could you support them in bettering their lot?

➤ Log on to www.paralosninos.org to see what one voice can do.

➤ Stand up for the foster children of America through First Star: www .firststar.org.

Executive Mentors

The past is a guidepost, not a hitching post.
—L. Thomas Holdcroft

Recently retired? Just because you're out of the workforce doesn't mean that you can't contribute to today's business world. One excellent use of your time, and your knowledge, is to become an executive mentor. These opportunities allow former executives to pass on their knowledge to the next generation of executives. As an executive mentor volunteer, you will be working with younger men and women, helping them up the corporate ladder, or you might be consulting on a specific project.

Some major corporations, such as Sun Microsystems, Hewlett-Packard, and General Mills, have established senior mentoring programs as part of their business models. The Service Corps of Retired Executives (SCORE) is a volunteer network of retirees who provide free mentoring advice to entrepreneurs throughout the United States. Some 8 million clients have worked with over eleven thousand volunteers who offer free, confidential advice on the phone or in person. The gold standard of executive mentors is the International Executive Service Corp (IESC), which maintains a database of executive volunteers and paid professionals. Founded in 1964 by David Rockefeller, IESC has placed more than twenty-five thousand former executives in over 130 countries. Whichever opportunity you pursue, you will surely be contributing to someone's personal business development or the continued growth of American and global business.

GETTING STARTED: Many alumni organizations at university business schools have mentoring programs. Contact your alumni-relations department and see if your alma mater offers one. If not, contact a local college/university or even community college or high school. The IESC has a very helpful Web site where you can register yourself and your pertinent skills: www.iesc.org, (202) 589–2600. Also visit the Service Core of Retired Executives (SCORE), which is funded by the U.S. Small Business Administration: www.score.org (800) 634–0245.

Caring for Our Girls

**The foundation of every state is
the education of its youth.**
—Diogenes Laërtius

Devawn, aged twelve, had nothing to do after school, and she was bored. When her mom was at work, she'd sit on the stoop and watch the boys cruise by on their bikes. But then a teacher suggested Girls Inc., and Devawn stopped by one day to check it out. It was an after-school program being held in the classrooms, labs, and gymnasium of a nearby high school. When she was there, Devawn was told she could be anything she wanted and that she should pursue the biggest dreams she could dream. This was an exciting idea to Devawn, who had never really thought about her dreams before.

Devawn started going to Girls Inc. every day after school. There was a class on economics she liked, and she started thinking maybe she'd own her own business when she grew up. (Although Devawn didn't yet know it, Girls Inc. offers a series of scholarships that might one day help her go to college—more than $2.3 million have been awarded since 1993.)

Girls Inc. is a national nonprofit youth organization dedicated to inspiring all girls to be strong, smart, and bold. Founded in 1864, Girls Inc. provides crucial learning programs to millions of American girls—particularly those in high-risk areas. (Of those they serve, 70 percent are girls of color, and 65 percent come from families earning $25,000 or less annually.)

Today, Girls Inc.'s innovative programs empower girls to reach their full potential and to understand, value, and assert their rights. Girls Inc. shows girls they can live successful, independent, and fulfilling lives.

Girls ages six to eighteen are offered after-school programs in areas such as science, math and technology, health and sexuality, financial literacy, leadership and advocacy. In 2007 Girls Inc. reached over 900,000 girls through their affiliates, their Web site, and educational products.

VISIT www.girlsinc.org.

Earthwatch Expeditions

We won't have a society if we destroy the environment.
—Margaret Mead

Instead of taking an ordinary vacation, if you choose an Earthwatch expedition, you'll spend a week or two as a volunteer directly assisting scientists with their field research. You might be studying climate change or endangered species or the state of the oceans; your project might be in an African wildlife reserve or on the Mongolian plains or aboard a ship at sea. No matter what the project or where it is, you'll return home with a better awareness of environmental issues and a renewed commitment to saving the only planet we have.

An Earthwatch expedition is a true scientific endeavor. It's not a guided tour or ecotourism, and the travel, living, and working conditions are sometimes primitive. You'll live, work, and eat as scientists do in the field. That means you'll work hard and find yourself doing things—and maybe eating things—you never imagined you could. Few volunteer opportunities offer as much of a chance to stretch your limits.

Most Earthwatch Institute expeditions are for adults only, but the Earthwatch Teen Teams program sends high-school juniors and seniors into the field as research assistants. Earthwatch Institute also offers family expeditions that aren't as rugged as the usual expeditions. Families with kids age ten and up spend half the day doing hands-on science with researchers in places like Kenya or British Columbia; the rest of the time is spent on family activities and outings.

When you go on an Earthwatch expedition, you're responsible for getting yourself to and from your research site. In addition to travel expenses, each volunteer opportunity has a minimum contribution, which goes to supporting the research and covering your housing, food, and other expenses while you're in the field.

IF YOU'RE READY for true volunteer adventure, contact:

Earthwatch Institute United States / 3 Clock Tower Place, Suite 100 / Maynard, MA 01754 / (800) 776–0188 / www.earthwatch.org

Collect Coins at Your Local Airport to Fight World Hunger

Life is something like a trumpet. If you don't put anything in, you won't get anything out.
—W. C. Handy, composer/singer

Many international airports have collection points where travelers can donate foreign currency they no longer need. UNICEF has raised over $60 million in their "Change for Good" program, launched in cooperation with airlines in 1987. However, the idea has not filtered down to local airports. It makes sense because many people are happy to get rid of loose change—U.S. or foreign—so as to speed their way through security.

Donate the change to antihunger organizations. Millions of people around the world, including in the United States, suffer from hunger. Airports overflowing with fast-food establishments are ideal places to educate people who may have time to kill while waiting for flights.

ACTION STEPS

LOCAL: Visit your local airport and pick out a few possible locations, outside of the security area, for your collection table. Contact the airport manager and ask if you and others can collect change and pass out literature. Usually the airport will have established policies; if you run into opposition, approach your mayor's office or state representatives. Tell them about your goals and ask for their help. Be persistent; ask for a trial period, and contact local media when your table is set up. Just a few hours a week will do for a start.

A good source of up-to-date information is the World Food Programme, www.wfp.org.

Here are a few other useful Web sites: www.bread.org • www.food forthepoor.org • www.oxfam.org

NATIONAL: See a national discussion of this fund-raising idea at www.whynot.net/ideas/43.

A Symbol of Influence

I'm not dying with AIDS, I'm living with AIDS.
—Patrick O'Connell, founding director of Visual AIDS, a group of
artists who developed the red ribbon; BBC interview

The red ribbon, which started it all, was for AIDS. Pink became the power color in fighting breast cancer, yellow for our troops. This is the power of a symbol. It did more for their causes than all the fact sheets in the world.

A yellow wristband—Livestrong: the fight against cancer from the Lance Armstrong Foundation does not mention the disease, yet we all know that's the cause. A symbol that rises above facts or figures and compels us to share our fellowship has value beyond valor. We want to wear the bracelet, race for the cure, and show that we stand side by side in the fight.

Creativity—it's the challenge to see the world differently, to see a ribbon as more than a ribbon but as a symbol of an epidemic—and even more so—of hope and life. Serve others by helping them see the world in more than one way. Act on your creative influence today. Know that you have the creativity to change the world.

ACTION STEPS

➤ You may have to work at your stroke of genius, experiment, and bang away at a symbol. Try this creative exercise: how many images can you see in three minutes of sky gazing?

➤ Play Twenty Questions with your cause. What are the questions you or anyone would consider related to your cause? The more you know, the better you can imagine and build a symbol that in the blink of an eye will say: I am working to change this, and you can join.

➤ There is an entire psychology associated to different colors. Every color has an emotional connection. Research color theory at major paint producer Web sites. One fun, detailed site, www.voiceofcolor.com, offers explanations on color theory and even a color sense online game to test your color intuitiveness.

Before Day's End

Beginning today, treat everyone you meet as if they were going to be dead by midnight. Extend to them all the care, kindness and understanding you can muster, and do it with no thought of any reward. Your life will never be the same again.
—Og Mandino

Wow. If you didn't have that reaction to the above quote, go back and read it again. Can you imagine the life-changing properties of such a practice? If you could really live in this manner, all impatience, frustration, and anger with others would simply vanish. What kind of person wouldn't extend all possible compassion to others on their last day on earth?

But as with all spiritual practices, there is the ideal and then there is the real. You will probably be good at remembering this quote at first. But then regular habits will slowly reassert themselves. And, fortunately, most people won't be dead by midnight, making it a challenge to treat them as such when you see them again and again each morning. As Confucius once said, in shooting for the stars, we hit the moon.

ACTION STEPS

➤ Before you go to bed tonight, copy this quote and place it by your alarm clock. Let it be the last thing you see as you turn off the light. When the alarm sounds, let it be the first thing you see tomorrow morning. Carry the slip of paper with you throughout the day to remind you how you want to behave toward others. Simply give Mandino's suggestion the best try you can. The most difficult thing at first is remembering to do it. So build in reminders: Have your work computer calendar pop up every hour with the message. Tape the quote to your phone so you see it each time you use it.

➤ If you find it impossible to continuously conduct your life like this, just devote one day a week to it. The Sabbath, whichever day of the week it is for you, comes to mind as a good day to act in this manner.

The Greater Good

**I must admit that I personally measure success
in terms of the contributions an individual
makes to his or her fellow human beings.**
—Margaret Mead

We always hear about society's ills: deranged individuals who shoot up schools and down airplanes, dictators who murder millions, greedy businesspeople who cause the collapse of economies while stuffing their own pockets. But did you know that there is an institute dedicated to the study of human goodness?

The Greater Good Science Center at the University of California–Berkeley is an interdisciplinary research center devoted to the scientific understanding of happy and compassionate individuals, strong social bonds, and altruism. Scientists in this institute hope that by studying people and their relationships, they will support well-being in society as a whole. They look to the social and biological roots of positive emotions.

The Center also publishes *Greater Good* magazine, a quarterly that supports people in applying its research findings to their lives. The magazine highlights the latest scientific research into the roots of altruistic behavior and includes stories of compassion in action.

The ultimate goal of the Greater Good Science Center is to support all of us in lighting each other up and becoming a more benevolent society.

ACTION STEPS
➤ What acts of altruism—contributions to the well-being of other human beings that do not benefit you—can you perform? What can you do to promote the greater good?

➤ Go to www.greatergood.berkeley.edu to find out about this unique organization. The Web site includes a sign-up for the Half Full Blog where parents are supported in raising happier, emotionally intelligent kids based on the latest scientific evidence.

Become a Doula

**Childbirth is more admirable than conquest,
more amazing than self-defense, and
as courageous as either one.**
—Gloria Steinem

Childbirth is by all accounts a miracle, and to be a part of someone else's experience is nothing short of breathtaking. A birth doula, or labor coach, offers expectant mothers and fathers a clear vision of the transition from couple to family that takes place during childbirth.

A birth doula is a knowledgeable, experienced companion who stays with the birthing mother and her partner through labor and birth, offering emotional support, encouragement, and wisdom. Birth doulas can assist childbirth during a home birth or in a hospital or birthing center. They work seamlessly with doctors, nurses, and midwives.

And while it might be enough just to be present for someone else, a real doula is professionally trained. Organizations like DONA International offer training, continuing education, and certification. They can prepare you for every scenario during birth, including how to handle the emotional as well as physical changes a birthing mother experiences.

There are many positive consequences of having a birth coach or doula present during childbirth. Numerous clinical studies have found that a doula's presence at birth can result in shorter labors with fewer complications. Mothers who use doulas or birth coaches make fewer requests for pain medication and epidurals.

A doula is usually a paid professional, though not everyone can afford one. This would be a tremendous volunteer service for you to take on, and the rewards would come with every birth you witnessed.

GETTING STARTED: DONA International is a leading trainer of doulas. For more information, visit their Web site, www.dona.org, or call (888) 788–DONA (3662). An excellent book that covers the roles of doulas and birth coaches is *Better Birth* by Denise Spatafora.

Honoring the Native People

Education is the best provision for old age.
—Aristotle

The name *Hopi* means "The Peaceful People," and the Hopi people have a rich and peaceful tradition of respecting all living things in accordance with Maasaw, the Creator of Earth. But along with the Navajo, the New Mexico Pueblo tribal communities, and countless other Native Americans, the Hopi have been marginalized since they were relegated to reservations.

And the ones who have suffered the most are the children. Three out of ten Native American schoolchildren drop out before graduating from high school—the highest drop-out rate of any ethnic group in the country. Schools on Native American reservations have the highest teacher turnover, and resources are severely limited. Less than 4 percent of Native Americans hold college degrees.

Futures for Children has stepped in, helping to ensure the right of Native American children to an education. The organization provides mentoring, training, and programs to more than sixteen thousand Native American students and their families. The result: 95 percent of Futures students graduate from high school, and 30 to 40 percent of them have enrolled in postsecondary education.

Futures for Children provides educational services through their Three Circles of Support: Mentorship, Youth Leadership, and Families in Action. More than 150 volunteers from tribal communities work with Futures for Children to deliver and monitor the programs and to encourage success for their children.

A high-school senior who was mentored since the second grade wrote, "My mentor has helped me get through tough times, and I'm glad that I have someone to talk to. I want to be a lawyer, like her."

The mentoring program costs $492 a year per child. A donation of $50 supports a youth leadership group in one of the Native American communities, and $100 supports training for Families in Action volunteers.

VISIT www.futuresforchildren.org or call (800) 545–6843.

Volunteer for a Medical Mission

I don't know what your destiny will be, but one thing I know: The only ones among you who will be really happy are those who have sought and found how to serve.
—Albert Schweitzer

As a healthcare professional, you went into medicine to help people. By volunteering for a medical mission, you can bring your skills and dedication to medically underserved communities.

A medical mission can be a professional and personal challenge. Medical supplies, lab tests, equipment, medicine, and even clean water can be in short supply. Along with your sincere desire to help and your medical or healthcare expertise, you'll also need ingenuity and flexibility. You'll be practicing your skills in ways and places you never imagined—and you'll discover again why it is that you went into healthcare.

Trained healthcare professionals have many options for going on a medical mission at home or overseas. Two good programs that need both trained healthcare personnel for treatment and training and ordinary volunteers for support and logistics are Global Volunteers and Remote Area Medical (RAM) Volunteer Corps.

Global Volunteers sends healthcare teams for short-term stints of one to three weeks in nearly twenty countries, including places as remote as the Cook Islands in the South Pacific. Volunteers go only where they have been invited by a local host organization, and they work under the direction of local people. RAM provides free healthcare, dental care, eye care, veterinary services, and technical and educational assistance to people in remote areas of the United States and in other countries. At its famed Reach Across America clinics, hundreds of RAM volunteers provide free care to tens of thousands of uninsured or underinsured people every year.

FOR INFORMATION:

Global Volunteers / 375 East Little Canada Road / St. Paul, MN 55117 / (651) 407–6100 / www.globalvolunteers.org • Remote Area Medical Foundation / 1834 Beech Street / Knoxville, TN 37920 / (865) 579–1530 / www.ramusa.org

Collect Used Books and Donate Them to Your Public Library

A good book is the precious lifeblood of a master spirit.
—John Milton

Many people discard books in the trash because they don't know what else to do with them. But most U.S. public libraries take book donations. Books donated to libraries are often sold to raise funds; such book sales are great gathering places for book lovers on a budget.

ACTION STEPS

LOCAL: First, check with your library for their policy on donations. Ask them what conditions of books they accept. You will also need to know the days and hours that donations are accepted and if there is a maximum number accepted per day.

Check local yard or garage sales listings; ask sellers if they will donate any books left at the end of the sale.

Designate a place for temporary storage—a clean, dry garage or attic will do. Never take in books with a strong musty or moldy smell—they will contaminate all the books! You might provide a tightly closed bin for these and take them to a paper recycling facility. Have strong boxes ready; these can be purchased at moving-supply stores or picked up for free at grocery or liquor shops. A person to provide regular transportation and one or two helpers to lift boxes will be useful.

For books that your library doesn't accept, contact thrift shops, senior centers, hospitals, homeless shelters, after-school programs, and prisons. There are also many Web sites that take book donations, such as www .bringmeabook.org and www.booksfirst.org.

NATIONAL: The American Library Association has tips for donating books: www.ala.org/library/fact12.cfm.

A list of organizations that accept books can be found at www.delicious .com/alalibrary/bookdonations.

Breaking Down Complexity

Don't let complexity stop you. Be activists.
Take on the big inequities. It will be one of
the great experiences of your lives.
—Bill Gates, Harvard University 2007 commencement

To turn our influence into action, we need to see a problem, imagine a solution, and envision its impact. And in our complex world, complexity often blocks all three steps.

However, even Bill Gates, the founder of Microsoft, manages a problem by breaking it down into four steps. In his Harvard University speech, he encouraged students to cut through complexity and fix the world's inequities by analyzing any problem in this manner: determine a goal, find the highest-leverage approach, discover the best technology for that approach, and make the smartest application of the technology available. He used malaria as an example of coming to a low-tech solution after breaking down a problem. The wide distribution of insecticide-treated bed nets has dramatically reduced mortality rates.

The most crucial thing is to never stop thinking and working—never surrender to the complexities of the world. Never quit. Each one of us has it in us to fight inequities large and small, to change our communities, and to influence the world.

ACTION STEPS

➤ Find a thinking partner. Engage smart people in helping you analyze, dissect, and solve the important problems you care most about. You can activate far more positive energy in the world by simply sharing not just your answers but your questions.

➤ Speak before a college class or with a club or even at a center for at-risk youth about the ability to make a difference that is in us all. Be passionate about the possibility of their personal impact, of their ability to influence the world, to give back, to serve others as you and so many—like Bill Gates—has discovered.

Compassion on the Menu

Epitaph for a dead waiter: God finally caught his eye.
—George S. Kaufman

If you've never worked in a restaurant, know that by the time you sit down for your meal, chances are good your server has already been insulted, barked at, and otherwise demeaned several times that day, oftentimes for things beyond his or her control.

This makes restaurants a prime opportunity for you to practice your particular brand of compassion. You can quite easily change a person's entire day from terrible to terrific with just a single side dish of kindness. You'll also find this to be an especially pleasant way to enjoy your own meal.

If you serve up a small helping of compassion to those who are serving you, you will find both your body and soul nourished by the time the check comes.

ACTION STEPS

➤ Set the right mood straightaway by using a little humor when your server arrives. If she says, "Hi, I'm Nancy, and I'll be your server tonight," answer with something like, "Hi, we're Chris and Michelle, and we'll be your favorite customers tonight."

➤ The government allows servers to be paid half the minimum wage because they're expected to make up the difference in tips. If you receive good service, the standard tip is 20 percent of the bill. If you think that's too high, go to a self-serve restaurant.

➤ Servers generally split a portion of their tips with bartenders, busboys, and dishwashers. Cooks, however, are usually left out of this equation. There once was a tradition of tipping the cook for a particularly good meal. Revive it by sending back five or ten dollars to the cook.

➤ At the end of their shifts, servers turn over their copies of all checks to their managers. Take the time to write a kind note on yours. Not only will your server see it, but so will his or her manager.

Practice Random Acts . . .

**You cannot do a kindness too soon, for you
never know how soon it will be too late.**
—Ralph Waldo Emerson

Astranger stops to give you directions because you seem lost. A co-worker provides comfort and a sense of calm during a turbulent time in your business. Your teenage son helps an elderly neighbor bring in her groceries—without your having to ask him! Your friend leaves food for your dog and fills her water dish while you are delayed at an out-of-town meeting. A woman finds your lost wallet and returns it to your home, wanting nothing in return.

There are so many supportive acts that we do for one another every day. But how do we support the continued proliferation of these kindnesses? The Kindness Project was started in 2005 by a group of friends to do just that. These friends realized that the less friendly strangers were to them, the less friendly they were in return. They felt they were becoming the cold, distant people they typically avoided. Adhering to the golden rule—do unto others as you would have them do unto you—they decided to use numbered tokens to recognize and support small kindnesses people do for one another.

The friends felt that if these small acts of kindness were recognized, people would be more motivated to reciprocate and to help others. The tokens are passed forward. Using their serial numbers, you can track the progress of your tokens online. Spread kindness around the world!

ACTION STEPS

➤ Pay attention to the small kindnesses that come your way daily. Keep a journal of how these generous acts make you feel. Record the kind acts you perform that support others.

➤ Log on to www.kindnessproject.com to find out about how to obtain and track kindness tokens. E-mail: info@kindnessproject.com. Phone: (512) 447–9993.

Man a Suicide/Crisis Hotline

Suicide is a permanent solution to a temporary problem.
—Phil Donahue

Every year, over thirty thousand Americans commit suicide. Many of these individuals believed there was nowhere for them to turn. But they were wrong. Fortunately there have been millions of people who have relied on the services of suicide hotlines, people who were able to save their own lives by reaching out for help.

By choosing this unique opportunity, you will be helping a wide range of people overcome one of the most critical times in their lives. You can provide the voice of reason in an otherwise unstable environment. Most important, you will literally be there for someone when they have no one else to count on or turn to.

If you are calm by nature, open-minded, and resourceful, this opportunity may be right for you. As a hotline volunteer, you will be trained to answer crisis calls for a variety of issues. Sometimes the calls will come from a person thinking of suicide; other calls will come from a family member or a friend. Frequently, volunteers provide support and guidance to those with issues of abuse or violence, economic problems, sexual-orientation issues, homelessness, substance abuse, physical illness, or even pervasive loneliness.

A second equally important way to volunteer is to help get the word out about suicide hotlines. There are local and national organizations that provide these services, but the hotlines are only effective if their telephone numbers are well known. Volunteers distribute wallet cards, flyers, and brochures that list the warning signs of suicide to doctors' offices, places of worship, senior centers, community centers, and other gathering spaces.

GETTING STARTED: The National Suicide Prevention Hotline has an updated list of hotlines across the country staffed by volunteers. For more information, visit www.suicidepreventionlifeline.org. Another Web site that promotes suicide prevention is www.save.org. They can provide printed materials for you to distribute.

A View of the World

Let your heart feel for the afflictions and distress of everyone, and let your hand give in proportion to your purse.
—George Washington

A disaster—a flood, a tidal wave, or a deadly epidemic—can strike at any time, without warning. World Vision, an international aid organization, serves close to 100 million people in nearly one hundred countries around the world (including the United States), responding quickly when disaster strikes. People they help include earthquake and hurricane survivors, survivors of famine and civil war, and refugees.

World Vision's Web site has a fun and dynamic "gift catalog" page, where you can choose exactly how much to give and what that donation will provide to people recovering from disaster. Examples include:

➤ **$25: TWO CHICKENS**

Fresh eggs raise the levels of protein and other nutrients in a family's diet, and the sale of extra eggs generates income.

➤ **$30: A BACKPACK AND SCHOOL SUPPLIES**
Basic school supplies can offer a chance of education to a child.

➤ **$35: FARMING TOOLS**
Supplies like seeds, fertilizer, hoes, harvest equipment, and irrigation kits offer hope to farming communities devastated by drought.

➤ **$75: A GOAT**
A goat provides a family with protein-rich milk, cheese, and yogurt. It also provides fertilizer that can dramatically increase crop yields.

➤ **$500: A DAIRY COW**
Capable of producing 120,000 glasses of milk in its lifetime, a cow boosts a family's protein and calcium intake, and both extra dairy products and the cow's offspring can be sold for extra income.

VISIT www.worldvision.org.

Give a Child a First Book

You have brains in your head. You have feet in your shoes. You can steer yourself, any direction you choose.
—Dr. Seuss

Do you remember the thrill you felt when you got your first brand-new book of your very own? One that you could read yourself? You probably still have fond memories of the person who gave it to you. That book made a difference to you. It opened the door to the magic of reading.

Too many kids in low-income populations never get their first book. In fact, in their homes and even in their schools, age-appropriate books are scarce. You can spread the reading magic by volunteering to give these kids books of their own.

The organization First Book aims to help solve the shortage of books in low-income areas by providing new books and other learning resources to children in preschools, shelters, day-care centers, and through other community organizations. Founded in 1992, First Book is a centralized network of more than twenty thousand local groups serving millions of children. So far, they have distributed more than 60 million new books to children from low-income families in thousands of communities. Volunteers help with the First Books mission by forming local advisory boards drawn from the community. These people come together and raise awareness and funds to provide new books to local literacy programs. Nationwide, there are about 275 advisory boards. Even if there isn't one near you (and even if you can't start one), volunteers are still needed at the First Book National Book Bank, which distributes new books donated by publishers. Volunteers are needed to help with sorting and distributing the titles. Anywhere from twenty-five to thirty giveaways are held every year in various places around the country, often in conjunction with the U.S. Coast Guard, which has made First Book its signature charity.

TO GIVE a child the gift of reading:

First Book / 1319 F Street NW, Suite 1000 / Washington, DC 20004–1155 / (866) 393–1222 / www.firstbook.org

Bring Fair Trade to Local Government

**If you let your fear of consequence prevent
you from following your deepest instinct, then
your life will be safe, expedient and thin.**
—Katharine Butler Hathaway

There is a growing movement toward using fair-trade materials in government operations. "Fair trade" means that producers (of paper, coffee, and fabrics, for instance) are fairly compensated and have safe and healthy working conditions. They may be nearby or far away. While we should all make an effort to buy such products, it is especially important that governments do so—because governments consume so much more and because they provide an example for citizens and local businesses.

Ask your local government to use fair-trade products at their facilities—such as the town hall, village police station, and public library. Buying habits may not be easy to change; current suppliers might be "traditional" or be used simply because they "have connections." But you can get a conversation going.

ACTION STEPS

LOCAL: With a little information, it really isn't difficult for local governments to do this. Check out some of the Web sites below. Using the directories and links on these sites, locate some convenient distributors of the materials. Send for literature or download it from their Web sites.

Choose a few products that seem promising for use by your local government. Then call your town or village offices; find out who's in charge of procurement. Make an appointment or, if that's not possible, write a letter. Explain why their using such materials matters to you. Pass along the literature, but don't stop there. Buy these products; write letters to the editor of your local paper; discuss the issue at your civic group.

NATIONAL: For information on fair-trade products: www.fairtrade resource.org • www.fairtradefederation.org • www.transfairusa.org • www.globalexchange.org/campaigns/fairtrade/coffee

The Courage to Act

The stories of past courage can define that ingredient—
they can teach, they can offer hope, they can provide
inspiration. But they cannot supply courage itself.
For this each man must look into his own soul.
—John F. Kennedy, *Profiles in Courage*

Influence: each of us has it—the power to be an agent of change, to be a doer of good things, even great things. We hold in our hands the courage to provoke change, to influence the future today. And yet we hesitate. We are timid. Immobile. We protest that we have no influence. What we mean is that we have no courage.

To provoke change, to have courage and to use the power of your influence—all this lies within. But one must act.

In 1961, then-president Kennedy had the vision to declare that the United States would put a man on the moon within a decade. But when it came down to the act, Neil Armstrong, on Apollo 11, on July 21, 1969, had to have the courage of his convictions. He had to venture that first step. Literally, he had to walk on the moon. And with these immortal words, he did: "That's one small step for man, one giant leap for mankind."

While we are not called every day to walk on the moon, we are called to face the extraordinary challenges of the twenty-first century. And for this we must summon the courage of our conscience and turbocharge the influence of our conviction in order to serve others. We must act, to take that first step—to make that giant leap—for ourselves and for all mankind.

ACTION STEPS

➤ Astronauts spend years in preparation for their journeys. Close your eyes. What preparation do you need for your journey of influence? Is there an expert, teacher, or mentor you need to talk with today? Break down the influence you need into key steps. Start with: my goal is _____. My big obstacle to influencing my goal is _____. Now, what is the first step in making your influence a reality?

Compassion for Yourself

It is possible to travel the whole world in search of one who is more worthy of compassion than oneself. No such person can be found.
—Buddha

If all the people who came into contact with you every day could clearly see the complete history of who you are, they would be both heartbroken and humbled by the hurt you have endured, the suffering you have borne, and, in spite of it all, the kind and decent person you have become. But the truth is, no one completely knows all that you've been through. No one but you.

For this very reason, you must learn to feel compassion for yourself. This is not to suggest that you should wallow in self-pity and get caught up in the pain of things past. This is to say, though, that you cannot begin to feel true compassion for others unless you are able to recognize that you are as worthy as anyone else on this planet of caring words and loving touches and kindnesses deserved and undeserved.

ACTION STEPS

➤ Take a piece of paper and begin writing down the things that have hurt you the most over the course of your lifetime. Don't hesitate in the least, just write freely.

➤ Once you're done, put the piece of paper away for a while in a place where you can't see it. Fix yourself a cup of tea, draw yourself a bath, or go for a walk. Make a bit of mental space between you and that paper.

➤ When you feel ready, come back to it, take it out, and read it. Don't see it as your writing—rather, consider it a letter from a close, personal friend. Finish it, and do exactly what you would do for a friend: say softly, "It's going to be okay."

School Opportunities

Education is not filling a bucket, but lighting a fire.
—William Butler Yeats

The federal government now mandates that 1 percent of a school district's Title 1 funding must be spent on programs for parents. This is based on Woodrow Wilson's belief that we own our public-school system. We pay for it, and as owners, we're responsible to participate in it. Parents, grandparents, and other caring adults are the best resources for today's ailing schools because they have a vested interest in the institutions and their children's success.

Surely you can volunteer a minimum of five hours per semester at your public school. What can you do to help? Plenty! Tutor a student or listen to small groups of kids read. If you're proficient in a foreign language, translate for children who are recent immigrants. Help a teacher with clerical work, prepare bulletin boards and posters, chaperone field trips. Share your interesting career, organize security, volunteer in the library or garden, do carpentry, photograph or videotape school activities, and help kids develop their computer skills.

The possibilities are endless from stuffing envelopes to providing snacks and sewing costumes for plays. All you need is the desire and the commitment to provide much-needed support.

ACTION STEPS

➤ Inquire at your school about parent/caring-adult programs. Is there a list of needs? If not, identify skills you can contribute. How might you support the educational environment for all the students, not just your own?

➤ Contact Project Appleseed, the foremost program for the involvement of parents, grandparents, and caring adults in our public schools: www.projectappleseed.org. Learn how to take responsibility for the safety and education of the children in your community.

Take Our Daughters and Sons to Work

Pleasure in the job puts perfection in the work.
—Aristotle

Many of us love our jobs. So what better way to show others what goes on at the office, store, barn, or school than to join the national program Take Our Daughters and Sons to Work. By showing young people exactly what you do, you are opening up myriad possibilities for their future, allowing them to begin to think creatively about what type of family and work life they would like to have.

A second goal of this program is to connect what children learn at school with the actual working world. You can show them how the math, science, writing, foreign language, or arts skills they are developing are used outside the classroom. They will also see how you strive or thrive in your job, giving them another insight into your own personal relationships. Not only will the child "shadow" you throughout the day, the experience offers a chance for the two of you to engage in a new conversation, answer questions, and creatively solve problems for both your workplace and their school day.

This program also offers opportunities to mentor beyond your own family. One nice idea is to bring a different child every year, or let your children attend with another adult at their workplace to expose them to even more employment possibilities. The recommended age range is eight to eighteen.

GETTING STARTED: The national date for the Take Our Daughters and Sons to Work program is the fourth Thursday in April. The national organization can be reached at www.daughtersandsonstowork.org, (800) 676–7780. If your place of work does not formally participate in the national program, ask your boss if you can bring your daughter, son, or other student to your workplace anyway. The Web site offers tons of activities and preparation materials that are applicable for this program, or if you are creating one for yourself.

Feeding the Hungry

**One cannot think well, love well, sleep
well, if one has not dined well.**
—Virginia Woolf

On San Francisco's Embarcadero, a well-dressed man sits looking out at the sweeping view of the bay while drinking champagne and eating Dungeness crab. On the other side of town, at a church-run shelter, a homeless man picks up a spoon to taste the soup he's just been served. What do these two men have in common? They are both eating food made at the acclaimed Fog City Diner, a donor in the Food Runners program.

Food Runners was the brainchild of Mary Risley, who runs the Tante Marie's Cooking School. For years, at the end of the day, she always had to decide—should she give the seven boneless, pâté-filled ducks she'd made in a demonstration to her employees or simply throw them away?

Then one day in the late eighties she saw a homeless man rummaging through a trash can for food, when it hit her. She thought, *Wait a minute: we have enough food to feed everybody!* With her new vision, she reached out to other chefs, restaurateurs, and local markets. Soon she had volunteers picking up perishable and prepared food all over the city and "running" it to homeless shelters. Today, Food Runners provides three thousand meals a week to 250 shelters and halfway houses. That is ten tons of food a week that would have been thrown away.

"Food is the way I can help," says Risley, who was named Humanitarian of the Year in 1999 by the James Beard Foundation. "I can't give money the way Bill Gates can, but I can give food."

Donors of $50 or more will receive their choice of a Food Runners T-shirt or apron, and those who contribute $500 or more will be invited to a dinner cooked by a well-known Bay Area chef (often in Mary Risley's private home!).

VISIT www.foodrunners.org. Or if you want to help feed the homeless in other cities, check out Philabundance, in Philadelphia (www.philabundance.org), or Fork It Over! in Portland (www.forkitover.org).

Hospice Care

Volunteers are the only human beings on the face of the earth who reflect this nation's compassion, unselfish caring, patience, and just plain love for one another.
—Erma Bombeck

The challenge of working with the dying as a volunteer isn't for everyone—and yet more than 400,000 volunteers work at hospices across the country. They're an essential part of the hospice philosophy of care, which sees dying as a meaningful personal experience, not a medical event. For hospice volunteers, the work is emotionally demanding, often exhausting, and deeply fulfilling.

Hospice care offers comfort, compassion, and dignity to those with a life-limiting illness. Hospice volunteers provide emotional and practical support for patients. They provide the simple companionship that can make a huge difference to a dying person. By visiting, helping patients go for walks and outings, and assisting with basic needs such as eating, volunteers provide the compassionate support that helps the patients and the family accept death with grace.

Hospice volunteers also provide much-needed respite and support for family members. When family members know they can leave their loved one in safe, caring hands for a few hours, they're willing to take that time to care for themselves and their own families.

Bereavement support groups are an important hospice function, one where many volunteers are needed. The jobs here range from leading the group—which may require special training—to preparing the coffee.

Because hospice work takes some special skills and can be so emotionally taxing, volunteers are asked to go through an extensive orientation and training program before beginning their assignments.

TO FIND a hospice near you and get details on their specific volunteer needs, contact:

Hospice Foundation of America / 1621 Connecticut Avenue NW, Suite 300 / Washington, DC 20009 / (800) 854–3402 / www.hospice foundation.org

Volunteer for a Political Campaign

All politics is local.
—Tip O'Neill

Getting involved in a campaign is a great way to learn more about issues affecting your community and meet others who have similar concerns. At a local level, you will get to know the candidate personally and quite possibly have input into areas that you feel he or she should address. If your candidate wins, you may be called upon to serve through a job or another volunteer position; certainly you can continue to keep him or her informed about a subject you are passionate about.

ACTION STEPS

LOCAL: Study the campaign issues that you care most about; which local candidate seems the most likely to support your views? The local chapter of the League of Women Voters will have detailed information on candidates' positions. Call his or her campaign office and ask to speak to the volunteer coordinator. Offer to do anything that is needed to get your foot in the door. Even if you are only licking envelopes at first, volunteers who show intelligence, creativity, and the ability to work hard often advance quickly into responsible positions. Find out where your elected officials stand at www.votesmart.org. Bring a speaker to your town to help get other citizens involved in politics: www.americaspeaks.org.

NATIONAL: Many political campaigns organize through the Internet and/or over the telephone. Even if you live far from Washington, DC, you can help a national candidate of your choice. You could also set up a local campaign office for a national candidate or help an existing local office set up events. Although you may not get to know your senator or representative personally, you will learn about the issues that your candidate represents and how to organize for change.

Join the League of Women Voters: www.lwv.org (it's for men too!).

Join a national organization that supports a cause you care about. They will help you focus local candidates on that subject.

Influence, Greened

**Holy Mother Earth, the trees and all nature are
witnesses of your thoughts and deeds.**
—American Indian adage

Every day, the average American produces four and a half pounds of trash, according to the Environmental Protection Agency. Take a swig of your bottled water and think of that. Wait a minute. That bottled water is one of the main culprits.

Americans gulp down approximately 50 billion bottles of bottled water and less than 25 percent of the plastic is recycled. An estimated 60 to 90 percent of all marine debris, and 90 percent of all floating debris is plastic. And when a plastic bottle is tossed into a landfill, it will take hundreds of years to break down.

But you have daily influence through your actions. Do you want to keep contributing to the waste? The essence of our green influence is in promoting and encouraging alternatives that are as convenient as the bad habits we've participated in most of our lives—and actively and visibly using the dollars in our pocket to bring about effective change.

ACTION STEPS

➤ Support new eco-friendly cartons of water coming onto the market, Plant It Water (www.plantitwater.com) for example. Adopt this water in a recycled carton, and this company will pay it forward immediately. "When you buy a carton, we plant a tree" is their pledge. The nonprofit Trees for the Future (www.treesftf.org) is their planting partner. They also love water and will make a donation, from every carton sold, to the nonprofit A Single Drop (www.asingledrop .org) for safe drinking water in developing countries.

➤ Go to your local grocery store. Suggest to the manager that a green section be set up for a special promotion in April, around Earth Day, highlighting for the entire community the convenience of going green. Stress that items should be competitively priced.

The Big House

**Never look down on anybody unless
you're helping him up.**
—Jesse Jackson

The United States places more of its citizens behind bars than any other country in the world. There are over 2 million people in our prisons. China has the next largest prison population of 1.5 million people doing time in its jails. But, of course, China has four times the population of the United States.

Why is this? Is there some defect in the American character that makes us more prone to criminality? Or is it more likely that we, as a country, believe that showing compassion to criminals makes us soft on crime?

If you said the latter, many would agree with you. But it's important to know that most American prisoners are behind bars for nonviolent crimes, such as drug possession and selling drugs to feed that addiction. Look at it this way—if we locked up everyone who was addicted to something—smokers, alcoholics, coffee drinkers, and the people who need six cans of diet cola to make it through a day—we would all be in the Big House.

Many religious traditions consider it an act of the utmost compassion to reach out to prisoners. As such, you'll find organizations as varied as Christian ministries and Buddhist prayer circles helping convicts. And who do you want coming out of prison at the end of a sentence—an angry, bitter ex-con, or someone who believes there are people looking out for him and invested in his success?

ACTION STEPS

➤ Court proceedings are almost always open to the public. Within the next month, make it a priority to sit in on parts of at least two trials. Except in the most heinous cases, it's hard not to be moved by the lives that have ended up in a courtroom.

➤ If you feel enough compassion to want to help, contact your local Salvation Army or United Way. Both can steer you to prisoner outreach programs.

Artistic Expression

**The arts incarnate the creativity of a free people.
When the creative impulse cannot flourish, when it
cannot freely select its methods and objects, when
it is deprived of spontaneity, then society suffers.**
—John F. Kennedy

There are so many impediments to the arts today. Shrinking government spending, dwindling donations, and loss of interest due to personal crises have jeopardized free artistic expression. "Starving artist" is no longer a metaphor since that "day job" may also be more elusive in these hard times. You may want to support the arts, but other than contributing to your local museum, opera, orchestra, or dance company, what can you do?

Fractured Atlas is a nonprofit organization that supports a national community of artists and arts organizations. Their services facilitate creative expression by offering support to its 7,500 members so they can function more effectively as businesses. With a $4.5 million budget, Fractured Atlas provides access to funding, healthcare, and insurance.

The founder, Adam Huttler, never intended to create an arts service organization. He wanted to start his own theater company but realized he was better suited to the business of art than its practice. He transformed his company into a nonprofit that helps artists so they can focus more exclusively on their own artistic expression. With this support, they may be less anxious about how to survive and more apt to produce objects of beauty or provocation.

ACTION STEPS

➤ Identify an arts organization in your community that needs support. Create or join a donors' circle to ensure that this group is getting the funds it needs to flourish.

➤ Contact Fractured Atlas at www.fracturedatlas.org to see how you can contribute to artists' creative expression. The Association of Performing Arts Presenters (http://artspresenters.org) supports performing artists.

Join the Peace Corps

The best way to find yourself is to lose yourself in the service of others.
—Mahatma Gandhi

The Peace Corps, started in 1960, is one of the most famous examples of government-sponsored volunteer service. More than 195,000 Americans have joined this esteemed organization, serving in Mexico and Central America, Africa, Europe, Asia, and the Inter-America and Pacific regions. Their mission is legendary: to expand world peace and friendship by creating a mutual understanding of diversity and cultures between the United States and the rest of the world.

Peace Corps volunteers are sent to remote corners of the world to help people craft better lives in the villages and communities that have often been forgotten. Volunteers bring American ingenuity, technology, and, most important, hope. Assignments include education, youth outreach, community development, business development, agriculture, environmental awareness, health, and information technology.

To qualify for service, you have to be at least eighteen years old and a physically healthy U.S. citizen. While most people think of the Peace Corps as something to do after graduating from college, there are plenty of volunteers who represent a range of ages and experiences, including retirees. All volunteers commit to twenty-seven months of training and service. Once you have been accepted into the program, you will be placed where your existing skills and experience are most needed. Then you will be living on your own and working independently. The program is both physically and emotionally challenging, but the rewards are many. For the majority who serve, they remain committed to the organization, and its mission, because they were able to see firsthand the profound changes they were able to make in the lives of others.

GETTING STARTED: Visit www.peacecorps.gov or call (800) 424–8580. The Web site also provides information on other related opportunities for kids and teens, including fund-raising.

Through Another's Eyes

**You are not here merely to make a living.
You are here in order to enable the world to
live more amply, with greater vision, with a
finer spirit of hope and achievement.**
—Woodrow Wilson

The Great Depression was a time of terrible hardship for many. In 1932 a volunteer named Julia Lawrence Terry was helping people get assistance from the Red Cross when she realized that many people could not even see well enough to fill out the application. So she collected used and unwanted eyeglasses in her neighborhood, brought them to the city in a shoebox, and handed them out. And so New Eyes for the Needy was born.

New Eyes for the Needy distributes glasses to those who need them both in this country and worldwide. In some countries, New Eyes for the Needy works with charities such as Physicians for Peace and Feed the Children, and to date they have distributed over 6.5 million pairs of glasses to people who need them. In this country, vouchers are given so that people can get new prescription glasses.

Having the right glasses can make the crucial difference that allows people to work, drive, and live productive and self-supporting lives. Aaron, a seventy-five-year-old client, said, "I cannot explain the relief I feel not having to make the choice between my medication and healing the strain on my eyes. Each day I feel the pressure from my eyes getting less and less. I cannot thank you enough."

Last year New Eyes for the Needy helped 5,200 people in this country get glasses who could not otherwise afford them. Unfortunately, another 1,600 people had to be turned away for a lack of funds.

A donation of $60 buys a person in this country a pair of prescription glasses. Donations of used glasses will be sent abroad. Donations of jewelry, crystal, china, and silver will be sold at New Eyes for the Needy's gift shop in New Jersey, with all proceeds benefiting the organization.

VISIT www.neweyesfortheneedy.org or call (973) 376–4903.

Frog Monitoring

**Frogs appear slow to make up their minds,
but then they act precipitately.**
—Henry David Thoreau

Frogs and other amphibians are sensitive indicators of environmental change. Because they depend on fresh water and wetlands to reproduce and live, pollution and climate change have serious impacts, and today frog species are in decline around the world.

Exactly how and where frogs are declining are crucial scientific questions that need to be answered in order to conserve amphibians. Gathering enough information to answer those questions needs the help of citizen scientists. To help conserve frogs and other amphibians, volunteer as a frog monitor with FrogWatch USA. By gathering information about the frogs in your area, you contribute to a long-running research project that can ultimately lead to better habitat protection and conservation of these important species. Your data allows researchers to get an accurate idea of how frog populations are doing.

Being a frog monitor is a lot of fun—and it's a great family activity, especially if you have a child who's in the frog stage (it usually comes soon after the bug stage). For older kids, frog monitoring brings science class to life and gives them an idea of what it's like to be a working scientist.

You don't need to be an expert on frogs to be a monitor—you don't ever have to touch one—and you don't need any special equipment. You can also live just about anywhere. Even deserts and densely urban areas have frogs. The only real requirements are that you learn to identify some frog calls for species in your area, agree to listen for frogs at a wetlands near you, and send in your data sheets. Monitoring takes only a few minutes. Ideally, you'll do it a couple of times a week during the spring breeding season, but data from even one three-minute monitoring session is still valuable.

TO SIGN UP as a frog monitor, contact:

FrogWatch USA Coordinator / Association of Zoos and Aquariums / 8403 Colesville Road, Suite 710 / Silver Spring, MD 20910 / (301) 562–0777 / www.frogwatch.org

Trace the Waste Stream of Your Family's Trash and Recyclables

At every step the child should be allowed to meet the real experience of life; the thorns should never be plucked from his roses.
—Ellen Key, Swedish writer/feminist

Kids love "yucky" subjects. As a school project, have them follow the journey of trash and recyclables from your home to the landfill, incinerator, or recycling facility where they end up. Are "recycled" glass, metal, paper, and plastics really being delivered to recycling facilities? If so, where do those facilities send them? The answers may be surprising! Some recyclables, for instance, end up in Third World countries, exposing workers to hazardous waste. Ask yourself and your kids: How far should our responsibilities for our waste extend?

ACTION STEPS

LOCAL: First, find out which government agencies are responsible for waste disposal in your locality. Kids can arrange an interview and even ask for tours of the facilities, perhaps take photographs. Some questions for them to ask: What percentage of our waste is recycled? What company handles the recycling? If the recycler sends these materials out of state, what happens to them then? What happens to the waste that is not recycled; if it is sent to a landfill or incinerator, are environmentally safe practices used there? Has our community considered using trash as biofuel? Is there a public campaign to get people to waste less, recycle more?

NATIONAL/INTERNATIONAL: To get kids interested in the national recycling effort, have them check out the U.S. Environmental Protection Agency's site for kids: www.epa.gov/kids.

Learn about international efforts to generate biodiesel fuel from waste materials at www.mefeedia.com/tags/ecofa. Send this information to your representatives in Washington.

The Personal Made Public

**C'mon, be cosmically conscious /
cosmically conscious with me—**
—lyrics written by Paul McCartney

What reunited Paul McCartney and Ringo Starr after seven years? What had comedian Jerry Seinfeld and the flutist Paul Horn debating who had done it the longest? Meditation. The April 2009 Carnegie Hall benefit brought out the stars in a loud way for a quiet cause, The David Lynch Foundation, which seeks to teach Transcendental Meditation to a million at-risk students worldwide.

Many of us know David Lynch from his mind-bending work as a filmmaker. As an artist, he has been candid about the tremendous creative benefits he has gained from his thirty-plus-year commitment to Transcendental Meditation. He has transported a ritual that inspires his life—meditation—out into the open, in public, particularly in the raucous, stressed-out student world.

"Every child should have one class period a day to dive within and experience the field of silence—bliss—the enormous reservoir of energy and intelligence within all of us," transmits the message from Lynch, on the David Lynch Foundation for Consciousness-Based Education and World Peace Web site: www.davidlynchfoundation.org.

ACTION STEPS

➤ Transcendental Meditation is a simple technique practiced silently. Try it today—with your child if possible—for fifteen minutes. For more about Transcendental Meditation, go to www.tm.org.

➤ Is there a daily act of creative inspiration that has grounded your life? How can you influence others to use this daily practice to enable a less stressful and more joyful life for others? Close your eyes, meditate for five minutes on your ability to reach out to others, and then write down your thoughts of what you can and must do.

Healing as High Art

**Everyone has a doctor in him or her; we
just have to help it in its work.**
—Hippocrates

Have you ever seen someone with leprosy? You may think of it as a long-gone biblical scourge, but there are still about 2 million people living with leprosy, now officially known as Hansen's disease. It's worth doing an Internet search on images of leprosy to see what a horribly disfiguring condition it can be.

A humble Albanian nun by the name of Mother Teresa knew about leprosy firsthand. She cared for many people with leprosy through her Missionaries of Charity organization based in Calcutta, India. Someone once said to her, "I wouldn't touch those lepers for one million dollars." Her reply, given her vow of poverty, was unsurprising. "Neither would I," she said.

Healing and compassion have a long, interwoven history. The best healers are highly compassionate. The highly compassionate are the best healers.

But the most important thing of all, as Mother Teresa herself often said, is that everyone is able to learn compassion and to practice the high art of healing. Including you.

ACTION STEPS

➤ The three pillars of healing are touch, listening, and prayer. The next time you encounter someone in need of healing, employ all three to the best of your ability.

➤ For emotional wounds, one of the best therapies is a pair of shoes. Take that person on a vigorous walk, followed by a slow meander. Make good use of your listening skills.

➤ It may seem prosaic compared to the loftier goals of the three pillars mentioned earlier, but learn whatever practical skills you can. Sign up for that CPR course you've been meaning to take. Find out about advanced first-aid classes. Go to your local Red Cross and get training.

Hamburger Haven

**Thinking is easy, acting is difficult, and
to put one's thoughts into action is the
most difficult thing in the world.**
—Johann Wolfgang von Goethe

Imagine receiving the diagnosis, "It's cancer." Now imagine it's your child who is ill. There can be no more devastating news. Families with a sick child, whether it's cancer or another illness that has stricken the child, need all the support they can get.

This was true of Fred Hill, a player for the Philadelphia Eagles. His daughter Kim was diagnosed with leukemia. He and his wife camped out at the hospital during her treatments—uncomfortable, frightened, and dislocated. It occurred to him that others were in the same position. Many lived hours from a children's hospital or specialized treatment center. Where would they stay? It was the Hills' need coupled with pediatric oncologist Dr. Audrey Evans's vision (and support from the Eagles and the McDonald's organizations) that launched the first Ronald McDonald House in Philadelphia, in 1974.

Today nearly three hundred Ronald McDonald Houses around the world support families while their children are hospitalized. Families stay near the treatment center and are comfortable and cared for in private bedrooms with home-cooked meals. Research shows that a family presence in the hospital helps children heal faster. Fred Hill's and Audrey Evans's good idea has grown into an international phenomenon.

ACTION STEPS

➤ If there is no Ronald McDonald House in your community, investigate how you can get one started at www.rmhc.org. If there is one, volunteer to help families cope during this very stressful time, acting as host, cooking meals, and providing a shoulder to lean on.

➤ Who has a child with an illness and needs support? Organize a network of helpers for this family. Ask the Starlight Foundation (www.starlight.org) for help.

Barter Your Stuff

Wealth is not his that has it, but his that enjoys it.
—Benjamin Franklin

While it's true that we all need stuff, we often don't need all of our stuff forever. When you're done with something, instead of throwing it away, pass it on! You might be able to get new stuff that you really want by giving away the stuff that you don't need, and you'll be helping someone else along the way.

One national organization that specializes in the disbursement of stuff is the Freecycle Network. Currently made up of close to five thousand groups with over 6 million members across the world, Freecycle is an entirely nonprofit movement that services people who are giving and getting stuff for free right in their own towns. The interactive Web site lets you post the stuff you don't want and find the stuff you need, all within your zip code or neighboring communities.

The Freecycle Network addresses many individual needs as well as larger social goals. First, it recycles your unwanted stuff: instead of filling up landfills, your things will go to someone who can use what you no longer need. You'll also find new ways to connect with others in your local community as your stuff gets passed around.

Freecycle is close in concept to the age-old practice of bartering, but with a twist. The definition of barter is the exchange of goods or services, meaning that you would get something for what you give. Freecycle allows you to get without giving, or give without receiving, literally passing stuff along and improving the lives (and closets) of others along the way.

GETTING STARTED: Visit www.freecycle.org, and enter your zip code once you join (for free). If there isn't a group in your area, you can start your own by placing ads for your unwanted stuff in local community gathering spots.

A Safe Place to Turn

Nothing good ever comes of violence.
—Martin Luther

Domestic violence is at an epidemic level in this country. Nearly one in four women has been raped and/or physically assaulted by a spouse or boyfriend at some time in her life. And at least three women are murdered by their husbands or boyfriends each day.

Many battered women feel helpless. But there *is* help available: the National Domestic Violence Hotline (NDVH), a nonprofit organization that provides crisis intervention and saves the lives of women in danger. Each day, more than six hundred people call the NDVH, looking to learn how to escape the terror and brutality of their lives.

Because just the act of reaching out can escalate the violence at home, the NDVH does everything it can to protect the caller. For example, hotline advocates can make calls for you so that the numbers do not show up on your phone bill. Also, their Web site gives safety instructions before you are even connected to the site, and there is a red "escape" button on the site so that you can quickly switch from the site to Google if someone suddenly comes into the room.

The NDVH is the only national domestic violence hotline in the United States. It is toll free, confidential, and anonymous. It operates 24/7 in more than 170 different languages (using interpreters).

For many, making the call is the first step in finding their way out of an abusive life. Many of the people who call—especially women with children but no income—feel that their situations are hopeless. The hotline offers them hope and helps them take action.

For $200, twenty-five calls to the hotline can be answered—meaning that twenty-five women who feel trapped and terrorized can know that there is a way out. "But even $25 is a significant gift," says Ann Dowdy, chief development officer, adding that every penny donated helps get battered women to safety.

VISIT www.ndvh.org.

Reading for the Blind

The remedy for all blunders, the cure of blindness, the cure of crime, is love.
—Ralph Waldo Emerson

In the early 1930s, the American Foundation for the Blind's (AFB) Talking Books department pioneered the development of recorded books for people who were blind or visually impaired. Since then, AFB has recorded tens of thousands of books—from textbooks and classic literature to bestsellers and children's books. These books are professionally produced, and they're available to the blind at no charge through the Library of Congress.

Even with all the technological advances being made, huge amounts of print material still aren't accessible to visually impaired people. Volunteers are badly needed to read these materials aloud, either directly to the individual or by creating a recording. Reading for the blind, especially for college students, is always near the top of any list of volunteer needs. That's not surprising—more than 20 million Americans have significant vision loss. You can give these people the joy of reading again.

Today anyone anywhere can contribute by recording the written material digitally and sending the file to the recipient's computer. The informal reader networks set up by individuals or through local social-services agencies now often operate at least in part in cyberspace.

State libraries are usually responsible for providing materials for their visually impaired residents. To do this, they rely heavily on local and distant volunteers. Some participate in person or electronically by reading aloud for a daily broadcast, picked up on special receivers, of current newspaper and magazine articles. Another major area for volunteers is in the studio, recording textbooks, books, government information, and other materials. In addition to readers, volunteers are needed to prepare the materials for the reader and to direct the recording process. It takes a lot of people and a lot of hours to get just one book recorded.

TO GET INVOLVED as a volunteer, contact your local librarian, who can put you in touch with the right department at your state library.

Develop a Healthy Lunch Program
for Your Local Schools

Eating is not merely a material pleasure. Eating well gives a spectacular joy to life and contributes immensely to goodwill and happy companionship. It is of great importance to the morale.
—Elsa Schiaparelli

Did you know that the food served in most school cafeterias is high in fat, salt, and sugar and low in nutrition? This contributes to the epidemic of childhood obesity and even affects kids' performance in class. But some schools are bucking the trend. In Appleton, Wisconsin, a high school for troubled youth stopped serving junk food and food with artificial ingredients and began emphasizing fresh whole foods. The kids' attendance, grades, and behavior improved substantially!

ACTION STEPS

LOCAL: Start by finding out what kids are eating at school now. Get a month's worth of menus from the local school office or your own kids. How many high fat/sugar items are served weekly? Are there any fresh fruits or vegetables? Visit the cafeteria—what do kids eat, and what do they leave on their trays? Are there vending machines selling junk food? Ask your kids and their friends what they think of the school food.

You don't have to be a dietitian; it's easy to learn which foods are healthy. See below for some helpful Web sites.

NATIONAL: The Edible Schoolyard is a pioneering program that helps schools grow their own healthy, organic food and get kids and their families interested in healthy eating. Their Web site, www.edibleschoolyard.org, has a list of books to read and other useful information.

The Alliance for a Healthier Generation is a national group fighting childhood obesity. Their Web site, www.healthiergeneration.org, has school food tips for parents, kids, and schools.

The Influence of the Busy Woman

**You just need to be a flea against injustice.
Enough committed fleas biting strategically
can make even the biggest dog uncomfortable
and transform even the biggest nation.**
—Marian Wright Edelman

She is a mom, an educator, and the head of the Concerned Citizens of the Plainview–Old Bethpage Community, a civic organization that has partnered with the local police, fought against overdevelopment, and for groundwater protection. Carol Meschkow helped turn a local issue of groundwater pollution into a statewide cleanup of the gasoline additive MTBE, which was leaking from gasoline stations into local aquifers.

"They say give a busy woman a job to do and it will be accomplished," remarked Meschkow, who serves, without pay, her community of about thirty-five thousand on Long Island, New York. "My community volunteer work will always be based on the motivation to do the right thing and serve as an educator and mentor for future generations."

The influence of busy people is that they know how to get the job done in the most effective and efficient manner. And they do so with the passion, which inspires others to rally around them. Every town needs a neighbor with the drive and dedication to keep fighting the good fight. One person's influence can infuse community spirit and encourage us all.

ACTION STEPS

➤ Enhance the outreach of your neighborhood group. High-tech action step: Create a community-wide e-mail database via social networking sites. Low tech: Ask the main grocery store in your town to dedicate a bulletin board for concerned-citizens' issues.

➤ Work with your neighborhood dynamo to set up a community blog. Organize a team of local watchdogs to attend community meetings and write about it on the blog.

Gifts Unseen

When you give to the poor, do not let your left hand know what your right hand is doing, so that your giving will be in secret; and your Father who sees what is done in secret will reward you.
—Matthew 6:3–4

When Jesus spoke of the importance of giving in secret in his Sermon on the Mount, it undoubtedly caused more than a few confused looks among those who thought that showing their compassion through charity was nothing to hide. The same would hold true today—most estimates place anonymous donations at about 1 percent of total charitable giving.

The ability to be anonymously compassionate removes all ulterior motives from your actions, allowing you to experience the pure nature of it. It is compassion for compassion's sake alone—the equivalent of unconditional love. And it can be just as spiritually profound.

ACTION STEPS

➤ Make at least some of your charitable giving anonymous. There are many ways to do this. Here's one particularly charming way: The next time you're at a restaurant, secretly pick up the tab of a young family. Since most young families are chronically short on cash, your action will be much appreciated.

➤ Over the Christmas holiday period, sign up for one two-hour time slot of ringing the bells for the Salvation Army at www.ringbells.org. Do it in a neighborhood where no one will know you. It's a fascinating and often surprising look at who in society feels compelled to give and who doesn't.

➤ The ultimate in anonymous giving is to sign an organ-donor card and make sure your family knows of your wishes so that they're followed. Let your last act on this earth be one of utter selflessness and compassion. Go to www.organdonor.gov for an overview and instructions on how to become a donor.

Giving Your All

**We drew strength when our firefighters ran up
stairs and risked their lives so that others might
live. . . . It was the worst day we have ever seen,
but it brought out the best in all of us.**
—Senator John Kerry on 9/11

Fighting a fire means strapping on many pounds of equipment and drag-
ging heavy hoses and axes while rushing into a burning building. It
means placing yourself in harm's way—overcoming the natural instinct to
run away when heat, smoke, and flames erupt. Yet today, there are 800,000
volunteer firefighters in this country. These individuals are fully trained and
certified just like members of paid departments, yet they do this work for
free. Their mission is to protect and give back to their hometowns—a most
selfless act of support. And dangers abound. Firefighters, whether paid or
volunteer, have been injured or killed in the line of duty. Indeed, one person
has said that volunteer firefighters have "hearts as big as buckets."

This is a grassroots operation—since the beginning of our nation's history, individuals in small towns have pitched in to help. Volunteer fire departments are widespread—in 75 percent of U.S. communities, these brave
individuals provide the only organized response team when a fire breaks
out. They elect a chief from within their ranks. He or she holds the awesome
responsibility for the lives of the team and the safety of the community.

Certainly these volunteer firefighters epitomize the themes of service
and support. And most certainly they also deserve our support in the
important and self-sacrificing work they do.

ACTION STEPS

➤ If you live in a community that has a volunteer firefighting force, find
out how you can help raise money and awareness. Inquire about their
needs and how you can fill them.

➤ If you're interested in becoming a volunteer firefighter, visit Web sites
www.firerescue1.com or www.volunteerfd.org for information.

Give Others Financial Advice

**Money isn't the most important thing in life,
but it's reasonably close to oxygen
on the "gotta have it" scale.**
—Zig Ziglar

The Great Recession has proven once again that the financial health of any economy can quickly go sour and that most of us aren't prepared. According to the Consumer Federation of America, more than 52 percent of Americans say they cannot afford to save or are saving inadequately. With the average household credit-card debt soaring to between $8,000 and $10,000 and unemployment numbers continuing to rise, Americans are collectively panicked and can't discern which from among the myriad of supposedly reliable sources they can count on.

If you have a solid background in financial management or have simply created a personal-finance program for yourself that continues to work despite these troubling times, sharing this information with others can be as important as throwing a lifeline to a drowning victim. Your best-practices approach can help someone else get their financial life in order now, so that they will be better prepared for the future. Now, more than ever, your skills can create new hope and a new beginning for others.

You can relay your information in a one-on-one setting or as a group lesson. Important topics that can be covered include personal credit counseling, debt management, housing and mortgage information, bankruptcy counseling, increasing savings, retirement planning, and more.

GETTING STARTED: Volunteer to teach a course at your local high school or continuing-education center. There are dozens of books that are great resources to help you create worksheets and handouts, especially if you have one particular area of expertise and need to learn more about other issues.

Helping Others Stay Mobile

The fact is that even if your body doesn't work the way it used to, the heart and the mind and the spirit are not diminished. It's as simple as that.
—Christopher Reeve

Tens of thousands of disabled Americans desperately need power wheelchairs. But with new chairs costing between $5,000 and $25,000 or more, they are far too expensive for many who need them—even people who have insurance (but who can be denied a chair by their insurance company if they can stand or walk even just a few steps).

At the same time, many once-useful power wheelchairs end up being discarded in landfills or junkyards or languish rusting and unused in garages or basements. But how do we get these chairs up and running again, and how do we get them to the people who need them so badly?

Enter David Heim. David was in a car accident and sustained a spinal cord injury. After several months of rehabilitation, he started working again (driving his power chair six miles every day to work) and realized how crucial his power wheelchair was to his continued employment, autonomy, and sense of self-esteem.

David, a skilled mechanic, began restoring and recycling used wheelchairs and offering them to those in need for a fraction of their cost (or, in some cases, for no cost at all).

"When you're trapped and can't get around, it's the worst feeling. Having a power chair and getting your independence back makes a big difference," David says.

Since its inception in January 1998, David's organization, The Wheelchair Recycler, Inc., has given away over five hundred power chairs and has repaired hundreds of others. However, with the success of the Wheelchair Recycler and the high demand for his services, David and his helpers are now running out of working space and funding for their daily operations including transportation (picking up and dropping off chairs).

VISIT www.wheelchairrecycler.org or call (508) 460–6328 to help.

Meals on Wheels

It is an eternal obligation toward the human being not to let him suffer from hunger when one has a chance of coming to his assistance.
—Simone Weil

Meals on Wheels is one of the most widely recognized names in senior services. This remarkable program dates back to 1954, when the first meals were delivered in Philadelphia. Today it still follows its original mission of delivering hot meals to the elderly and disabled in their own homes.

The thousands of local organizations that make up the Meals on Wheels network often provide additional help to seniors, such as assistance with grocery shopping and getting to medical appointments. Amazingly, the vast national Meals on Wheels network relies largely on volunteer help to deliver millions of meals each week. In the Minneapolis metro area alone, for instance, about forty separate Meals on Wheels programs serve the elderly population, using nearly four hundred volunteers to serve four thousand meals a week.

Clearly, the biggest volunteer need at Meals on Wheels programs everywhere is people to deliver meals and spend a few friendly moments chatting with the recipients. Many regular Meals on Wheels volunteers deliver to the same clients for years. The close ties they form are just as important as the food they deliver.

All it takes to volunteer as a food deliverer is an hour or two of your time at midday, as often or as infrequently as you want. Volunteers generally pick up the meals at a catering kitchen near their home or work. They use their own vehicles to deliver them to local residents—often their own neighbors. With so many programs nationwide, there's bound to be one near you.

CHECK with your local senior-services organizations, or contact the national headquarters of Meals on Wheels to find the program nearest you:

Meals on Wheels Association of America / 203 South Union Street / Alexandria, VA 22314 / (703) 548–5558 / www.mowaa.org

Help Start a Model UN Club at Your Local High School

I believe that we are here on the planet Earth to live, grow up and do what we can to make this world a better place for all people to enjoy freedom.
—Rosa Parks

Model United Nations is an exciting program in which young people take the roles of diplomats, working in simulated sessions of the General Assembly, Security Council, or other UN bodies. This is a valuable way for students to learn about international relations, globalization, and diplomacy. Kids have fun while developing research, writing, negotiation, leadership, and public-speaking skills. They travel to conferences and meet other like-minded students.

ACTION STEPS

LOCAL: Study Model UN programs (see resources below). Approach your local high-school administration about cosponsoring a Model UN club. Speak with interested counselors or teachers. Ask them individually and then meet with them as a group. Estimate how many of their students might be interested; discuss ways to get kids involved. Set up a time for the initial student meeting, and spread word of it around school. At the student meeting, present the full scope of Model UN programs. The kids can then take over: electing officers, volunteering for committees, and dividing tasks like research and fund-raising among themselves. At least one of the adult sponsors should attend each student meeting and be available when needed for encouragement and support.

NATIONAL/INTERNATIONAL: United Nations Model UN headquarters: www.un.org/cyberschoolbus/modelun/index.asp • UN-USA clearing house of Model UN resources: www.unausa.org/modelun • Model UN resources from Stanford University: www.stanford.edu/group/Jonsson/mun.html

The Influence of Kim

**But if the while I think on thee, dear friend /
All losses are restor'd and sorrows end.**
—William Shakespeare, "Sonnet 30"

Kim knows the best doctors and most likely knows someone who knows someone if you need a recommendation. She's the friend who remembers your birthday when you want to forget it. Her birthday parties are mixers designed for everyone to meet a new friend. She's the person with the old-fashioned address book, a Rolodex, the precursor to LinkedIn and MySpace. She's a one-person social network, a superconnector.

"What excites me is bringing great people together with other great people," says Kim. She's also the go-to friend if something is wrong. She will connect you to a friend with a similar problem, or because she is Kim, she will connect you to herself.

We should all have the influence of a Kim, a superconnector in our lives. However, many of us don't. Maybe it's our busy lives, long commutes, working two jobs, and overall exhaustion that lead us away from friends. A landmark study, "Social Isolation in America," from the *American Sociological Association,* noted that the number of people saying there is no one with whom they discuss important matters nearly tripled from 1985 to 2004. Yet study after study shows that friends, especially as we age, keep us healthy—and alive.

ACTION STEPS

➤ Be a "Kim." Introduce your friends to one another—do this electronically or the old-fashioned way—face-to-face.

➤ National Friendship Day is the first Sunday in August. Use it as a reason to organize a neighborhood meet-and-mingle block party—organize teens to set up a friendship-bracelet table to weave bracelets for old and new friends. Find out how to make the basic friendship bracelet at www.parentingteens.about.com.

A Hook to Hang a Hat On

**Home is the place where when you go
there, they have to take you in.**
—Robert Frost

For thousands of years, until the establishment of the independent state of Israel in 1948, Jews lived without a homeland. Not surprisingly, they were exceedingly aware of the importance of feeling welcome in the homes of others.

This sense of obligation in caring for travelers and wanderers is a central tenet of Judaism. In fact, during the Middle Ages, many Jewish villages maintained a guest house where the traveling indigent could stay at no cost. In the Talmud, the Jewish collection of sayings and discussions of ancient rabbis, one of its writers goes so far as to say that welcoming guests is more important than welcoming God through the study of the Torah, Judaism's most holy book.

The duty of caring for others continues in Jewish communities today. You would be very hard-pressed to find someone sleeping on the streets of a Jewish neighborhood because he had nowhere else to go.

Join in this tradition that dates back to Abraham, the first Jew. Do whatever you can to make sure everyone has a roof over his or her head on your watch.

ACTION STEPS

➤ Become known as the place friends and relatives can count on if they ever need a place to stay. Keep a guest room or a foldout bed always prepared. This doesn't mean you have to let people move in with you. Just provide emergency shelter until you can help them find a place of their own.

➤ If you own a second property or a vacation home, set aside a week or two each year to allow someone to use it free of charge.

➤ Visit www.edar.org, where $500 gives a man, a woman, or a child a basic roof.

Special Children

Special Olympics is more than just a program of sports training and competition; ultimately it's a strong statement of optimism about human life. It says that every human being can learn and grow and contribute to the society we all share.
—Bill Clinton

Special children have special needs. Those with intellectual disabilities such as Down syndrome face particular challenges that can include shyness, social withdrawal, and coordination issues. Parents of special-needs children have challenges of their own as they struggle to find the right educational and social environment for their offspring.

One international organization supports many children with intellectual disabilities in finding success and self-esteem. The Special Olympics, founded in 1967 by Eunice Kennedy Shriver, seeks to reinforce dignity, equality, and opportunity for all people through their involvement in sports. Athletes compete in a wide variety of sports including alpine skiing, football, gymnastics, cycling, and figure skating. From this they gain skills that transcend the playing field—leadership, teamwork, persistence, and self-esteem. Their young-athletes program has enrolled ten thousand children between the ages of two and seven, supporting their motor, social, emotional, and communication development. Those who find their way into this program walk a path that leads to empowerment, competence, acceptance, joy, and friendship.

ACTION STEPS

➤ If someone in your circle has a child with Down syndrome or another intellectual disability, support them in contacting Special Olympics: www.specialolympics.org.

➤ Volunteer as a coach, a key component to the program's goal of building self-esteem. You will be trained, and no experience is required—just a willingness to watch children flourish.

Collect and Recycle Baby Clothes and/or Equipment

Real generosity toward the future lies in giving all to the present.
—Albert Camus

When baby arrives, the credit card comes out. And with each exciting stage of development, out go the old clothes and equipment to make room for the new. Bassinets, strollers, prams, high chairs, car seats, bouncy chairs, and more all have a usefulness of about one year. Once your kids have grown out of each, don't throw them away or let them gather dust in the garage! There are many others who can use these important items for their own growing families.

There is also a tremendous need for donations of diapers and gently used children's clothing. In 2007 the *New York Times* reported that one of the biggest needs of those living below the poverty line is diapers. While food stamps cover many foods, diapers are classified as "disallowed purchases," along with cigarettes and alcohol. The cost of diapers is enormous: the average baby goes through ten diapers a day, which can cost almost $700 a year. Organizations like the Diaper Bank of Southern Arizona need volunteers not only to donate diapers, but to collect, sort, and distribute them to local agencies, day-care centers, and even individual families.

By getting involved in these vital causes, you are helping families get through the difficult, and expensive, first years of child-rearing.

GETTING STARTED: Contact your local Goodwill (www.goodwill.org) or Salvation Army (www.salvationarmyusa.org). If you don't have a local outlet, find out if your local hospital or religious group organizes a clothing or equipment drive. Or throw a mothers-helping-mothers baby shower for someone expecting a child. Consider collecting new items and donating these as well. You can also explore if your community has a diaper bank, and if not, start one. For more information on finding or starting a nonprofit in this realm, see www.diaperbank.org or www.newhavendiaperbank.org.

A Laptop in Every Lap

I do not fear computers. I fear the lack of them.
—Isaac Asimov

It's easy to think that if a child is attending school, he or she is doing fine. However, what "being in school" means in many developing countries is very different than what it means in the United States. Children in remote rural villages often attend school for only a couple of hours a day, because they are needed to work in the fields or in factories to help support their families. And the typical expenditure on public education is $200 to $250 per child (compared to $10,000 per child in the United States).

Enter One Laptop per Child (OLPC), a nonprofit organization that distributes XO laptop computers to schoolchildren around the world. The XO laptop is a very low-cost, child-friendly laptop computer that can deliver a quantum leap in the education and potential of a child. Studies have shown that children who have their own laptops are more expressive and read more than children who can only access computers through labs or Internet cafés. And having a laptop can provide a badly-needed connection to others for children who live in remote areas.

The XO laptop is about the size of a small textbook and has a unique screen that is readable under direct sunlight for children who go to "school" outdoors. It's made to survive extreme environmental conditions, is very energy efficient, and, perhaps most important, it's really fun.

To date, OLPC has distributed nearly 1 million XO laptops in nineteen languages in thirty-one countries, such as Rwanda, Nepal, Mongolia, Haiti, Peru, and Uruguay, and teachers across the board have given the program rave reviews. Once the laptops are given to the children, school attendance goes way up, and behavior problems go way down. And, in many cases, the children go home after school and teach their parents how to use the computer, thus furthering global computer literacy.

A donation of $199 will buy a schoolchild a XO laptop; $1,990 will buy ten.

VISIT www.laptop.org.

USO: Serving Those Who Serve

**I just think it's my responsibility as a human
being and an entertainer to see the soldiers.**
—Coolio

Think of the USO, and you inevitably think of entertainers such as Bob Hope, who travel the world volunteering their time, often under combat conditions, to bring some entertainment to those serving their country.

You're probably not a famous entertainer, but you can still volunteer to help the USO. A private, nonprofit organization whose mission is to support the troops by providing morale, welfare, and recreation services, the USO operates more than 135 centers worldwide, including in Germany, South Korea, Kuwait, and Afghanistan. Service members and their families visit USO centers nearly 7 million times a year for activities, advice, help, and just a friendly face offering a touch of home.

All that activity takes a small army of volunteers—about twenty-five thousand of them every year. A major area for USO volunteers is greeting and supporting the three thousand troops who arrive each day at airports in the United States as they return home on leave or depart again. Two special programs have developed from the current American presence in Iraq and Afghanistan: Operation USO Care Package and USO Operation Phone Home. Care packages send badly needed items such as lip balm, sunscreen, reading material, and more to combat troops stationed overseas—more than 1.5 million boxes since the program began in 2002. Operation Phone Home distributes free international calling cards to soldiers at home and overseas—more than 2.2 million cards since the program began in 2003.

Volunteers are always needed at USO centers and at the greeting desks the USO runs at airports for troops in transit. Help is also needed to provide care packages and phone cards by organizing a local drive or volunteering to help pack and ship the boxes.

FOR INFORMATION contact:

USO World Headquarters / Box 96860 / Washington, DC 20090–6860 / (888) 484–3876 / www.uso.org

Get Involved in "Green" Planning for Your County or State Fair

You should keep on learning as long as there is something you do not know.
—Seneca, Roman philosopher and statesman

Everyone loves a fair, and local fairs are a great place to demonstrate green initiatives to people of all ages. Organic gardening and farming, environmentally sound livestock management, recycling, and conserving natural resources can all be featured in fairs' booths, exhibits, and competitions.

ACTION STEPS

LOCAL: Find out who's in charge of planning your county or state fair. Ask them to work with you on creating more "green" exhibits. Learn about the application process for exhibitors. Talk to local farmers, 4-H clubs, county extension agents, and cooking and garden clubs to find out who has exhibited before. Ask them for help.

Using the resources below, find farmers in your area who use organic or sustainable methods. Approach them about exhibiting at the fair. Explain how that will help promote these ideas as well as their businesses.

Consider participating with your school, youth group, or club. Kids could develop exhibits on composting, recycling, or energy conservation. Cooks could compete for the best whole-food recipes.

NATIONAL: Directory of state and county fairs in the United States and Canada: www.fairsandexpos.com/associations.aspx.

Searchable database of local farms: www.localharvest.org.

See what some local fairs are doing: www.tennesseestatefair.org/mustsee/green.asp • http://nevadacountyfair.blogspot.com/2008/08/going-green-at-nevada-county-fair.html • www.co.dakota.mn.us/countygovernment/news/archive/easygreen.htm

Live Light . . . Live Right Influences

A healthy future is our gift to our children.
—U.S. Surgeon General's pledge

The waiting room is packed, even more so because all the mothers have in hand their "little" children, who are fifty, one hundred, or more pounds overweight. This is ground zero of our nation's obesity crisis.

These families are awaiting the weekly clinic at the Live Light . . . Live Right program. Based in one of the toughest neighborhoods in our country, the Brownsville–East New York section of Brooklyn, New York. This innovative program was launched by Dr. Sarita Dhuper, after a study she conducted confirmed her worst fears. In this community, the incidence of obesity is two to three times the rates of obesity nationwide.

The Office of U.S. Surgeon General sees the crisis across the country. In 2009, an estimated 12.5 million children were overweight—more than 17 percent of all kids.

Live Light . . . Live Right, a nonprofit, community-based partnership is working hard to reverse this trend through education. At the heart of Dr. Dhuper's multidisciplinary team is Dr. Sherry Sakowitz and senior patient coordinator, Susan Blech. A family-based approach influences and informs all their thinking. Their program, free to those who qualify, empowers children and their families with the knowledge and support to help them make healthy choices in food and fitness to last a lifetime.

"This is the first generation that will not live longer than their parents if we do not do something about the obesity crisis," notes Blech. "Save one kid from obesity, and you save the future."

ACTION STEPS
➤ Take the U.S. Surgeon General's Healthy Future Pledge at www.surgeongeneral.gov/obesityprevention.
➤ Go through your family's refrigerator and pantry. Are you influencing the healthiest choices for your family? For inspiration go to Live Right . . . Live Light at www.livelightobesity.org.

The Fine Art of Criticism

I am returning this otherwise good piece of paper to you because someone has written gibberish all over it and put your name at the top.
—Anonymous English professor

Let's put one persistent myth to rest: compassionate people should know that there is no such thing as constructive criticism. All criticism, by its very nature, is destructive. People criticize others primarily because they want them to change some sort of behavior. But here's the thing: animal behaviorists have found that the best way to train animals is to praise them heartily when they perform a desired behavior and simply ignore undesirable behavior.

And guess what? This works with humans too. There's a great apocryphal tale about a psychology professor who was teaching his class about the principle of positive reinforcement. The class, unbeknownst to him, decided to conduct a little experiment of their own.

When the professor stood in one corner of the stage, they all made eye contact, nodded approvingly at whatever he said, and became engaged in the lecture. When he moved away from that spot, they buried their heads in textbooks. In short order, and quite unconsciously, the professor was speaking exclusively from the small corner of the stage.

Here's how you can influence people's behavior, in a compassionate way.

ACTION STEPS

➤ When you have to let people know they did a substandard job, try to employ humor as the English professor did in the quote above. Make it an inside joke to be shared rather than a criticism to be levied.

➤ Whenever possible, let mistakes slide. Give people opportunities to succeed, and lavish sincere praise on them when they do.

➤ For a pitch-perfect example of this principle in action, visit the *New York Times* Web site, www.nytimes.com, and search for the story "What Shamu Taught Me About a Happy Marriage."

187

Supporting a Young Business

Are entrepreneurs born or made?
—Brigham Young

To answer Brigham Young's question, perhaps it's a little of both—with timing and luck thrown in to boot. Young entrepreneurs must have a propensity for risk taking or they would never begin their businesses. But they also need support: financial assistance from family or the bank, networking opportunities, a business plan, and morale boosters.

Several organizations support young entrepreneurs in gaining a foothold in the business world. The Entrepreneurs' Organization was founded in 1987. Today, it's a global network of more than seven thousand business owners in thirty-eight countries that enables entrepreneurs to learn and grow from one another. It also sponsors the Global Student Entrepreneur Awards, which rewards undergraduate students who own and run a business while still in college. The Small Business Administration is an excellent resource for small-business owners or those who want to start a business. This federal agency assists with business plans, loans, licensing, and finding organizations, such as the Renaissance Entrepreneurship Center in San Francisco, which provide an incubator for fledgling businesses, offering access to tools, information, networks, and resources.

All of these resources will support a natural-born entrepreneur stepping into his or her future.

ACTION STEPS

➤ If you know young entrepreneurs who could benefit from tips on how to move their companies forward, help them connect to the Entrepreneurs' Organization (www.eonetwork.org) or a business incubator like San Francisco's Renaissance Entrepreneurship Center (www.rencenter .org). The Small Business Administration (www.sba.gov) will help you find one in your community.

➤ The National Foundation to Teach Entrepreneurship (www.nfte.com) trains teachers and laypeople to teach high school students to become entrepreneurs.

Donate Your "Once in a Lifetime" Dresses

**I have never been a believer that nice clothes
should only be for people with money.**
—Jaclyn Smith

Your wedding dress, your prom dress, the bridesmaid's dress you loved
or loathed. After the music from these wonderful evenings was over,
you knew right then that these exquisite dresses would certainly never be
worn again. Why not donate them to someone who needs them?

There are a myriad of charities that will put these dresses to much
better use than sitting in the back of your closet. Some will repurpose the
dress for a different life-cycle event; others will pass it on to someone who
cannot afford her own. Still others will use your gowns to raise money for
worthy causes. What they all have in common is that you will have the
opportunity to think about your own life events in a whole new way, by
sharing your garments that represent your passages with another.

Brides Against Breast Cancer is looking for donations of wedding
gowns from 2000 until the present. You send them your dress, and they
will resell it, with all proceeds going to provide a wish for women who
are losing their battle with breast cancer. The dresses are sold significantly below market value, making them available to women who could
not otherwise afford them.

Donate My Dress is the first national network of local dress drives.
They will take your prom dress or other event dress and donate it to
someone who needs a dress but can't afford one. The site features a directory of local dress drives across the United States to help you find out
where you can donate a dress.

GETTING STARTED: Depending on the type of dress you can donate,
see the following Web sites: www.bridesagainstbreastcancer.org or call
(503) 491–8091; www.donatemydress.org. It could be fun to have a
tea party after your event and have your friends each bring a dress to
donate.

Caring for the Apes

**An animal's eyes have the power to
speak a great language.**
—Martin Buber

The orangutan is an animal many people see as being akin to human. According to animal behaviorists, orangutans are extremely intelligent and can learn and problem solve even better than chimpanzees. One study of orangutans revealed that they could problem solve by using leaves to make rain hats and roofs to keep out the rain over where they sleep.

Ten thousand years ago, orangutans were found throughout Southeast Asia. Their populations probably numbered in the hundreds of thousands. Now orangutans are an endangered species because their rainforest habitat is being destroyed.

Today the species is found only on the islands of Borneo and Sumatra. In the past decade the wild population may have been cut in half. Estimates of the current population are less than sixty thousand. Despite their being protected as an endangered species, experts predict that wild orangutans could become extinct within the next twenty years.

The mission of the Orangutan Foundation International (OFI) is to support the conservation and understanding of the orangutan and its rainforest habitat while caring for ex-captive orangutans as they make their way back to the forest. Among its many programs, the OFI runs a care center in Borneo for orangutans who need medical attention, such as babies whose mothers have died, and where humans can sometimes interact with the animals. (A little boy from this country visited the care center, where one orangutan was very interested in him, an OFI employee recounts. When the child returned several years later, the orangutan clearly remembered him.)

A donation of $75 feeds a baby orangutan for one month at the care center through the organization's "fostering" program. A donation of $560 will pay for twelve police officers in guard posts and on chartered boats to protect Tanjung Puting National Park for one day.

VISIT www.orangutan.org or call (310) 820–4906.

Volunteer on a Sabbatical

Time is the coin of your life. It is the only coin you have, and only you can determine how it will be spent. Be careful lest you let other people spend it for you.
—Carl Sandburg

Taking a sabbatical—a planned period of leave from your job—is a way to recharge, reenergize, and rethink. A sabbatical isn't a vacation, though it can certainly be relaxing and fun. There's no reason not to spend it cruising the Caribbean if that's what you want, but many people fortunate enough to have a sabbatical decide to spend that time giving back. They commit to spending some or all of their sabbatical as a full-time volunteer.

In today's world the traditional sabbatical—a full year of paid time off—isn't very common. Not too many of us can manage a year off from work, especially if it's unpaid, but many employers are now open to the idea of giving valued employees an unpaid job pause (with benefits) for anywhere from one to six months or even longer. And if you're between jobs, a volunteer commitment can give you some valuable perspective on exactly what you'd like your next job to be.

How to spend your volunteer sabbatical time? Look around your community—perhaps it's time to start that youth organization or go on that church mission, or spend more time with a volunteer project you've been involved with all along. Or perhaps you'd like to take that time to see more of the world *and* do some good. Many organizations are eager for dedicated volunteers who can spend a month or more in one place on a long-term assignment. Your volunteer sabbatical doesn't have to be all work, though. An assignment overseas, where you might teach English or work on a development project or do field research for an environmental group, will probably still leave you time for sightseeing. And because your basic living expenses are usually covered, you'll have extra money to enjoy your host country.

TO FIND a sabbatical opportunity, contact: VolunteerMatch / www .volunteermatch.org.

Change the Focus of Kids' Sports in Your Town

The important thing is to learn a lesson every time you lose.
—John McEnroe

Youth athletics should be about exercise and enjoyment—not pressure and competition. Yet almost three-quarters of children who register for sports teams in the United States stop playing by the time they're thirteen—mainly because it just isn't fun anymore. Adults often emphasize "winning at any cost." A more relaxed approach can be healthier for everyone.

ACTION STEPS

LOCAL: Take an honest look at the athletic programs in your community. What is the atmosphere at games—calm and friendly, or are adults yelling at players and one another? Are kids participating even with injuries? Do they seem tense before, during, and after a game?

If you have a child involved in sports, ask yourself if he or she really enjoys playing or is just going along with your wishes. Then ask your child. Say that you really want to know how he feels and you won't be angry, whatever the answer. Speak with other adults. Reach out to parents with kids on opposing teams; recommend that they look at the readings below. Examine coaches' behaviors. If you agree that a coach is pushing too hard, or being unsportsmanlike, approach him or her. If necessary, raise these issues with the school or team sponsor.

Is the success of youth teams a big part of your community's image? Start a public conversation about what that might be doing to kids.

NATIONAL: More information about kids' sports:

Mark Hyman, *Until It Hurts: America's Obsession with Youth Sports and How It Harms Our Kids*.

Positive Coaching Alliance: www.positivecoach.org.

www.aacap.org/cs/root/facts_for_families/children_and_sports.

Everyone Eighteen Years and Older Has This Influence

The ballot is stronger than the bullet.
—Abraham Lincoln

Once you had to own land to do it, then you could only do it if you were a white male, then being male would do it, and eventually females were let into the club. But you still had to be twenty-one. In the midst of the Vietnam War, in 1971, the 26th Amendment to the United States Constitution lowered the voting age from twenty-one to eighteen. Now any eighteen-year-old who is a U. S. citizen can influence the most powerful democracy in the world—by the power of the vote—by the cast of his or her ballot.

An estimated 23 million young Americans under the age of thirty voted in the 2008 presidential election, 3.4 million more votes as compared to 2004, representing approximately 52 percent of potential voters under the age of thirty. Young women voted more than young men; black women much more than black men; those with some college education most of all. The influence of these "millennium" voters was huge. But what about the other 48 percent of eighteen-to-nineteen-year-olds, who didn't vote? What's one of the big reasons people give for not serving this country with their vote? They say they don't know how.

ACTION STEPS

➤ Want to find out how to register to vote in your state? Go to www .vote411.org, an effort by the League of Women Voters to inform voters how to vote, or www.rockthevote.com, which seeks to empower young people to vote.

➤ Use your influence, your e-mail list, your text messages, your social network, or Twitter to get five friends to register to vote with you today.

The Honor of Work

**Derive happiness in oneself from a good day's work,
from illuminating the fog that surrounds us.**
—Henri Matisse

There's an old story about a traveler who comes upon a great cathedral under construction. He asks the first person he encounters, a carpenter, what he's doing. "I'm carving figures on a door," the man answers. He asks the next person, a stonemason, what he's doing. "I'm shaping this block so it will fit in that wall," the mason responds. The traveler then meets a woman sweeping up work debris and asks the same question. "Me?" she says. "I'm building a cathedral to the glory of Almighty God."

Even today, we often discount what we classify as menial work. Think about your own reactions when finding out what someone does for a living. If she says she's a university professor, you likely respond with far greater interest than if she's an office worker.

Compassionate people don't measure value by what someone does for a living, except to ask whether or not it makes that person happy. They understand that any job offers a chance to "build a cathedral" and serve others by doing your best work.

ACTION STEPS

➤ Refrain from ever asking someone, "So, what do you do?" Get to know the person for his own merits instead of slotting him into a particular category based on his job.

➤ Carefully monitor your own actions to ensure you are just as respectful to a company janitor as to a company president.

➤ Next time you're at a function where you'll likely never see these people again, try this experiment: when people ask what you do for a living, give varying answers to see how differently people treat you based on how you respond. If you get tripped up in your experiment, come clean and explain what you were doing. This can lead to a fascinating conversation.

Touched by Autism

There are no hopeless situations; there are only men who have grown hopeless about them.
—Clare Boothe Luce, American playwright

The diagnosis of autism can terrify any parent. Autism is a complex neurobiological disorder that manifests uniquely in each autistic child. It can interfere with the capacity to understand emotional expression, to talk to or relate to others. Some children with autism practice rigid routines and repetitive behaviors like counting or obsessively arranging toys. Symptoms vary from mild to severe. Today, 1 in 150 children is diagnosed with the disorder. It occurs in all racial, ethnic, and social groups though it is four times more prevalent in boys than girls.

Although the cause and cure for autism have not been found, this doesn't mean the situation is hopeless. Through Autism Speaks, parents have banded together to raise money for biomedical research into these areas as well as into prevention and treatments. They raise public awareness about the effects of this disorder on individuals, families, and society. Autism Speaks aims to bring hope to everyone who faces the challenges of this disorder, providing resource lists for support groups in which parents and grandparents share their struggles and triumphs. The organization advocates for best practices in treatment, education, and services, providing supportive information on its Web site.

ACTION STEPS

➤ If someone in your circle has a child with autism or another lifelong disorder, become a shoulder to cry on—parents under duress need someone to focus on them. They also need respite—a break from their child's constant needs. If you step in to give them a break, be sure the parents have explained what to expect and how to handle situations.

➤ Support the family in contacting Autism Speaks at www.autism speaks.org. There they will find kindred spirits to comfort them as well as those whose passion pushes them toward finding a cure.

Mentoring Doctoral Candidates

**Mentoring is a brain to pick, an ear to listen,
and a push in the right direction.**
—John Crosby

As unbelievable as it sounds, studies show that 50 percent of all people who begin a doctoral program drop out at the dissertation stage, with even higher rates for women of color. Dropping out puts the end to a dream that many have worked for years to complete, leaving them with less earning potential as compared to those who actually finish their degree. The literature strongly suggests that if these people—particularly women of color—had more support during the writing process, they would complete their degrees. If you have a doctorate, and understand this process, helping another candidate complete her dissertation is a unique opportunity to help someone achieve her goal.

Enter the organization SisterMentors. This Washington, DC–based group has already helped more than thirty women of color earn their doctorates. Currently they have a waiting list of women looking for mentors to help them. The organization specifically recruits other women of color for these mentor positions. They are trying to create a network of role models who have already achieved academic success despite the odds.

The mentees are then required to create their own community within the organization. They are asked to encourage one another by reviewing participants' work and sharing resources. Each mentee is also required to be a mentor to a middle-school or high-school girl in her local area, providing another opportunity to serve as a role model.

GETTING STARTED: To volunteer with this unique program as either a mentor or a mentee, visit their Web site at www.sistermentors.org, or call (202) 778–6424. You can also offer your services through your own alumni groups, thereby helping others in your own particular specialty.

Helping a Child in Need

If our American way of life fails the child, it fails us all.
—Pearl S. Buck

A.J. was a bright eight-year-old boy who was taking a class with Draw-Bridge, an organization that provides art programs for homeless children. Being homeless was very upsetting to A.J., and at one class, he wrapped himself entirely in tape, mummifying himself, then said, "I want to find a big lake; I want to jump in and drown!" Children can often express in art or action what they can't say in words, and A.J. was saying how trapped he felt. But then he tore himself out of the tape and said with happiness and relief, "Now I have become a beautiful butterfly!" He still had hope that his life might change for the better.

Homeless parents are often so overwhelmed with day-to-day problems that they can't be there emotionally for their children. And homeless children are far more likely than nonhomeless children to feel they need to shoulder adult responsibility, such as figuring out how to find money for food. Trying to control what we can't makes all of us—even kids—feel angry, depressed, and hopeless. And having no chance to vent these feelings can cause some kids to act out, such as misbehaving or doing poorly at school.

By supplying both trained facilitators and beautiful, brand-new art supplies, DrawBridge gives homeless children like A.J. a chance to express difficult emotions in a safe and loving setting, without having to fear they will be judged or ridiculed. Besides the simple joy any child feels when given a fresh box of crayons, homeless children at DrawBridge also get a chance to be heard by an understanding adult, which can help them regain a sense of control in an out-of-control world.

You can support DrawBridge by buying the T-shirts, tote bags, posters, and greeting cards made with images produced by the children. Donations of money and art supplies are also appreciated.

VISIT www.drawbridge.org.

Breast-Cancer Awareness

I've been a rock star since you were very young. But I've never encountered anything as powerful as cancer.
—Melissa Etheridge

You know the statistic: one in eight women will develop breast cancer at some time in her life. That means if you know eight women, yourself included, breast cancer is an issue for you.

When breast cancer is detected early, before it's had a chance to spread, the five-year survival rate is better than 95 percent, but even so, forty thousand American women die of breast cancer every year. If more women were aware of the risks and knew the steps to take to reduce their risk and find breast cancer early, the death rate would drop. You can help by volunteering to spread the word about early detection.

Public education is the greatest tool for improving breast-cancer awareness. This is an area where volunteers can be tremendously helpful. Local affiliates of national breast-cancer organizations such as the Susan G. Komen Foundation and Network for Strength can often provide a free speaker who will come to your workplace for a brown-bag seminar on early detection. They'll also happily come speak at schools, for organizations and clubs, and at community centers. You can volunteer to set up the meeting, or you could even volunteer to be the speaker.

Another major public education area is reminding women to get mammograms. Hospitals with breast-cancer centers often do drives that provide free mammograms for the uninsured—and volunteers are always needed to help with the organization and publicity.

You can make a difference just by ordering free breast self-exam instruction cards and handing them out to your friends and family. You could also contact organizations for women and offer to provide the cards and arrange for a speaker.

TO GET FREE breast self-exam shower cards, contact:

National Women's Health Resource Center / 157 Broad Street, Suite 106 / Red Bank, NJ 07701 / (877) 986–9472 / www.healthywomen.org

Create Your Own Show for Public Access TV

The ultimate value of life depends upon awareness, and the power of contemplation rather than upon mere survival.
—Aristotle

Are you passionate about a local issue? Public Access TV can draw attention to your cause. Producing a PATV show requires more knowledge than using YouTube, but the potential rewards are greater. Your presentations will have a focused, local audience. With a bit of publicity, your viewership can grow. If you are fair and ask thoughtful questions, local experts, politicians, and businesspeople will more likely grant interviews.

Cable television companies are legally required to provide PATV facilities and equipment for the general public on a first-come/first-served basis. Details are negotiated by local governments and vary from place to place, so begin by learning about access where you live.

ACTION STEPS

LOCAL: Ask your local cable TV provider if they have a public-access studio and training classes. Be persistent; it may take a while before you reach the person in charge. If there is a studio but no classes, get the names of some shows' producers, and volunteer to help; you can learn by doing. If classes are offered, you can soon be learning production basics. Crew on existing shows to practice your new skills. Keep in touch with other students, producers, and crew, because you will need their help for your own show. In the meantime, research your subject area. When you are ready, with input from experienced producers, submit a proposal for your show to the station. Before long you will be ready to roll!

NATIONAL: Check out these resources: The Global Village CAT: www.communitymedia.se/cat • Producer's Handbook and Community Media Resource Directory: http://ourchannels.org/books.html • Alliance for Community Media: www.ourchannels.org/?page_id=11

Start a Chain Reaction

I am sure that my codes of life may be very different from yours, but how do you know that trust, compassion, and beauty will not make this world a better place to be in and this life a better place to live?
—Rachel Scott from her essay "My Ethics, My Code of Life"

Rachel Scott's essay "My Ethics, My Code of Life" was written a month before she was murdered at Columbine High School in one of the worst school massacres in U.S. history, on April 20, 1999. Yet the desire for a more honest and compassionate world expressed in her writing would inspire her father to form Rachel's Challenge.

In the ten years since that fateful day, her father, Darrell Scott, has told the story of his daughter's life, death, and legacy in thousands of school assemblies, community workshops, and outreach programs, spreading a message of tolerance and helping to shape positive school environments. In 2009, he expanded Rachel's Challenge into the corporate world with a focus on hope and compassion within the workplace.

Rachel culminated her essay with a challenge to us all, "My codes may seem like a fantasy that can never be reached, but test them for yourself, and see the kind of effect they have in the lives of people around you. You may just start a chain reaction." Rachel's spirit and influence lives on. Her words have proved mightier than any act of violence.

ACTION STEPS
➤ Become an F.O.R. ("Friend of Rachel") by reading and accepting "Rachel's Challenge" at www.rachelschallenge.com, which begins with challenge No. 1: "Eliminate Prejudice by Looking for the Best in Others."

➤ Approach your local PTA and help to organize a kindness club, especially among elementary school students, in order to begin teaching tolerance in the most formative years.

Do as I Do

A perfect summer day is when the sun is shining, the breeze is blowing, the birds are singing, and the lawn mower is broken.
—James Dent

One day a woman came to the famous Indian spiritual leader Mohandas Gandhi with her overweight son in tow. She said, "My son won't give up eating sweets. Please tell him to stop. He will listen to you."

Gandhi looked at the boy and his mother and told them to come back in one week. Seven days later, the woman again approached the great man with her son. Gandhi said to the boy, "Please do not eat any more sweets."

The woman thanked Gandhi, then asked: "We have had such a long walk, Bapu. Why not tell him this a week ago?"

Gandhi answered, "Because a week ago, I was still eating sweets."

When we tell people to do things, whether it's our children or our employees, it's essential to do so in a compassionate way. That's impossible unless we know what we're asking for based on firsthand experience.

When we order our teenager to mow the lawn immediately, do we take into consideration that the sun is shining for the first time in a week and he's exhausted from schoolwork? When we tell a subordinate that a deadline is absolute, do we understand that it means she'll be at the office every evening and weekend for the next month?

If you make compassion a part of every request, you will gain greater compliance, and earn the respect of those whom you are asking.

ACTION STEPS
➤ Just before you issue your next set of marching orders, be sure you've done the task yourself at least once. If you do know what you're asking and you know it's a daunting thing, pitch in for as long as you can.

➤ Always, always end your request by asking something along the lines of, "Is there anything that will help you in getting this done?"

Local Heroes

To have no heroes is to have no aspiration, to live on the momentum of the past, to be thrown back upon routine, sensuality, and the narrow self.
—Charles Horton Cooley, American sociologist

We all need heroes to look up to, to emulate, to inspire us to greatness. And there are myriad heroes among us who deserve our support—the police officer on the beat, the shopkeeper who becomes an agent of change, the wife who tends to her family while her husband is away at war.

Our environment also needs heroes—people who champion its cause despite great personal hardship and even peril. Often, these individuals go unrecognized. Yet their efforts to protect the world's natural resources are increasingly critical to our planet's well-being. In 1990 San Francisco philanthropists Richard and Rhoda Goldman created the Goldman Environmental Prize to recognize grassroots environmental heroes from the six inhabited continental regions of the world. Each winner receives $150,000 for his or her efforts toward positive change. The prize hopes to inspire and support other ordinary citizens to take extraordinary measures that protect the natural world.

These local heroes are often men and women from isolated villages or inner cities. In 2009 their work encompassed eliminating poisonous agricultural chemicals in the environment in the former Soviet Union, protecting the rain forest in the Congo and Suriname, and creating waste solutions in Bali. The prize amplifies these heroes' voices, gives them visibility, and provides financial support so they can continue their work.

ACTION STEPS

➤ Identify local heroes who could use your moral, financial, and hands-on support. What can you do to further their causes?

➤ Log on to the Goldman Environmental Prize Web site (www.goldmanprize.org) to learn more about these extraordinary/ordinary individuals. Find out how you can support this worthy cause.

Big Brothers Big Sisters of America

The road to a friend's house is never long.
—Danish proverb

Big Brothers Big Sisters is the oldest and largest youth-mentoring organization in the United States. By linking disadvantaged children with caring adults and teens, this program creates lasting relationships that can transform the lives—at the earliest stages—for those who need companions, guides, and friends the most.

The organization was started in 1904 by a New York City court clerk named Ernest Coulter, who believed that caring adults could help many of the felonious boys coming through his courtroom stay out of trouble. At around the same time, another New York organization, Ladies of Charity, began mentoring equally troubled girls. The two groups continued to work independently until 1977, when Big Brothers of America and Big Sisters International joined forces and became Big Brothers Big Sisters of America.

Today there are thousands of volunteers in communities across the country, including yours. With neighborhood offices in all fifty states, and twelve additional countries, there are literally hundreds of children between the ages of six and eighteen who are ready and waiting to be matched with an adult who can enhance their lives.

Volunteers are referred to as Bigs, and the children they mentor are Littles. Each Big is carefully matched with a Little. The average Big volunteers four hours a month—just one hour a week—and is supported by rigorous standards and trained personnel. The agency also provides ongoing supervision to the Big, the Little, and the Little's family.

Big Brothers Big Sisters is always looking to create new matches, especially with men. By joining this program, you'll share the invaluable gift of friendship, creating a relationship with lasting results.

GETTING STARTED: Check out the national Web site at www.bbbsa .org, where you can enter your zip code and find the BBBSA location closest to you. You can also call the national office in Philadelphia at (215) 567–7000 for more information.

The Healing Love of an Animal

No matter how little money and how few possessions you own, having a dog makes you rich.
—Louis Sabin

"Patches has been my main support ever since I was diagnosed with HIV," a woman says of her Boston terrier. "I was shunned by a lot of people, and I got really depressed. But he loves me unconditionally."

"Molly gives me a reason to live," says a man of his springer spaniel. "When I was in the hospital with pneumonia, I knew I needed to get well so I could get home to her, and that's what got me through."

Many of us intuitively know that the love of our pets helps keep us healthy, and now scientific studies have shown that animals improve human cardiovascular health, reduce stress, and decrease loneliness and depression. And nobody knows that better than the people at PAWS.

PAWS (Pets Are Wonderful Support) started in San Francisco in the mideighties in response to the HIV/AIDS epidemic when volunteers at a food bank realized that clients were going hungry so they could give the food to their pets. They decided more must be done to support pet owners who were facing medical and financial challenges.

PAWS offers in-home pet care, including dog walking, litter-box cleaning, general pet grooming, and emergency foster care. They give out free pet food and flea medications and supplies. They provide subsidized veterinary care, including annual wellness exams and veterinary vouchers to cover ongoing and emergency services. PAWS provides advocacy for disabled persons with service animals who are facing a housing crisis such as eviction. In short, they do everything they can to see that the elderly, people with HIV and other life-threatening illnesses, and those who are on limited incomes are able to keep their beloved animal companions.

A gift of $35 will provide a PAWS client with one month's pet food for one dog or two cats; $100 will provide veterinary visits for the pets of eight PAWS clients.

VISIT www.pawssf.org or call (415) 979–9550.

Become a Master Gardener

Everything that slows us down and forces patience, everything that sets us back into the slow circles of nature, is a help. Gardening is an instrument of grace.
—May Sarton

If you're a passionate gardener, you probably already have a reputation among your friends, relatives, garden club pals, and neighbors as the go-to person for garden questions. Your gardening wisdom and love of horticulture make you an ideal candidate to become a Master Gardener. This popular volunteer program began in Seattle back in 1972 at the local cooperative extension office. The overwhelmed extension agents asked the gardening community for help. As gardeners tend to do, they responded enthusiastically, and within a few years the program was national.

State cooperative extension services were created in 1914 as a division of the U.S. Department of Agriculture. The agents work closely with both farmers and backyard gardeners to provide information and advice. During World War II, for instance, the service ran the Victory Garden Program. Extension agents provided seeds, gardening tools, and advice—and by 1943, some 20 million victory gardens were in production.

Because modern victory gardening is popular, Master Gardener volunteers are needed more than ever to be garden experts for the public. Master Gardeners staff the garden hotline, visit gardeners to give advice, make presentations at public events, and participate in community gardening. It's a wonderful way to bring your love for gardening to your community.

TO LOCATE the cooperative extension service in your county, check the government pages section of your local phone book. Ask to speak to the Master Gardener coordinator. Alternatively, contact the Cooperative State Research, Education, and Extension Service (as it's officially known) at:

United States Department of Agriculture / Cooperative State Research, Education, and Extension Service / 1400 Independence Avenue SW, Stop 2201 / Washington, DC 20250 / (202) 720–4423 / www.csrees.usda.gov

Recycle Electronics

The purpose of life is a life of purpose.
—Robert Byrne, chess grandmaster

Often computers and other electronic equipment are discarded just because they aren't the "latest thing." Meanwhile, schools, nonprofit organizations, and lower-income families are desperately in need of working equipment. You can help by getting used electronics to those who can use them.

ACTION STEPS

LOCAL: Donate used equipment through a charity such as www .computerswithcauses.org. You can also take the initiative to gather electronics equipment for donation. You will need a clean, dry place to store gathered equipment; someone to pick up donated material, and a person to log in the equipment. At least one "geek" would be handy to test and fix equipment. (This could be an IT person from your office or a student from a nearby technical school.)

A flyer can advertise your goal; distribute it to businesses, schools, and civic groups that would have used equipment.

Many of the donated items may not be operable, but you will at least be removing them from the waste stream. Recyclers can dismantle such items so the materials can be reused. Some electronics manufacturers take back used products for recycling; these are either mailed back or brought to a local retailer. For information about local recyclers and collection events, visit EIA Environment Consumer Education Initiative at www.eiae.org and My Green Electronics at www.mygreen electronics.org.

NATIONAL: The U.S. Environmental Protection Agency has started a "Plug-In to eCycling" campaign. For more info: www.epa.gov/osw/ partnerships/plugin.

The Player's Influence

Life is not a spectator sport. If you're going to spend your whole life in the grandstand just watching what goes on, in my opinion you're wasting your life.
—Jackie Robinson

He was born in Cairo, Georgia, the heart of the segregated South, in 1919, the grandson of a slave and the son of sharecroppers. Yet he changed America when he shattered baseball's color barrier on April 18, 1946, and became the first black player in Major League Baseball. And by September of his rookie season, Jackie Robinson had become a national phenomenon.

A postseason poll would name him the second most popular man in America. Only crooner Bing Crosby received more votes. On September 22, with the Brooklyn Dodgers in first place, Robinson won baseball's first Rookie of the Year Award. Forty years later, the annual prize would be renamed the Jackie Robinson Rookie of the Year Award.

Robinson was called by his teammate Duke Snider, "the greatest competitor I have ever seen." He opened the doors for the talent and diversity that defines baseball—and sports in America—today.

On November 4, 1972, Jackie Robinson suffered a fatal heart attack. The quote on his tombstone stresses our duty to be a player. "A life is not important except in the impact it has on other lives."

ACTION STEPS

➤ Take a moment to think about what sports would look like—and play like—without the diversity found on fields today.

➤ Jackie Robinson's family continues to serve others through the Jackie Robinson Foundation, a public, nonprofit organization founded by his wife, Rachel Robinson. Scholarships and support via the foundation's Education and Leadership Development program are available for minority youths. More at www.jackierobinson.org.

Bad News

Afflict the comfortable and comfort the afflicted.
—H. L. Mencken

It used to be the sworn duty of American journalists to go after the big guy and stick up for the little guy. Sadly, these are very different days in the world of journalism than when famed Baltimore newspaperman H. L. Mencken penned the above words as a reporter's creed.

While there is still some good work being done, the institution of American journalism is a pale shadow of the days when it brought down a corrupt president, rallied to the cause of civil rights, and challenged even the most entrenched authorities. Newspapers are closing at record rates, TV newscasts are losing viewers, and online news sites struggle.

That's incredibly unfortunate because at the root of all the greatest works of American journalism is a deep and abiding sense of compassion and the desire to set things right.

ACTION STEPS

➤ Go to the nearest computer or library and read the First Amendment. Or go to whitehouse.gov and click on "Our Government" to see it in the full context of the U.S. Constitution. Not only does the First Amendment guarantee the right to a free press, it gives you the right of free speech, the right to assemble and petition your government, and the freedom of religion. It's important that you fully understand the power of that amendment and its rarity among governments.

➤ Use every last inch of it to inspire you to right wrongs, speak up to injustice, and, by golly, afflict the comfortable and comfort the afflicted. You don't need to have a press card to do all these things.

➤ If you have something to say, seek out avenues to say it. Small weekly newspapers often take on local columnists (sometimes without pay unfortunately). Or start a blog on local affairs. Or just write letters to the editor on topics that matter to you.

Be Someone's Eyes

**The eyes are not responsible when
the mind does the seeing.**
—Publilius Syrus, first-century BC Roman author

We have all seen the sign-language interpreter beside the stage, helping hearing-impaired people follow a lecture, play, or speech. But what if someone is blind or partially sighted? How can they follow the action?

A relatively new service is now being offered to people who are visually impaired to solve this problem. Trained "audio describers" make live theatrical, opera, and dance productions more accessible to people with vision problems by narrating the action on the stage. The describer sits in the back of the theater (or on the catwalk or elsewhere), wearing a special microphone that transmits the narration to the patron through an earpiece connected to a handheld receiver. The listener is guided through the presentation with descriptions of new scenes, settings, costumes, body language, and sight gags they would otherwise miss. The narration is carefully slipped between the dialogue or songs. During an opera, the superscript is also added. The service is provided free to the arts patron through designated programs. Some museums, such as the Getty Museum in Los Angeles, also provide audio describers.

Those of us who are sighted may take for granted the rich visual environment in which we live. This service, now mandated by the Americans with Disabilities Act (ADA), opens a new world of enjoyment for people who would otherwise be left in the dark. It is a profound way to support their participation in the arts and in life.

ACTION STEPS

➤ The ADA requires that individuals with disabilities have full access. If someone in your circle is blind or partially sighted, ask at your theater whether audio description services are available. If not, be a catalyst to get them started. For more information on how an audio description service works contact www.artsaccessinc.org.

Help a Friend Get Fit

Thou shouldst eat to live; not live to eat.
—Socrates

You've heard it all before: obesity is running rampant. According to the National Institutes of Health, about two-thirds of adults in the United States are overweight, and almost one-third are obese. The life-threatening diseases linked to obesity are an ever-growing list and now include diabetes, heart disease, metabolic syndrome, and even cancer. So the implications of this are quite clear: chances are you or someone you know needs to lose weight, and fast.

The problem is that dieting rarely works in a vacuum. It is difficult to lose weight, and often depressing, when you try to do it alone. That's why organizations like Weight Watchers thrive: they offer a community-based program based on the tenets of mentoring. However, these programs can be costly and often have a commercial agenda (for example, buy their products to help you lose weight).

If you have lost weight successfully and have kept the pounds off for at least a year, why not help those you love as a diet mentor? In this role you can be there for those who need your support. At the same time, you can provide them with dieting advice that has worked for you. You can exercise with them, eat with them, and even cheer them on as the pounds come off.

Or if you need to lose weight, join the buddy system and support a friend to reach your mutual goals. Together you just might be able to meet the challenge and become a thinner, healthier pair.

GETTING STARTED: There are a myriad of responsible diet books and Web sites to turn to for accurate advice to share. But go to an established, medical reference like the Mayo Clinic (www.mayoclinic.com) or National Institutes of Health (http://win.niddk.nih.gov) for solid advice that is not linked to a commercial agenda.

Looking the Part

**The man who has confidence in himself
gains the confidence of others.**
—Hasidic saying

It's not always easy to make a fresh start if you've made a mistake, suffered a setback, or had a run of bad luck. You may be out of money, or your ego may have taken a bruising—both can keep you from moving forward in your career.

Career Gear understands this and is here to help. Since 1999 Career Gear has helped men—including public-welfare recipients, recovering addicts and alcoholics, boys coming out of foster care, recent immigrants, and men who have been incarcerated—transition to a better life.

The men that Career Gear invests in have already started to turn their lives around by completing a job-training program and securing a job interview, and Career Gear helps the men prepare for that interview. As well as getting interviewing tips, each man receives a business suit, a dress shirt, a tie, a belt, and shoes. (Ninety percent of the suits are brand new, donated by Brooks Brothers and Men's Wearhouse.)

"Having a new suit is a huge confidence boost; it makes the men feel that they deserve the job," says Leta Malloy, director of strategic initiatives. Once they have secured the job (and 82 percent do), the men can then join a Career Gear retention program, which helps them focus on keeping the job while taking workshops on subjects like financial literacy, paying child support, networking, résumé writing, and nutrition. They are given a voucher for another piece of clothing every week so they can accrue a working wardrobe.

In the past decade, Career Gear has outfitted more than 17,500 men but has had to turn away others. While the new business suits get all the press and attention, it's actually the retention program that can really help a man establish a career and make the greatest difference in his life. Fifty dollars will keep one man in the retention program for one semester.

VISIT www.careergear.org.

Volunteer for Animal Welfare

Animals love happiness almost as much as we do.
—Colette

Nationwide, the need for volunteers at animal shelters and animal-rescue operations is large and growing larger. Budget cutbacks mean the shelters can't afford many paid staff members, even at a time when people who can't afford their pets any longer are dropping them off at the shelters.

Animal welfare is one of the top areas for volunteering. Little is more rewarding than rescuing an animal from a bad situation and finding it a good home. The American Society for the Prevention of Cruelty to Animals (ASPCA) runs many shelters; others are operated by local or regional groups. Animal shelters always need volunteers. It takes a lot of caring people to feed the animals, clean the kennels, walk the dogs, and give them all some attention and love. Extra volunteers are needed for special events, like adoption days. Your local animal shelter will be very welcoming of your offer to volunteer.

Breed-rescue organizations also need volunteers nationwide. These groups are dedicated to a particular animal breed—cocker spaniels or Burmese cats, for instance—and help find new homes for animals that are in bad situations or have been orphaned in some way. Most volunteers are lovers of that particular breed, but anyone is welcome to help.

You can also become a pet foster parent. You volunteer to provide a temporary home for pets that need love and care until a permanent home can be found for them. Sometimes fostering also involves training the animal to resolve behavioral problems that would prevent adoption. Pet fostering can last for just a few days or up to several months (or permanently if you decide to keep the animal yourself).

TO BECOME a fostering volunteer, check with your local animal shelter or a breed-rescue group. Nationwide, there are more than 3,000 animal shelters run by the ASPCA, humane societies, and animal control organizations. To find one near you, check the ASPCA national database at www.aspca.org or call (212) 876–7700.

Get Kids Involved in Protecting Community Water Resources

**Life consists in penetrating the unknown,
and fashioning our actions in accord with
the new knowledge thus acquired.**
—Leo Tolstoy

From 1950 to 2000, the U.S. population almost doubled, but public demand for water more than tripled! Safe water supplies are an endangered resource worldwide; according to the EPA, at least thirty-six U.S. states predict some shortages by 2013. It's especially important to teach young people about caring for our water.

ACTION STEPS

LOCAL: Ask your schools to include caring for water resources in the curriculum; encourage kids to tackle the subject as a debate topic or science project.

Investigate some of the resources below; there are dozens of ways that kids can learn about water protection and conservation. They can also roll up their sleeves and actually help improve watersheds.

The EPA's "Adopt Your Watershed" campaign has activities like watershed testing, cleanup, and restoration: www.epa.gov/adopt.

Through volunteer programs nationwide, kids can check the condition of local groundwater and waterways: www.epa.gov/volunteer.

World Water Monitoring Day is an annual international event. Students can test a stream, lake, bay, or wetland for dissolved oxygen, temperature, water clarity, and acidity: www.worldwatermonitoringday.org.

Girl Scouts can earn a Water Drop Patch: www.girlscouts.org/program/gs_central/insignia/online/participation_patches/water_drop.

NATIONAL/INTERNATIONAL: Global water news: www.circleofblue.org/waternews

The Beginning of Life

Children begin by loving their parents. After a time
they judge them. Rarely, if ever, do they forgive them.
—Oscar Wilde

Does your influence as a parent start the moment that precious baby is placed in your hands? Does it start with his or her first look into your eyes? Vital organs start forming as early as four weeks into the pregnancy, before many a woman even knows she's pregnant.

As you envision the life you are creating, review the following highlights from the prenatal checklist of the March of Dimes, whose mission today is to improve the health of babies by preventing birth defects and infant mortality:

➤ Get a medical checkup, including a dental checkup.

➤ Eat healthy food, maintain a healthy weight, and get fit.

➤ Stop smoking and avoid secondhand smoke.

➤ Stop drinking alcohol and don't use illegal drugs.

➤ Talk to your doctor about your family history and genetics.

➤ Woman! Take a multivitamin with folic acid every day before pregnancy. Foods with folate, the natural form of the vitamin, include fortified breakfast cereals, dried beans, leafy green vegetables, and orange juice.

All pregnant parents start their influence for the next generation now— and every negative behavior changed influences the life of the child they are nurturing.

ACTION STEPS

➤ Review a full prenatal checklist: go to the Pregnancy & Newborn Health Education Center at www.marchofdimes.com.

➤ March of Dimes is renowned for its fund-raising walks to support their advocacy on behalf of children's health—organize or join one in your area. Get fit, and do good today.

On the Backs of Babes

Children are the hands by which we take hold of heaven.
—Henry Ward Beecher

On the first day of school in the fall of 2007, a ninth-grader wore a pink polo shirt to his new high school in the small Canadian community of Cambridge, Nova Scotia. In the mid-1980s, he would have been lauded for his fashion sense. Not so this time.

Bullies immediately harassed the freshman, calling him disparaging names, and threatening to beat him up. This could have been the start of a terrible year for the boy. But unbeknownst to him, two twelfth-grade students heard what had happened and decided to do something about it.

That evening, they bought fifty pink shirts from a discount store and sent an e-mail to all their classmates, asking them to wear them to school the next day in a show of support for the new kid. The next day, the school was awash in pink, with hundreds of kids wearing either the discount shirts or their own pink outfits, some head to toe.

Our children aren't only the hope for the future—they're the hope for a hopeful future. They are born with the capacity for goodness and compassion stamped right on their souls. Our task is to give them every possible opportunity to express it.

ACTION STEPS

➤ Catch kids doing something compassionate. We're often overly concerned with correcting our children's behavior. Instead, go out of your way to notice when they show even the smallest act of kindness.

➤ Become a block parent. Not only does this make your house a safe haven for lost or endangered kids, but it sets a powerful example for your own children.

➤ Look into foster parenting. Kids in the foster system are in desperate need of safe, loving homes. You don't have to do it full-time. Many foster parents act as respite workers, providing a home for short-term emergency placements or to cover for the vacations of foster parents.

Taking Care of the Caregiver

I have seen so many people who have suffered from always having to take care of another. . . . Caregivers give so much of themselves and sometimes receive so very little in return.
—Rosalynn Carter

Caring for a sick relative can tax you emotionally, financially, and physically. It can disturb sleep, limit your privacy, and affect your health. Research has shown that long-term caregivers suffer from impaired immunity for as long as three years after their role ends. If you care for a loved one with a chronic illness, you may be at increased risk for developing your own serious health problems, including cardiovascular disease.

There are psychological issues too. Depression can set in—you may become unmotivated; you may suffer from insomnia, headaches, and lethargy or feel frustrated and angry—all signs of burnout.

It's hard to be supportive if you're suffering too. But help is available. The National Family Caregivers Association provides a Caregiver Community Action Network. Experienced caregivers provide information and support to those struggling in their role. The Caregiver Story Project, e-communities, and message boards help caregivers feel supported.

"Lotsa Helping Hands," a project affiliated with the National Alliance for Caregiving supports family caregivers in coordinating meals, shopping, respite, and transportation. Caregiving is difficult but with enough support, many people thrive in the role, especially if they feel they are helping a loved one through a difficult time.

ACTION STEPS

➤ With 50 million Americans giving care, most likely a caregiver is in your circle. Ask, "What could I do to ease your load?"

➤ If you know a struggling caregiver, help that person connect to the National Alliance for Caregiving (www.caregiving.org) and the National Family Caregivers Association (www.nfcacares.org).

Sponsor Someone at a Twelve-Step Program

All glory comes from daring to begin.
—Eugene F. Ware

Breaking a bad habit requires recognizing that you have a problem and then actively deciding to change your ways. One profoundly positive method that many people use to cast off a multitude of personal habits is recovery programs, which offer a community of others who have gone through the same issues you are facing and are willing to help you through your ordeal. The most popular format of recovery programs is the twelve-step model first introduced almost eighty years ago with Alcoholics Anonymous.

Today, there are twelve-step programs for a wide variety of issues, including addiction, compulsion, overeating, gambling, and more. Members are encouraged to regularly attend meetings and to work with a sponsor. The sponsor is a current member of the group who has more experience in the recovery process. In twelve-step parlance, "Sponsors share their experience, strength, and hope with their sponsees. . . . A sponsor's role is not that of a legal adviser, a banker, a parent, a marriage counselor, or a social worker. Nor is a sponsor a therapist offering some sort of professional advice. A sponsor is simply another addict in recovery who is willing to share his or her journey."

As a sponsor, you are taking on the responsibility of helping someone during a particularly trying time and at specific points during the twelve steps. You agree to support another's efforts in recovery and to be there for the person emotionally, physically, and spiritually. It is a gift of great personal sacrifice, but the rewards are great, especially if you have been through these same problems.

GETTING STARTED: Before you choose to sponsor someone in your own twelve-step group, it might be wise to read up on your particular issue. Take some time to remember what it was like when you were first eliminating your habit. A great resource for learning how to be an effective sponsor is the book *A Sponsorship Guide for 12-Step Programs* by M. T.

A Way Out

Dime con quién estás y te dire quién eres. (Tell me
who you are with, and I will tell you who you are.)
—Mexican saying

Rico wanted to become a member of the Marianna Maravilla Diablos,
one of an estimated 1,100 Los Angeles gangs. His father, a heroin
addict, was a member of the Maravilla gang, and so is his older brother.
Rico, fourteen, has been shot several times, and his older brother's best
friend was paralyzed in a shooting. Rico is putting in "work" (beating
people up, robbing stores, etc.) to gain entry to the gang.

If he keeps going in this direction, one of two things awaits Rico: *la
torcida* (prison) or death. But there aren't many alternatives: East L.A.,
where he lives, has one of the highest school drop-out rates. Youth unemployment is at about 75 percent, and teen pregnancy is high.

What can be done for young men like Rico? Father Gregory Boyle answered this question in 1988 by creating Homeboy Industries, an alternative to gang life for young men (and women) who are either in gangs
or at risk of joining one. Homeboy Industries started as a jobs program
and soon added a small bakery and then a tortilla stand as places for
young men to learn job skills. Today, Homeboy also helps young people
to get a GED, to write a résumé, or to remove a gang tattoo. Homeboy's businesses now include Homeboy Silkscreen, which prints logos on
clothing, Homeboy Maintenance, which provides landscaping and maintenance services, and Homeboy Merchandise, which sells items with the
Homeboy logo. A new program, Homeboy Press, where kids can learn
computer skills, has just published its first literary magazine.

A gift of $250 will pay for job-skills training for a worker at the
Homeboy Bakery, $125 will pay for one session of gang tattoo removal,
$100 will pay for five students to attend a semester of the Homeboy cre-
ative writing class, and $35 will pay for the production of ten *Homeboy
Review* literary magazines.

VISIT www.homeboy-industries.org.

Tap Your Professional Skills

**Philanthropy is almost the only virtue which
is sufficiently appreciated by mankind.**
—Henry David Thoreau

As a working professional, you don't have a lot of extra time to spend on volunteer work—yet your professional skills are exactly what a lot of nonprofit and community organizations really need. There's a way around this conundrum. The Taproot Foundation brings together professionals who want to help with organizations who need their particular skills. If you work for a company that wants to do pro-bono work, so much the better—you could be paid for your time while you volunteer.

Taproot links up the expertise of individuals with the specific needs of carefully selected nonprofits—an approach that means you're much more likely to be a good fit with the organization and be able to maximize your impact. You agree to volunteer your professional services for about three to five hours a week, usually on a pro-bono project that lasts about six months. Most of your assignment will be done as part of a team of other volunteers. You'll have a weekly conference with your team and a monthly face-to-face meeting with your nonprofit client.

The Taproot Foundation screens hundreds of requests each year to select nonprofit clients that can use professional volunteers most effectively. Volunteers are needed in the strategic areas of the arts, education, social service, environment, and health. The skills needed include project management, marketing, creative services, human resources, information technology, and strategy management. Chances are good that Taproot can match your professional abilities and availability with a nonprofit that needs you. Because your volunteer work will help the nonprofit build stability and capacity and serve its clients better, your impact will be felt long after you've completed your project and moved on.

TO REGISTER with Taproot, contact:

Taproot Foundation National Headquarters / 466 Geary Street, Suite 200 / San Francisco, CA 94102 / (415) 359–1423 / www.taprootfoundation.org

Create a Green Map of Your Community

Satisfaction of one's curiosity is one of the greatest sources of happiness in life.
—Linus Pauling

Green Maps have been made in over fifty countries since 1995. Each Green Map is created by a team of people from the community. They pinpoint a wide variety of places related to green living, such as parks, farmers' markets, nature walks, thrift stores, recycling centers, and retailers of green products. Some also list environmental problem areas. Green Maps come in many forms: they may be published digitally or printed, put online, painted on a wall, or posted on a bulletin board. However, they all use universal icons, which can be understood by people worldwide. The mapmakers communicate with one another and receive guidance through the Green Maps Web site.

ACTION STEPS

LOCAL: Log on to the Green Map Web site, www.greenmap.org, to see if there is an existing project in your locality. If so, volunteer! If not, first decide what area your map should cover. It might or might not follow political boundaries. It could just as easily cover a natural area, such as a river valley, or encompass several towns.

Go to the Green Map FAQ page to learn about community participation: www.greenmap.org/greenhouse/en/participate/FAQ_makers#1554. Decide on the audience for your map (such as tourists, families, newcomers, or kids). Decide who the potential mapmakers are. Green Mapmaking is open to any age, background, or technological skills level. Download information from the Green Map Web site. Meet with leaders of your local school, community center, or environmental group; share the information, and ask for their help in setting up a project in your selected area. After your group registers with the Green Map System, you will learn about team development and funding, and you'll receive guidance as you research, design, and produce your map.

A Snapshot of Influence

**All should be encouraged to reveal themselves,
their perceptions and emotions, and to
build confidence in the creative spirit.**
—Ansel Adams

In the "first act" of our lives, many of us chose practicality over creativity in our occupations. One successful corporate executive knew that path all too well. She climbed to the top of her field in television research. She measured, analyzed, and dissected research data, giving her corporate bosses snapshots of major trends. She thought it too late to venture down another path.

Then one day she took up a camera. Drawn to urban street scenes, to interpreting the graffiti markings, this was more than dabbling or hobby time. It was fresh. New. This was art. Charlene Weisler is now showing her photography at galleries around the world (www.charleneweisler .com).

It is never too late to embrace another path, perhaps a creative one, and go where it takes us. Focus on the world through experienced eyes; see it new once more. We can serve others through the beauty and thought-provoking nature of our ageless art.

ACTION STEPS

➤ Take a picture of yourself. Who do you see there? What is the creative influence behind the photo?

➤ Bring together a "hot" new selection of local artists, all over a certain age. Organize a gallery show or literary reading at your local library or community college. Have the artists each write statements about their work to post at the event and online—and demonstrate to all how we influence the arts and the world as we take the stage for our second acts.

Disagreeing Agreeably

I started writing down people's conversations as they sat around the bar. When I put them together I found some music hiding in there.
—Tom Waits

The skill Tom Waits used to make his trademark brand of music, psychologist Marshall Rosenberg would have recognized as nonviolent communication, also called compassionate communication. Rosenberg, after all, pioneered the concept.

Compassionate communication requires one thing most of all—the ability to observe in as empathetic a way as possible, trying honestly to understand the true meaning of what the other person is saying and not focusing on the specific words or manner it comes in. That's hard to do at first, because people can catch you off guard with angry words, and, out of habit, you respond in kind.

When you communicate in this fashion, you use compassion as your main motivator, not guilt or fear or shame or any of the other ways people try to get their own way. And it can transform the way you deal with others, both to your benefit and theirs.

ACTION STEPS

➤ The next time you enter a charged conversation, stop and commit to the idea that you can both get your needs met. Listen intently to what the person is saying, without judgment. When you think you understand, tell that person what you heard. If you misheard, ask the person to start over. This repetition also serves to cool you both down. Once you understand, clearly explain your position. Ask if there's any way you can both get what you want. Almost always, there is.

➤ When you get good at this form of communication, consider running with it in larger ways by becoming a professional mediator, either part-time or full-time, paid or volunteer. Learn more through the Association for Conflict Resolution, www.acrnet.org.

The Encore Career

If we boomers decide to use our retirement to change the world, rather than our golf game, our dodderdom will have consequences for society every bit as profound as our youth did.
—Nicholas Kristof, *New York Times* columnist

You've heard of Bill and Melinda Gates's largess. Having retired from one of the most lucrative careers in history, Bill and Melinda have devoted themselves to finding solutions to world health problems—an encore career. But have you heard of Rob Mather? A British management consultant, he came across the story of a five-year-old girl with severe burns all over her body. He thought a fund-raising swim would help raise money for her treatments. His relentless quest eventually engaged ten thousand people in seventy-three countries and raised hundreds of thousands of dollars.

Inspired by the possibilities, the following year, Mr. Mather organized a swim to fight malaria. For that event, 250,000 people participated worldwide, prompting him to leave business for an encore career. He created Against Malaria, which has raised nearly $4 million to buy 886,000 bed nets to prevent the mosquito-borne disease.

Helping others is also good for your health and can help you enjoy a longer and fuller life in retirement. Research has shown that altruism helps asthma, cardiovascular disease, weight loss, and insomnia. When former cardiac patients at Duke University Medical Center were asked to listen to and support current patients, the volunteers had improved health after their heart attacks. Other research shows that seniors who give tend to live longer. With an encore career, you can do good and also feel good.

ACTION STEPS
➤ Define what problems in your community are calling for remediation. Rank them in order of importance. Now commit yourself to becoming involved in the first two on your list. What encore career can you create around these issues?

Mentoring Cancer Patients

Learn from yesterday, live for today, hope for tomorrow.
—Albert Einstein

Cancer, or any other life-threatening disease, puts people in a terribly lonely emotional place. Many survivors credit their success to those who helped them during their sickness. While it's important to be surrounded by excellent medical caregivers, friends, and family, it would also be of great assistance to be able to turn to someone who has been there.

Scott Hamilton, Olympic figure-skating champion, came to this conclusion after conquering his own battle with testicular cancer. Since his remission, he has launched the CARES Initiative, which stands for the Cancer Alliance for Research Education and Survivorship at the Cleveland Clinic in Ohio. One of the initiative's primary components is called the 4th Angel Mentoring Program, whereby a cancer survivor is trained in peer counseling and then serves as a mentor to either a cancer patient or a caregiver of a cancer patient. These mentors offer comfort, reassurance, information, and practical advice. Each mentor is paired as closely as possible with respect to diagnosis, gender, and age.

As a mentor, you can pass on your own experiences with disease and the strategies you used that helped you cope with uncertainty, fear, and sadness. By doing so, you will be able to give current patients hope, which is known to be a key component in any recovery. At the same time, you are creating an opportunity for a frank and honest conversation with someone who is on a difficult passage.

GETTING STARTED: You can learn more about the remarkable 4th Angel Program by visiting the Web site for the Cleveland Clinic, www .clevelandclinic.org, or calling them at (800) 223–2273, ext. 52573. To start this type of service where you live, contact your local hospital.

The Foundation for Jewish Culture

There is just one life for each of us: our own.
—Euripedes

The Foundation for Jewish Culture invests in creative individuals (whether Jewish or not) who are exploring the Jewish experience. Through its various grant programs including documentary film, theater, scholarship, the Goldberg Prize for New Jewish Fiction, and the Six Points Fellowship for Emerging Jewish Artists, the foundation supports those artists and scholars who envision the future while honoring the past.

Each program is structured differently, tailored to the needs of the field; for example, the Lynn and Jules Kroll Fund for Jewish Documentary Film is a completion grant given to complete the last stages of a project, often for films that are 95 percent done and just need a small push across the finish line. The Doctoral Dissertation Fund provides significant support for living and research expenses, and the New Theatre Projects Program funds the creation of new work. In addition to financial support, the foundation provides professional development, networking opportunities, and a community for its grantees.

"When people ask, 'Why is culture important?'" says Andrew Horwitz, director, strategic partnerships of the Foundation for Jewish Culture, "I answer that every great American accomplishment, insight, and innovation that has enriched our lives, every new way of seeing or hearing that has changed the world, we've had to dream up for ourselves, and it's artists who do the dreaming.

"Right now is an amazing moment in the Jewish world," he adds. "We are in many ways reinventing Jewish life in America. At the foundation we are deeply committed to both maintaining and innovating Jewish life so that it remains meaningful to many people."

A donation will help the foundation build that meaningful life.

VISIT www.jewishculture.org.

Family Volunteering

Can you imagine anything more energizing, more unifying, more filled with satisfaction than working with members of your family to accomplish something that really makes a difference in the world?
—Stephen Covey

Finding enough time for both your family and for volunteering is a problem with an easy solution: volunteer as a family. There's no better way to create genuine quality family time than by sharing in a volunteer project. There's also no better way to teach your children that volunteer work is meaningful *and* enjoyable.

The challenging part of family volunteering is finding a project that's suitable for all family members, from grandparents to little kids. The project doesn't have to be a major commitment. In fact, if younger kids are involved, short stints of just an hour are preferable. Start by having discussions about what's important to you as a family. Are you animal lovers? Look into helping out at a local animal shelter. Do you want your kids to realize that there are people less fortunate than they? Volunteer at a food pantry or soup kitchen. Are you interested in environmental issues? Help at a local stream cleanup.

Almost as important as the volunteering itself is what comes after it. Discussing the experience and reflecting on it helps all family members appreciate what they have and helps put problems into perspective.

Every year in mid-November, the Points of Light Foundation and the Volunteer Center National Network sponsor Family Volunteer Day to highlight the benefits of family volunteering. It's a great target date for your first family effort, and it's also a great way to find local opportunities that are right for your family.

TO LEARN more:

Points of Light Foundation / 1875 K Street NW, 5th Floor / Washington, DC 20006 / (202) 729–8000 / www.pointsoflight.org

Pull Together Your Neighbors
to Start a Food Pantry

**Generosity is giving more than you can, and
pride is taking less than you need.**
—Kahlil Gibran

Chances are there are hungry families in your town. In which areas is the need most acute? It's not always in the poorest-looking neighborhoods—especially in these times, such people might live anywhere. Get your faith or community group involved in feeding those in need.

ACTION STEPS

LOCAL: If you don't immediately know where the need is the greatest, ask around. Often elementary-school teachers or school counselors know which kids come to school hungry. Where do those families live? Additional information might come from social-service organizations (private or government-run), and medical or dental clinics. Although specific data on their clients is confidential, these sources should be willing to tell you which neighborhoods have the greatest need for food.

A food pantry is the simplest thing to start, because no kitchen is needed. Approach houses of worship and community centers for an easily accessible space. Advertise for volunteers, and begin to collect donations; these can be cash or packaged, nonperishable foods. Set up a registration system for recipient families and one distribution day per week.

Your group will need to keep donations flowing, because families will come to depend on you. Ask an established food pantry in another part of town for advice. Find out about available government support or grants.

Advice for setting up food pantries can be found on many Web sites, including www.cofchrist.org/hunger/pantry/default.asp and www.ehow.com/how_2244181_start-community-outreach-food-pantry.html.

NATIONAL: Learn more about hunger in the United States at www.feedingamerica.org.

The Influence of Every American Citizen

**The first requisite of a good citizen in this Republic of
ours is that he shall be able and willing to pull his weight.**
—Theodore Roosevelt

One of the greatest influences we have in our country is the right to
speak directly to those in power. And today, in this time of great
change and with technology available to us, our government representatives want to hear from us. And they are easier to reach than ever in
history with e-mail and Web sites; some Twitter, and even our president
carries a BlackBerry.

You can reach the White House at www.whitehouse.gov or at White
House, 1600 Pennsylvania Ave, NW, Washington, DC 20500, or by calling: (202) 456–1111.

Any member of the Senate can be contacted via www.senate.gov. To
send your senator a letter, the proper address is: The Honorable Sen. [Full
Name Here], United States Senate, Washington, DC 20510. The House
of Representatives also makes it easy to reach its members at www.house
.gov and at: The Honorable Rep. [Full Name Here], United States House
of Representatives, Washington, DC 20515. The Capitol switchboard
connects you to your representatives: (202) 224–3121.

ACTION STEPS

➤ Organize a local schoolwide letter-writing campaign. With pen and
paper, address a government official on an issue that the students believe serves the greater good of all Americans. Seal, mail, and bring to
the post office today.

➤ As a follow-up to the letter-writing campaign, arrange for a visit to
the school from a local government official. The more local the office-
holder, the more likely he or she will come speak to the students.

Solace, with a Due Date

A library book, I imagine, is a happy book.
—Cornelia Funke

For much of human history, libraries were places only a select few could enter—the rich, the powerful, the educated. In other words, those who could read. And their secrets were closely guarded by the political and religious elites.

Then, about 150 years ago in England, a magical era began—the dawn of the free, public library. Since then, libraries have taken on many roles in modern society beyond that of merely archiving manuscripts. They are gathering places for community groups, champions of freedom of speech, tireless researchers for countless projects. And we flock to them in droves: the American Library Association points out that Americans visited libraries nearly 1.3 billion times in the past year.

But libraries are also something else—they are places of healing and comfort. We seek them out when we need quiet to think. We slowly walk the stacks looking for just the right book to soothe the hurt we feel. We sit at length in a chair overlooking a park, knowing no one expects us to hurriedly move along. They are havens for troubled souls.

In short, libraries are the perfect place for you to practice compassion.

ACTION STEPS

➤ Peruse books in the library and pick six from which people might be seeking solace. A few possibilities: *Why Bad Things Happen to Good People*, or *The Year of Magical Thinking*, or *A Woman's Guide to Healing the Heartbreak of Divorce*. Use your own experiences to guide your choices.

➤ Leave a handwritten note in each book for the next borrower to find. It could read something like, "I know you've picked up this book in a time of great need. Please understanding that even strangers are praying for you." Be sure to say that prayer!

Imagine the Possibilities

We can't solve problems by using the same kind of thinking we used when we created them.
—Albert Einstein

Only the dreamers among us, the budding scientists of tomorrow, will formulate inconceivable solutions to our current societal ills. How can you support the sciences and young scientists in the making? One way is to advocate for continued funding of science education in our schools. What better investment can we make for future generations?

Kids are eager to learn about the natural world. They observe worms in the garden and rocks while they're hiking. They want to understand where rain comes from and why magnets push and pull. Computer technology opens vast new areas for curious exploration.

Entering the local Science Fair is a great way to have your child think about contributing to society. One junior-high student drew so much attention for his project on ionic propulsion that two judges offered him summer internships. Another boy designed a novel configuration for solar panels that produces energy more efficiently. Young scientists like these may eventually make it to the Intel International Science and Engineering Fair, the largest precollege research competition in the world, where their new ideas can change the world for all of us.

ACTION STEPS

➤ Encourage your child's curiosity about the natural world by spending time in nature, but also allow space for daydreaming and tinkering. Competitions for youngsters exist. The Discovery Channel Young Scientist Challenge is open to children in the fifth through ninth grades: www.youngscientistchallenge.com.

➤ To support science education, contact the Society for Science and the Public (www.societyforscience.org).

Blog It!: Write About Your Experiences to Share with Others

A blog is in many ways a continuing conversation.
—Andrew Sullivan, blogger for the *Daily Dish*

One of the most intriguing parts of the Internet is blogs. At any moment in time, someone somewhere is sharing with the rest of the world what they've accomplished, what they've eaten, thought of, or experienced. Sometimes these are self-serving, but many are excellent ways to share your knowledge with others who can learn from your experiences. You can help others get through their own struggles as you share your own life story.

For example, blogs on medical Web sites like WebMD are provided by doctors, free of charge (and the doctors provide this service for free as well). As a reader, you can ask a doctor for an opinion on a variety of medical topics and get a fast and accurate response. As the doctor, you are able to provide advice and compassion from the comfort of your home. You can even contribute to a conversation as a layperson by joining in on the community response.

Other blogs are less corporate and more personal, but they can still attract a wide audience. You can set up a blog so that search engines like Google can find you. There are written blogs and video blogs (called vlogs) and lots of free programs on the Internet to get you started. Some of the most helpful have been on medical topics (surviving cancer, for example), dating, or parenting. You might find that it's easier to help others when you don't have to face their problems head on. The bottom line is this: write about whatever you wish, whenever you want; someone will benefit no matter what.

GETTING STARTED: WebMD offers an easy-to-access community bulletin board: www.webmd.com/community. If you want to create your own blog, try www.blogger.com, which is a free service provided by Google.

Lending an Ear

**Kindness is a language that the deaf
can hear and the blind can see.**
—Mark Twain

Imagine your frustration at not being able to hear the phone ring or someone knocking at the door. Now imagine the comfort of having someone—say, someone four legged and furry—in your home to alert you to sounds. Dogs for the Deaf rescues dogs from shelters—dogs who otherwise might be put down—and trains them to serve the deaf and hard of hearing. The organization finds dogs in shelters, quarantines them, gets them all their shots, spays and neuters them, gets them micro-chipped, and puts them through an extensive, professional four- to six-month training program.

"We give the dogs not just a second chance at life, but the chance to become somebody's hero," says Dogs for the Deaf's Pam Slater.

The dogs are taught to alert their human partners to a knock at the door, a doorbell, a name call, and the sound of the telephone, oven timer, smoke alarm, or alarm clock. In households with small children, they are also taught to alert to the sound of a baby's cry. In over thirty years, Dogs for the Deaf has rescued and placed over three thousand dogs in homes across the United States. The dogs who don't make it through the program to become hearing dogs instead become "miracle mutts" and join the homes of people living with special challenges such as depression, cerebral palsy, Alzheimer's, or who have had strokes.

Having a hearing dog can transform a life. A deaf woman who lives alone says, "I have had so many firsts since I got Haddie: the first time I knew someone was knocking at the door, the first time I knew the cookies were ready to come out of the oven, the first time I felt safe in my own home."

The wait period for a Dogs for the Deaf hearing dog is more than four years, because the need is so great and funds are limited. A gift of $100 provides vaccinations; $200 rescues a dog from a shelter; $500 provides evaluation, spaying, and neutering.

VISIT www.dogsforthedeaf.org or call (541) 826–9220.

Feed the Hungry

As a nation we must prevent hunger and cold to those of our people who are in honest difficulties.
—Herbert Hoover

More and more people in America today are facing food insecurity. They simply can't afford to buy enough food to feed themselves and their families. Soup kitchens and food pantries have traditionally helped these people, and the need for volunteers and donations is now greater than ever.

Volunteering at a local soup kitchen is something you might already have done, perhaps on Thanksgiving or Christmas. On those holidays so associated with abundance, your help was appreciated, but what about all the other, ordinary days of the year? There are just as many hungry people then—and volunteers are a lot scarcer.

Your help at a soup kitchen can take many forms. Food preparation is one area (often augmented by professional help); setting up, welcoming guests, and helping them get served, and cleaning up afterward are others. Behind the scenes, volunteers are also needed to solicit donations of food, money, and other community support to help keep the program going. For many soup kitchens operating on a shoestring, that's perhaps the most important job of all.

Food pantries are another way for a community to help feed its hungry. Food and other items, such as cleaning supplies, come from both donations and purchases; it's distributed at no cost. Food pantries usually have designated distribution days once or twice a week. The work to prepare for the distribution is ongoing, however, as is the endless need to ask for donations.

MANY FOOD programs operate very quietly in their communities, and you may be surprised to find that they even exist when you start looking for a place to volunteer. Even an hour of your time once a week can make a difference and help keep the doors open. VolunteerMatch can help you find a local group at www.volunteermatch.org.

Start a Movement in Your Community to Ban Plastic Bags

Learning is a lifelong process of keeping abreast of change.
—Peter Drucker, writer/educator

Plastic bags are a common part of our everyday lives, but many people don't realize how destructive they are. Their manufacture contributes to greenhouse gases; they clog landfills and storm drains, litter streets and streams, and kill wildlife. Thousands of sea creatures consume them by mistake and die as a result. Woodlands are defaced by bags hanging on trees.

But the "green" movement is fighting back, and winning. Over 700,000 bags, mostly plastic, were collected during a 2009 coastal cleanup in the United States and one hundred other countries (www.rte .ie/news/2009/0410/waste.html). In 2008, China announced a ban on the thinnest bags and a tax on others. A number of African countries now have such laws, and European countries are following suit.

Here in the United States, San Francisco and Oakland, California, have antibag laws in place, and many other cities are considering them. The time is right to bring pressure on public officials in your locality.

ACTION STEPS

LOCAL: Find out what some communities are doing about plastic bags at http://news.nationalgeographic.com/news/2008/04/080404-plastic-bags .html • www.chelseagreen.com/content/watch-the-scourge-of-plastic-bags-save-the-bay-campaign

NATIONAL/INTERNATIONAL: You can join the National Plastic Bag Campaign on Facebook: www.facebook.com/group.php?gid=180920260000.

The international Ban Plastic Bags Campaign aims to eliminate the worldwide use of plastic bags: www.earthshipsummit.com/info/sponsors_ plastic_en.php.

Grow Your Influence

Keep a green tree in your heart and perhaps the singing bird will come.
—Chinese proverb

She's the Divine Miss M. "Her audaciously theatrical delivery and campy taste-zapping zest for life can still strike a listener like a cold slap in the face," notes the *New Rolling Stone Album Guide* on this outlandishly wonderful entertainer. And she picks up litter. Cleans up parks. Plants trees. A million is the goal in New York City.

What makes her influence startlingly different and divine is the dichotomy of Bette Midler. How many of us see ourselves as one thing? An accountant or lawyer? A mechanic or nurse? A teacher or an actress? We see ourselves as rooted to one identity, and in seeing ourselves this way, we may limit our influence.

Ms. Midler must see herself as a tree with many strong, sturdy branches. As the founder of the New York Restoration Project, she stood alongside the mayor of New York City in the fall of 2007 and poetically urged every New Yorker to join the MillionTreesNYC effort. "To walk under the branches of a tree that you have planted connects you to the roots of our past and the aspirations of our future."

ACTION STEPS

➤ Plant a tree.

➤ Draw a tree. Each branch is one part of your identity. Label them. Dig into how you can use your influence to make a larger impact if you draw on the different parts of your life. Start planting ideas from the seeds of this tree. Find out how the Divine Miss M. does it: www.nyrp.org.

➤ Graft the Divine Miss M. to your influence. Be outlandish. Have a May Day community clean-up day with all the kids—and adults. Make it fun for everyone.

The Age of Compassion

**How far you go in life depends on your being
tender with the young, compassionate with the
aged, sympathetic with the striving and tolerant
of the weak and strong. Because someday in
your life you will have been all of these.**
—George Washington Carver

Over the wide, long course of human history, most cultures have traditionally paid great respect to the elders of their communities. In part, that was probably because the aged were so rare—for most of our time on this planet, people were lucky to make it to the age of thirty.

But now there are many old people as average life expectancy approaches eighty years here in the United States. Our respect for them wavers, if not outright falters, on those days that it seems they're all in front of us trying to figure out the ATM or griping about how their property taxes keep going up to pay for schools their kids haven't used in half a century. And, honestly, when was the last time you saw a Boy Scout helping a little old lady across the street?

ACTION STEPS

➤ Perhaps the best way to show compassion for the aged is to do your part in returning to a culture of respectfulness. Stand when they enter a room. Offer them your seat on a bus or in a waiting area. Give them your place in line. Call them Sir or Ma'am. They've earned it.

➤ Visit the graves of your forebearers with the elders of your family. Show them that they will never be forgotten. Ask them to tell you about those whose lives have led to your own.

➤ Ask their advice. It may seem odd that asking someone for something is compassionate, but elders have experienced the fullness of life and are anxious to pass it on. You can ask the advice of an older person you know, or you can ask advice from seniors who volunteer their time. Go to Web sites such as www.elderwisdomcircle.org.

The "Juno" Factor

It is said that the present is pregnant with the future.
—Voltaire

If you saw the movie *Juno,* you might have been surprised at the equanimity with which Juno's parents greeted the news of their teen's unplanned pregnancy. Not so long ago, an "unwed mother" shamed her family. She was sent to a home for months where she bore and relinquished the child in secrecy, ever to bury the sorrow of her loss.

Despite society's new openness, a woman who becomes pregnant at an importunate time needs support. Crucial decisions must be made: Should she keep the baby and become a single mom, relinquish the child for adoption, terminate the pregnancy, marry the father? Some choices are inevitable depending on one's religion, age, and relationship with the dad. Nevertheless, each holds difficulties.

A single mother is engaged in a juggling act that may require family to pitch in with babysitting and financial support. A woman who relinquishes her baby to adoption as well as one who terminates the pregnancy may long for the child she will never know. If she bears no more children in her lifetime, this loss can become acute. The one who marries the child's father may be plunging prematurely into marriage.

In each case, the woman must be surrounded by love and caring. Bearing a child is hard enough. Doing so under these circumstances can alter her life trajectory as well as her child's.

ACTION STEPS

➤ If someone you know is struggling with a decision about an unplanned pregnancy, support her choice, no matter what it is. Have faith that this is the right decision, and do all you can to help.

➤ For information and advice on options, contact Planned Parenthood at www.plannedparenthood.org or consult with your clergyperson.

Offer Travelers Aid

**Stand still. The trees ahead and bush
beside you are not lost.**
—Albert Einstein

In the mid-nineteenth century, St. Louis, Missouri, was a struggling gateway to the West. Mayor Bryan Mullanphy could barely meet the needs of travelers, who were plagued by unreliable stagecoaches, sickness, and delays that left them stranded in his city. Upon his death, Mullanphy left the city what was then a princely sum of half a million dollars to "aid travelers going West."

Although transportation options have improved, the needs of travelers have not. More than 150 years later, Travelers Aid International continues to aid the stranded in close to 50 communities across the country (including Puerto Rico), Canada, and Australia, serving 6.5 million people each year. Travelers Aid aims to help people who encounter crises via a network of service provider programs and their own volunteers. Their offices are most frequently found at transportation centers, including airports, bus, and train stations.

As a volunteer with this organization, you will not only be a friendly face to someone in desperate times, you will also become part of American history. Travelers Aid is the oldest nonsectarian social welfare organization in the United States. It has helped newly arrived immigrants get settled, and displaced workers return to their homes. Travelers Aid was one of the original USO agencies formed during World War II.

By volunteering your time at one of their centers, you can provide reassurance as well as information to every type of traveler: from the elderly to runaways, from the disabled to the infirm, or anyone who needs extra attention. Whether you assist in an arrival or a departure, you will be making a difference for someone along their journey.

GETTING STARTED: Visit www.travelersaid.org or call (202) 546–1127 to see if there is an office in your community. If there isn't, you can also contact them about starting a new branch where you live.

An Ounce of Prevention

Keeping your body healthy is an expression of gratitude to the whole cosmos—the trees, the clouds, everything.
—Thich Nhat Hanh

In 2005 Dr. Kay Taylor, a retired gynecologist, was invited to Honduras on a medical mission to care for young women who were at risk of becoming victims of human trafficking. During her two weeks in Honduras, she saw three cases of cervical cancer, which was more than she had seen in her entire career in the United States. Researching the disease, Dr. Taylor discovered that 300,000 women in underdeveloped countries die of cervical cancer every year, a statistic that astonished her, since it is the most preventable cancer in the world.

In the United States and Europe, cervical cancer deaths have been reduced to just over 2 per 100,000, but in Third World countries it is the number one cancer killer simply because there is so little reproductive healthcare available, especially in rural areas. At particular risk are the more than 1 million women and girls who are forced into prostitution worldwide every year. Many of these girls and women are also at high risk of contracting HIV, which in turn puts them at increased risk of cancer.

In response to this crisis, Dr. Taylor founded PINCC (Prevention International: No Cervical Cancer). Along with other medical volunteers, Dr. Taylor travels to remote areas of Central America and Africa (and soon India) to provide culturally sensitive education in the local language to both patients and healthcare workers. PINCC donates medical equipment and trains doctors and nurses at hospitals and clinics to diagnose and treat the precursors of cervical cancer, so that even after the PINCC team has left, women can continue to get care. (Some women are so determined to get screening and treatment that they will walk for miles or travel for days to reach a clinic.)

A gift of $150 will pay for ten women to be treated, $250 will pay to train one doctor or nurse, and $600 will buy exam equipment for a clinic.

VISIT www.pincc.org.

Lawyers Helping the Arts

**Life beats down and crushes the soul and
art reminds you that you have one.**
—Stella Adler

In an ideal world, a creative artist would never have to think about the legal issues relating to his or her work. In the real world we all live in, the law often intersects with artistic pursuits. Since 1969, Volunteer Lawyers for the Arts (VLA) has been helping artists resolve these issues.

Rapidly changing technology means rapidly changing legal and business issues for artists. To help them keep up, VLA offers bootcamps for filmmakers, musicians, Web designers, bloggers, and anyone else working in interactive media. These intensive all-day workshops cover issues such as intellectual property and sponsorship models—issues that today are more important, and more controversial, than ever for working artists.

Volunteer lawyers also lead shorter programs that help educate artists, cultural institutions, and creative organizations about legal and business issues that affect them. The goal is to help these artists avoid costly, time-consuming problems that distract them from their creative work. And VLA volunteers participate in mediation efforts to help resolve arts-related disputes outside the traditional legal framework.

VLA lawyers also advocate on behalf of the arts, including First Amendment and free-speech issues, artist taxation, and protecting the integrity of artists' works.

Most VLA lawyers volunteer by using their pro-bono time at their law firms to participate in the program—their firm allows them the unbillable hours, as it helps meet the ethical requirement to work at no charge on behalf of the community. Others volunteer their skills directly, even when their hours aren't counted toward pro-bono work. VLA is a model for similar volunteer programs.

TO LEARN more:

Volunteer Lawyers for the Arts / The Paley Building / 1 East 53rd Street, 6th Floor / New York, NY 10022 / (212) 319–2787 / www.vlany.org

Record the Wisdom of Your Town's Elders

**To know oneself is wisdom, but to
know one's neighbor is genius.**
—Norman Douglas

Interviewing older people in your community is a great way to record local history and let older people know that their lives and contributions are valued. It's easy to publish their stories with an online self-publishing program. The storyteller gets one free copy to keep, and one is donated to your local library or historical society. You can make additional copies available to others in the community (with permission of the subject) at a small profit, which can help to support the project. When you have accumulated a number of stories, set up booths at community events to sell copies and generate even more interest.

ACTION STEPS

LOCAL: Start by making a sample; interview a member of your own family. Tape the interview and make a transcript; go over it with the interviewee for additions and corrections. Organize the memories into chapters. Then design and print a small book using an online publishing service such as Picaboo (www.picaboo.com). You can readily add digital photos, including old photos than have been scanned by you or a local photo shop. One copy of a book will cost $30 to $100 to print.

With your sample in hand, approach local senior centers about giving a presentation to their members. Everyone loves to tell their story, and you will most likely be deluged with requests wherever you speak. For interviewing, develop a list of simple questions to ask, and learn to redirect the conversation gently if the speaker wanders. It may help to focus on one topic, such as an historic local event or a specific period of time. You will soon accumulate a valuable library of reminiscences.

NATIONAL: The Association of Personal Historians (www.personal historians.org) offers assistance, ideas, and resources for recording personal histories.

Out of the Box

Somewhere, something incredible is waiting to be known.
—Carl Sagan

Up to one-third of children living in inner-city public housing have allergic asthma, and overall it's one of the most common chronic diseases in America today. Hundreds of scientists have spent countless hours in pristine laboratories studying the cause and effect of asthma.

But when one team from the Boston University School of Medicine announced they had found the allergen, the cause of asthma, it was their unorthodox method that made news. This scientific team ventured into inner-city public housing, and using an old-time data-collection instrument—the common vacuum cleaner—solved the puzzle of asthma's cause.

The brilliant and telling key to their influence, which recharged the efforts to find a cure for this debilitating disease, was to think outside the confines of their laboratory. To think outside the box—to embrace unconventional, creative, smart thinking.

And the cause of childhood asthma? As reported in the *New York Times* in April 2009, after the team collected the house dust, added water, and spun the "junk" out of it, the extract was filled with proteins from *Blatella germanica*—the common cockroach—whose exoskeletons and droppings became airborne after death. The next step for the scientists is to build treatments based on their findings.

ACTION STEPS

➤ Solve the "nine dots" puzzle. The challenge is to connect the dots by drawing four straight, continuous lines, and never lifting the pencil from the paper. Draw three rows of dots, three across (nine dots). Many theorize that the origin of the phrase "thinking outside the box" comes from this puzzle, and that's a hint to solving it too!

➤ For one minute, imagine yourself stepping outside the confines of your living space or workplace or psychically outside your comfort zone. What challenge would you step toward?

Doing Nothing Is Really Something

Sometimes I sits and thinks and sometimes I just sits.
—Satchel Paige

The soil in which compassion grows is best made of quietness and contemplation. But it's not easy for us to just sit and think, let alone just sit. Our society's work ethic discourages downtime.

This is because we are an industrious people, something that every survey on the topic bears out. We consistently rank among the world's highest in worker productivity. We also rank among the lowest in vacation days taken and other forms of time off work. The Protestant work ethic, as it has been called, is important to us.

This also makes us harshly judge the co-worker who sits staring out the window as we clatter away at a keyboard. We reprimand the child who is watching the clouds go by when he or she is supposed to be doing chores. We get angry at spouses who kick back in recliners when there are a hundred and one things to be done.

But famed baseball pitcher Satchel Paige knew what he was talking about. Quietness and contemplation allowed him to stoically face the racism rampant in the days when he made the transition from the former Negro League to Major League Baseball. No one could accuse him of laziness: He started in 29 games one month. And fellow baseball great Joe DiMaggio called him "the best and fastest pitcher I've ever faced."

ACTION STEPS

➤ Who is the person you consider laziest? Your teen? Your spouse? Do something that will both shock them and build compassion in you: The next time you see them doing nothing, join them.

➤ Schedule "nothing" days for yourself at least once a month.

➤ While you're scheduling your "nothing" days, pen in "something" days to fall a day or two later. You will find that many issues come to your attention on "nothing" days, issues that require compassion to resolve. Use your "something" days to address these issues.

Keeping It Close to Home

**I love my hometown. I have freckles and
oversized ears. I'm a geek. I have tried not to
hide who I am or what matters to me.**
—Clay Aiken, *American Idol* runner-up

We've been advised to buy locally. Other than the well-known positive effects on the environment and the freshness of the produce, many other reasons compel us to do so. Local businesses use much more of your money to buy from other local businesses, service providers, and farms. This positive loop maintains your community's unique nature while it strengthens its economy. And local businesses support local non-profits, which receive an average 250 percent more support from smaller businesses than from large corporations.

This need is so important that the mayor of Orlando, Florida, decided to do something about it. Buddy Dyer recently created Buy Local Orlando. He personally asked downtown businesses to participate, and within five weeks more than one hundred vendors signed up. Orlando's residents receive a plastic card that entitles them to discounts from participating businesses. Even local franchise operations that have local owners (such as Arby's) participate. Our mom-and-pop stores are a dying breed. When you shop at a megastore, you may get lower prices, but in the long run, you undercut the economic stability of your hometown. Local artisans also need your support. They live from their artistic creations and struggle to make ends meet.

ACTION STEPS

➤ Organize a Buy Local day, week, or month in your community. Go to www.buylocalday.org to find out how. At www.localharvest.org you can locate farmers' markets, family farms, and other sources of sustainably grown food in your area.

➤ While vacationing, watch for artisans' shops on the road. Even buying from a roadside fruit stand supports the local economy.

Mentoring High-School Students

Teaching is the greatest act of optimism.
—Colleen Wilcox

High school is difficult under the best of circumstances. The social and academic pressures are intimidating. And when you add to the mix the stress of getting into a college or university, some students simply cannot handle the load. Volunteering as a high-school tutor or mentor, is an important way to help young people through this very tough time in their lives. In our complex world filled with the trappings of social-networking sites, "sexting" on cell phones, teenage drinking and drug use, high-school students need mentors now more than ever before.

As a mentor, you can provide help on so many levels, aside from academics. Young people are often confused about which classes are best for college applications and which colleges are realistic to apply to. You can also help them manage social distractions and ensure that they understand the implications of their actions.

While you can walk into any high school and offer your services, one established program worth checking out is called College Track. This after-school program is run at centers located in the San Francisco Bay Area and in New Orleans. The program begins during the summer before high school and features a rigorous after-school program: students are expected to come for a few hours several days a week. The tutors and mentors are all volunteers, working in specific areas: academics, college choices, career paths, and community service. Their goal is to help students with their coursework while they are still in high school and then teach them how to make good decisions about class enrollment and the college-application process. A program like this really can make a difference, getting high-school students onto the right path.

GETTING STARTED: Check out the College Track Web site at www .collegetrack.org to see how an established program operates. Then take their best practices into your local high school and see if they would be interested in setting up a similar program.

Making the Ground Safe

I cannot believe that the purpose of life is to be happy. I think the purpose of life is to be useful, to be responsible, to be compassionate. It is, above all to matter, to count, to stand for something, to have made some difference that you lived at all.
—Leo Rosten

If you are trying to walk somewhere and want to cut across a field, you probably do so without much thought. This is not the case in many parts of the world, where people trying to go about their daily lives are never sure where to step, for fear of being maimed or killed by a landmine. It is estimated that between fifteen and twenty thousand people are killed by landmines each year. And most of the people who die are not soldiers at war—they are civilians who live in countries that are now at peace.

Although we often think of landmines as a thing of the past, they are still being manufactured, stockpiled, and planted today. Unfortunately, the United States has not signed the Ottawa Convention (the Mine Ban Treaty), which has been signed by 122 other governments.

The U.S. Campaign to Ban Landmines (USCBL) is one of ninety country campaigns that comprise the International Campaign to Ban Landmines—winner of the 1997 Nobel Peace Prize. The USCBL works to ban the use, production, and export of antipersonnel landmines and cluster bombs by the United States. It also lobbies the U.S. government to join the 1997 Mine Ban Treaty and to support programs for victims of landmines, cluster bombs, and other unexploded remnants of war.

"Donations to the U.S. Campaign to Ban Landmines will help save countless lives," says Lora Lumpe of USCBL. "We don't get corporate support—we rely on individual contributions. Needless to say, the U.S. government does not support our work, so donations by individuals are critical."

VISIT www.banminesusa.org.

Special-Needs Summer Camp

Summer afternoon, summer afternoon; to me those have always been the two most beautiful words in the English language.
—Henry James

Kids with special needs often feel out of place. Try as we might to help them fit in, acceptance can be elusive. But at a summer camp designed just for children with a particular need, these kids find other kids who are just like them. They realize they're not alone.

Summer camp for special-needs kids benefits families as well. Families get a respite from the stresses of caregiving, while kids gain self-confidence and make new friends. At many special-needs summer camps, kids also learn about self-care and how to better manage their disabilities.

To make summer camp for kids with special needs a safe and happy place, lots of staff members are needed. Depending on the camp, teens and college students are welcome to volunteer alongside the adult staff. Volunteers usually participate for anywhere from a week to the whole summer in exchange for room and board and perhaps a small stipend.

Why do so many people give up all or part of their summer to work with special-needs kids? For the fun and satisfaction, of course, but also because they learn what it's like to have a handicap or chronic disease. They gain insight into what these kids live with every day.

Camps for special-needs kids especially need trained healthcare providers, mental-health workers, dietitians, and others who can help the campers learn to manage better. But the camps also need people to work in the office, be counselors, activity leaders, waterfront staff, and even just to direct traffic on opening and closing days.

TO VOLUNTEER, check with organizations that serve kids with special needs, such as the American Diabetes Association, Easter Seals, or the Muscular Dystrophy Association. Volunteer spots can fill up with surprising speed—start your search well before the summer camping season begins.

Start a "Sister City" Project with a Town in Another Country

**I look upon every day to be lost, in which
I do not make a new acquaintance.**
—Samuel Johnson

A "sister city" partnership is a close relationship between a U.S. city or town and one in another country. Through a sister-city relationship, many in your community will expand their horizons, developing an international perspective so important in today's world. Communities have a variety of reasons for becoming sister cities; cultural exchanges, environmental initiatives, humanitarian assistance, business development, women's empowerment, and programs for young people are some participants' interests. In any case, people on both sides usually report that they have learned more and benefited more than they could ever have imagined.

ACTION STEPS

LOCAL: Sister Cities International is the nonprofit network that creates and coordinates these partnerships in the United States. To get started, visit their Web site, www.sister-cities.org. The site contains clear, step-by-step information for those exploring the sister-city concept. Sister Cities International will guide you through the entire process of choosing, approaching, and working with a sister city. Through their Web site, you will also be able to communicate with other U.S. sister cities and gain from their experiences.

NATIONAL: Sister Cities International: www.sister-cities.org; (202) 347–8630 • Sister Cities of Los Angeles: www.lasistercities.com • Chicago Sister Cities: www.chicagosistercities.com • "Town twinning": www.absoluteastronomy.com/topics/Town_twinning

The Flow of Influence

**Drive a nail home and clinch it so faithfully that
you can wake up in the night and think of your
work with satisfaction—a work at which you
would not be ashamed to invoke The Muse.**
—Henry David Thoreau

When we delve into our work, lose ourselves in our efforts, when time sweeps by and we look up and an hour or two has sped by, we have caused our spirit to soar to another level. This state of mind has been described by the legendary social scientist Mihaly Csikszentmihalyi as "flow," also the name of his groundbreaking work, *Flow: The Psychology of Optimal Experience*. "Any activity can do it. Working on a challenging job, riding the crest of a tremendous wave and teaching one's child the letters of the alphabet are the kinds of experiences that focus our whole being in a harmonious rush of energy."

Flow—being involved, concentrating, absorbed—is when the mind and body are in full partnership with each other to achieve the task at hand. Being in the flow is a rare state of consciousness. When we are in the flow, the impact of any task, no matter how small, is large for those we serve. Why? Because when we are fully there, our influence is wholly engaged, serving with total involvement and joy.

ACTION STEPS

➤ For sixty seconds, concentrate on a lit candle. Clear your mind. Do you want to write? Draw? Map out a new project? The point is to practice concentrating fully on the immediate and invoke the Muse—and the flow.

➤ Drive a nail in faithfully: Get a board and nails. For ten minutes, immerse yourself body and soul into the details of hammering the name in straight. Let it flow. Take that energy and concentration out into the world as you use your influence in the spirit of service.

The Power of Ten

Be kind, for everyone you meet is fighting a hard battle.
—Plato

A young child quickly learns that if he ignores the hisses of a cat that has hidden itself in the back of a closet to birth its kittens, he will get a fearsome scratching. When the boy grows up, he does not blame the cat for what it did—he knows that almost all creatures will lash out when they are suffering, even at a hand that means them no harm.

Yet we often forget to extend that understanding to our family, our friends, and our co-workers. We forget to see the battle lines on their faces and the suffering in their souls. And when they lash out—often unfairly—we respond in kind. Jobs, friendships, and, saddest of all, marriages often collapse under the weight of so many hurled hurts.

ACTION STEPS

➤ Whoever first suggested to count to ten when you are angry is a saint whose name is lost to the mists of time. But he or she was absolutely right. Unlike any other animal on this planet, we humans have the ability to insert a pause between action and reaction, in this case a ten-count. Use that pause to bring compassion into the equation, and ask yourself if it is possible that the person is lashing out as a result of unseen pain.

➤ If yes, then respond with kindness in the face of harshness. Forgive the hurt or insult immediately as you would if an injured animal bit your hand. Few people can miss the contrast of a caring response to an angry outburst. If appropriate, try to find out the source of the pain. Oftentimes, the person won't even realize that he or she has been harsh or unfair to you.

➤ A select few people are just jerks by nature. In such cases, stand your ground and release any negative emotions after the encounter. Whisper a compassionate wish for them to better see how their behavior affects others.

Groupthink

**Great teamwork is the only way we create the
breakthroughs that define our careers.**
—Pat Riley, coach of the Los Angeles Lakers

According to gender specialists Drs. Pat Heim and Susan Murphy, girls grow up in flat societies in which they feel relatively equal—there's no head doll-player, and a girl who stands out is often called "bossy" and rejected. Boys, on the other hand, grow up in more hierarchical societies—sparring with one another to become top dog. Think of a sports metaphor—there's the coach and lead players and then the rest of the team.

As adults, women continue this pattern. They coalesce into informal support groups, helping one another with babysitting and enjoying group lunches where boyfriends are discussed. Sewing circles, book or bridge clubs, and writers' groups also provide support and enlightenment. These leaderless groups help women get along in the world.

However, you may be called upon to join a team patterned on male society in which you must adjust to hierarchical rules. This can feel uncomfortable at first, but learning to function on such a team helps you navigate the world of business, because it too is structured as a pyramid. In fact, it may be useful to volunteer for a team to learn skills that make hierarchical groups work. This can also enhance your career and teach you another way to effectively get things done in order to help others.

ACTION STEPS

➤ Join a group whose mission you believe in. Volunteer for a committee that interests you or matches your skill set. Or seek out a new experience in order to expand your horizons while supporting your cause.

➤ To learn more about gender dynamics and mutual support, read *In the Company of Women* by Pat Heim and Susan Murphy. *The Starfish and the Spider: The Unstoppable Power of Leaderless Organizations* by Ori Brafman and Rod Beckstrom explains group dynamics and how people form successful action groups.

Convert Your Car to Biodiesel

Humanity is living off its ecological credit card and can only do this by liquidating the planet's natural resources.
—Mathis Wackernagel, Global Footprint Network

You've seen the movie and read the books: global warming, now known as "climate change," is here. We can no longer wait for our government to solve this problem. We can reverse the trend by taking matters into our own hands. Whether you're a fan or a foe of Big Oil, one thing you can do to help save this planet so that we'll be able to pass on the lifestyle we've come to know and love to our children, and their children, is to start driving more-fuel-efficient cars.

➤ The easy first step is to trade in your gas guzzler for something smaller and lighter. Or, consider buying a car with a diesel engine. A 2007 study conducted by the Rand Corporation shows that diesel engines get better fuel economy than even the cutest, smallest, gas-electric hybrids.

➤ If you want to take the challenge one step further, there are DIY kits that can help you convert an existing diesel engine to something cleaner, greener, and cheaper: vegetable oil. A kit sells for about $600, and, according to *Budget Living* magazine, one user claims that she made her money back in only nine months. Once your engine has been converted, you'll need only the smallest amount of diesel gas to run your car: the rest of your fuel will come from used food grease that restaurants are dying to get rid of anyway. Many users are making arrangements with restaurants who are only too happy to get rid of it for free.

GETTING STARTED: Check out www.greasel.com or www.greasecar.com, which are the suppliers for the conversion kits. Joshua Tickell's book, *From the Fryer to Fuel Tank,* gives all the "been there, done that" advice you'll need.

Bringing the Joy of Art to All

**Art is a collaboration between God and the
artist, and the less the artist does the better.**
—Andre Gide

Just a few decades ago there was no arts education for children with developmental, emotional, cognitive, or physical disabilities. Believing that *all* people should participate in and enjoy the arts, in 1974 Ambassador Jean Kennedy Smith created *VSA arts,* an international, nonprofit organization that supports artists with disabilities at all stages of their careers.

A young man named Chris is a great example of how *VSA arts* can help establish an artist. Chris first heard of *VSA arts* from his college theater professor, who encouraged him to apply for the *VSA arts* apprenticeship at the Williamstown Theatre Festival. Chris applied and was named the inaugural *VSA arts* apprentice at the prestigious summer theater, an experience he later called "life changing."

Chris, who has cerebral palsy, connected with *VSA arts* again two years later as a participant in *Inside/Out . . . voices from the disability community,* a world premiere theatrical production that was commissioned by *VSA arts* and performed at the Kennedy Center. Through Chris's work on that production, *VSA arts* was able to sponsor his membership in the professional actors' union, Actors' Equity Association, which opened the door to Chris's career as a professional actor.

Every year more than 5 million people like Chris across the globe participate in *VSA arts* programs. *VSA arts* shares their tools and resources for teachers, arts professionals, and parents in classrooms and cultural centers, as well as in homes and communities, and provides opportunities in and through the arts for people with disabilities. Donations made to *VSA arts* help support and showcase the work of established and emerging disabled artists through exhibitions and performances—support that can be life-changing for an artist. Potential donors can earmark funds to any part of *VSA arts* programming that they wish to support.

VISIT www.vsarts.org or call (800) 933–8721.

Sing Out! The Music National Service Initiative

Music can change the world because it can change people.
—Bono

Imagine a version of the Peace Corps that focused on bringing the joy of music to schools and communities across America. That's exactly what the new Music National Service Initiative (MNSI) is designed to do. Through its innovative MusicianCorps program, MNSI deploys trained musicians who commit to one to two years of service.

As school systems struggle, "frills" such as music education are often the first to go. Community centers and after-school programs face the same financial pressures. At the same time, studies show that youth who participate in music programs do better academically and are much more likely to graduate from high school.

MusicianCorps Fellows aim to reverse the counterproductive elimination of music education. They bring music and all its benefits back to public schools and community programs. By helping community-based organizations offer music programs, MusicianCorps Fellows provide urgently needed after-school activities.

The pool of potential MusicianCorps volunteers is large—every year, more than fifty thousand students graduate from music programs. Musician Corps offers these new graduates a wonderful way to use their training and passion for music-based public service. MusicianCorps Fellows receive a living stipend, health insurance, training, and lots of support throughout their service. The funds come from the Music National Service Initiative, which in turn has received significant start-up funding from major foundations.

TO LEARN more about becoming a MusicianCorps Fellow, contact:

Music National Service Initiative / 280 Granville Way / San Francisco, CA 94127 / www.musicnationalservice.org

Change a Life Through Reading

Knowing you'll have something good to read before bed is among the most pleasurable of sensations.
—Vladimir Nabokov

A surprising number of adults in the United States (about 30 million) are fully or functionally illiterate. The United States, the richest country in the world, ranks only fifth in reading skills compared to other industrialized nations. Most local libraries and/or school systems have literacy programs. Volunteer! You will be trained and receive plenty of support in your work to give adults this life-changing skill.

By helping someone to become literate, you may also improve the life of an entire family. Studies show that parental literacy is one of the biggest indicators of children's success. And women who are literate are less likely to suffer from abuse, and more likely to be economically independent.

Local adult literacy programs exist in all parts of the country. The National Institute for Literacy Hotline, (800) 228–8813, can put you in contact with agencies or groups in your area that offer adult literacy programs. Your local United Way agency may also have links to local social-services agencies that offer adult literacy classes. You can also try your local library or public-school district office, which might offer continuing education classes for parents of current students. You can even talk with your local religious leaders, who might be able to put you in direct contact with an individual who needs help.

GETTING STARTED: ProLiteracy is a resource where volunteers can get the resources and training they need to help others master reading in the United States and around the world. Check out their Web sites at www.proliteracy.org, (888) 528–2224, where you can enter your zip code and find the Literacy Program closest to you. Literacy Connections is another resource that gives advice and useful tips for volunteer tutors and teachers: www.literacyconnections.com.

Visible Influence

Live with your head in the lion's mouth.
—*Invisible Man*

"**I** am an invisible man . . . I am invisible, understand, simply because people refuse to see me." Ralph Ellison's groundbreaking novel, *Invisible Man,* won the National Book Award in 1953, the first work by an African American to do so. Our first African American president cites this novel as a major influence on his personal evolution.

Invisible Man powerfully questions race and identity and what we see and refuse to see in our country. Influential artists and their work always ask the big questions about life and purpose and society. They challenge us to live life in the lion's mouth.

And the greatest artists reflect a groundswell for change. In 1954, *Brown v. Board of Education,* striking down school segregation, followed Ellison's work, and in the 1960s, even more major civil-rights legislation led the way to change.

Yet, Ellison's *Invisible Man* challenges us even today to think about the divides in American society. The message of all important and vital and great art transcends its time and place, touching us through the ages. And the arts, at their best, influence all of us to make the invisible visible.

ACTION STEPS

➤ What work of art has influenced you? Specifically, what question has it asked you to reconsider? About gender? class? race?

➤ What classic novel has changed your perceptions of America? Go to one of the many online book-review sites, and add a review about the novel you chose. Focus on why its influence is still relevant. Help make this classic a new influence for the next generation.

➤ Read *Invisible Man* by Ralph Ellison.

➤ Recommend an influential book to a friend—or, better yet, share the wealth by giving a book to others who might be similarly affected or inspired.

The Lyrical Voice of God

**For me music is a vehicle to bring our pain to
the surface, getting it back to that humble
and tender spot where, with luck, it can lose
its anger and become compassion again.**
—Paula Cole

Music has an incredibly important role to play in the development and
maintenance of compassion. Our brains are hardwired to respond
to music in a way that even the smartest neuroscientists don't yet understand. Some people put aside scientific explanations and simply see music
as God's way of speaking.

As life gets more and more rushed, we've learned to treat music in the
same way we treat food—we choose items that we can consume faster
and on the run. Hence, the only time we get to listen to music is on our
commute or while we're doing something else, such as housework.

But music listened to for its own sake, with our full ability to hear
and nothing else going on, no other purpose in mind, is a powerful spiritual practice that can feed the soul. A deep soulful connection is often a
gateway to compassion.

ACTION STEPS

➤ Stand in front of your CD collection or dial up your iPod menu.
Which is the album that immediately transports you to a thoughtful,
even emotional place? Choose that one.

➤ Find a private place where you won't be disturbed for the next hour or
so and put your headphones on. Get comfortable and close your eyes.

➤ Listen to the album with complete focus. Pay attention to each instrument and what it's doing. Follow one through the melody for a while.
Then listen to how all parts come together into one body of work. Let
yourself completely feel what the music brings up in you, even if it's
sorrowful. When you're done, just sit quietly for a while until you're
ready to rejoin the world.

Support, Education, and Hope for Cancer Patients

The goal is to live a full, productive life even with all that ambiguity. No matter what happens, whether the cancer never flares up again or whether you die, the important thing is that the days that you have had you will have lived.
—Gilda Radner

A diagnosis of cancer universally brings a sense of doom. You wonder, is this a death sentence? Will the treatment be devastating? In years past, both were true. But today, with more than 12 million survivors in the United States, cancer is becoming a chronic illness. The trick is to live well with the disease and enjoy the life ahead.

Often this means seeking support. Many people turn to family, friends, and clergy for comfort. But sometimes this isn't enough, especially if the person with cancer is afraid to worry loved ones with his or her concerns. Communication can break down. In the presence of others with cancer, however, a kinship can evolve that may not exist among those who are well. Harold Benjamin, the founder of The Wellness Community, among the largest cancer support organizations in the world, has said, "There is no other person a cancer patient wants to see more than a cancer survivor."

People with cancer often experience unwanted aloneness, loss of hope, and loss of control. Organizations like The Wellness Community help counter these stressors by encouraging participants to become active in their fight for recovery.

ACTION STEPS

➤ If someone you love has cancer and you're feeling overwhelmed and frightened, help them seek free support from The Wellness Community, which has facilities or affiliates in over 50 cities worldwide.

➤ Contact them at www.thewellnesscommunity.org or call (888) 793–WELL (9355).

Teach Others to Express Themselves

**Better than a thousand days of diligent
study is one day with a great teacher.**
—Japanese proverb

High-school girls often stop following their dreams in order to "fit in."
This might mean dropping soccer, even if they were the best on the
team, or giving up playing a musical instrument they were once proficient in. The result is a disparity of talents among men and women later
in life. Mentoring organizations that focus on young girls try to dissuade
this decision to drop something and augment the skills many of these
girls already have, and truly enjoy.

One such program is called WriteGirl. Based in Los Angeles, it was
started in 2001 in an effort to bring together professional women writers (novelists, songwriters, poets, screenwriters, editors, and others) to act
as mentors. Volunteers meet with the girls individually and at monthly
workshops. Their goal is to introduce girls to a wide variety of writing
opportunities, teach them better writing and critical-analysis skills, and
help them explore and develop their creative talents. Along the way, they
are also promoting healthy behaviors and life choices through positive
mentoring relationships. At the end of each season, they publish a book
of the girl's writing and have a reading at a local bookstore.

This opportunity can be modified for whatever skill set you possess.
Your goal doesn't have to be to work with girls and writing, although it
is a very good cause. But if you can keep a girl on the soccer field, or in
the art studio, or the orchestra, you are not only encouraging her talent,
but inspiring her to explore a career based on it. At the same time, you
are giving her the opportunity to work with an adult and to learn more
about addressing the challenges she may face day to day.

GETTING STARTED: The WriteGirl Web site (www.writegirl.org) is
loaded with great ideas about this organization and how you can start
one of your own. Their recent book, *Lines of Velocity,* is an inspiring example of what can be accomplished.

A Home for Everyone

**Home is not where you live, but
where they understand you.**
—Christian Morgenstern

The Partnership for the Homeless was founded in 1983 in response to what was thought to be a short-term emergency—the growing number of homeless on the streets of New York City. But, of course, the problem did not turn out to be short-term. In January 2009, there were over thirty-five thousand people—including over eight thousand families and almost fifteen thousand children—in New York City shelters, and those numbers are expected to continue to increase with the bad economy.

The best safeguard against homelessness is a person's connection to community. For example, if a person with substance-abuse issues has people checking in on him, who make sure he does not spend his disability check on alcohol or drugs instead of the rent, he is at lesser risk of becoming homeless. For this reason, as well as trying to get people housed quickly, Partnership for the Homeless helps people establish connections to their communities, such as through churches or synagogues, senior centers, or other social services. At the same time, Partnership for the Homeless also monitors public policy concerning issues crucial to lower-income people, such as quality housing, quality education, and good healthcare—which are all preventative factors against homelessness.

Partnership focuses particularly on homeless seniors, people with an illness such as HIV, and families with children. Providing homes for these people is crucial. But just the act of reaching out to somebody who's homeless and showing concern makes a powerful statement.

"A big part of what people are faced with when they become homeless is a sense of invisibility," says Scott Cotenoff of the Partnership. "When people step up and say, 'We value you enough that we think you are entitled to a home, and we are going to help get you one,' the homeless person knows that he or she is not actually invisible after all."

VISIT www.partnershipforthehomeless.org.

Hotline Counseling

**People used what they called a telephone
because they hated being close together
and they were scared of being alone.**
—Chuck Palahniuk

A friendly, supportive voice can make all the difference to someone in crisis. That's what hotlines are all about—a phone number anyone can call at any time and be certain of getting an answer and some help

Crisis centers operate hotlines—telephones and also Web sites—for drug abuse, sexual assault, runaways, AIDS, depression, and many other social or health concerns. Crisis hotlines are usually staffed around the clock by volunteers, often in conjunction with mental-health professionals, social workers, and other professionals.

Counseling is a tremendous responsibility for a volunteer—but helping people in such serious trouble is also tremendously rewarding. What makes a good hotline volunteer? Excellent listening skills, a strong desire to help, empathy, self-knowledge, and perhaps most of all, not being judgmental or rigid. Whatever organization you decide to work with will have to do a background check. You'll then be asked to complete training in crisis intervention (you can often do this online) before you can take calls.

There are a number of national hotlines, such as Covenant House hotline for teens in crisis and United Way runs many hotlines through its networks of state and local organizations—check www.liveunited.org or call (703) 836–7112 to find volunteer opportunities near you. Other hotlines are run by local or regional volunteer networks that focus on a particular area, such as child abuse or domestic violence.

TO VOLUNTEER for a hotline that's right for you, start with your local phone book—hotlines by definition are listed there. United Way also sponsors 211 phone service for finding community and human services, including crisis intervention hotlines, in your area. The person who answers can tell you who to contact about volunteer opportunities.

Start a Peer-Mediation Program
at Your Local School

**Hate is too great a burden to bear. It injures
the hater more than it injures the hated.**
—Coretta Scott King

Peer mediation is a form of conflict resolution in which young people, trained and supervised by qualified adults, help with everyday disputes among their peers. There are thousands of these valuable programs nationwide. They teach skills such as active listening, appreciating differences, empathy, impulse control, problem solving, and anger management; and they strengthen the schools and the communities they serve.

ACTION STEPS

LOCAL: Read and print the conflict-resolution standards at www .mediate.com/acreducation. Then contact your school administration. Say that it's important for the future of your community that as many young people as possible learn about conflict resolution. Volunteer to work with the school to get a peer-mediation program started. Explain that such programs are voluntary and do not get involved with illegal or dangerous situations. They deal with issues such as gossiping, name-calling, and poor sportsmanship.

Discuss funding. If such a program seems beyond the reach of the school's budget, say you will look into support from other sources.

Through the contacts below, find schools that already have peer-mediation programs for support and guidance. Ask them where training for teachers and coordinators is available in your area.

NATIONAL/INTERNATIONAL: School Mediation Associates: www .schoolmediation.com • Association for Conflict Resolution: http:// acrnet.org/acrlibrary/more.php?id=6_0_1_0_M • Where Peace Lives: www.wherepeacelives.org

A Ninety-Five-Year-Old's Greatest Influence

Do not follow people that stand still.
—Woodrow Wilson

We all have events in our lives that change us forever. The day we meet our life partner. The birth of a child. Other turning points in our lives that influence us forever after. Or consider traumatic events in which the world changes around us, and we change with it. For one generation, the day then-president John F. Kennedy was shot, November 22, 1963; for another generation, September 11, 2001.

"1920." That's what ninety-five-year-old Grandma Ray said to her granddaughter. "November 2, 1920. Everything changed after that."

1920?

That was the year women won the right to vote, and Grandma Ray marched out to cast her first ballot. The statement it made on her ability to direct her life, to work outside the home, to encourage her daughter to pursue advanced degrees, influenced her forevermore. Voting changed everything for her and millions of American women who followed. It was the defining moment, the greatest influence, in her life.

What is yours?

ACTION STEPS

➤ Start a personal time capsule with writings, articles, and memorabilia. "Bury" it in the attic or a top closet shelf to open and add to at significant future anniversaries.

➤ StoryCorps is undertaking a major oral history project to preserve the experiences of ordinary Americans. Record your story (you don't need to be ninety-five years old!) at a local StoryBooth. Or arrange to sponsor an on-site recording session anywhere at the location of your choice. Every person who participates receives a free CD. A copy of each story is also sent to the Library of Congress to be preserved for future generations. Since 2003, over fifty thousand people have shared their life stories. More at www.storycorps.org.

For Better or Worse (But Go Easy on the Worse)

There's only one way to have a happy marriage and as soon as I learn what it is, I'll get married again.
—Clint Eastwood

Maybe Dirty Harry should have paid more attention to the Japanese generation known as the Issei. Prior to the establishment of Japan as an economic powerhouse, huge waves of its citizens left for other countries in search of a better life. The first generation of each family to arrive in a foreign land was known as the Issei.

Alone in a foreign land, married Issei couples usually had only each other to cling to. Years later, in studying the happiness (or lack thereof) in these marriages, researchers found that the most harmonious marriages were also the ones where compassion was displayed most often.

It's true that the person most difficult to feel empathy for is often your spouse. After a certain number of years pass, you've heard all the complaints and the excuses, and they get tiresome. The little spats and big arguments stack up like cords of aging wood, so dry that they can easily be set alight. But the Issei found the secret, and it is compassion.

ACTION STEPS

➤ The Issei knew that a marriage involved the binding of two families together, not just two people. The best marriages were ones where each spouse treated the other's family with respect and compassion. Vow to do the same in your own family.

➤ Issei husbands who were happiest had wives who did not criticize them. Criticism and compassion are mortal enemies. Eliminate criticism from your marriage. Issei wives called their husbands "esteemed." Treat the other person in your marriage with kindness and compassion, especially at times when it is hardest to do so.

Be Kind to Your Mother

**It is evident in the world around us that very
dramatic changes are taking place.**
—Al Gore, *An Inconvenient Truth*

After watching videos of a twenty-five-mile-long ice shelf shattering in the Antarctic and catastrophic hurricanes like Katrina, it's becoming clear that the time has passed for debating global warming. It is upon us. We need to pull together to support our planet—or we face dire consequences.

You may shrug and say, "What can I do? I'm just one among billions." That's true. But if you start changing your habits, you may influence your children and friends . . . who will influence their own circles.

Some actions are easy and inexpensive. In fact, they'll save you money. Use cloth towels instead of paper—you'll spend less and save some trees. Instead of drinking bottled water and tossing the plastic, use refillable bottles. Barring that, be sure to recycle. While you're at it, recycle glass, plastic, aluminum, paper, and cardboard. Many cities provide bins for trash-collection day. Use them! It'll make you feel virtuous. Some cities even provide composting bins. This reduces the amount of methane—a potent greenhouse gas. If you don't have access to bins, create your own compost heap, and bring recyclable bottles and cans to the market for a refund. Tote your own reusable bags to the grocery. Some give credit for every bag you bring. Use public transportation. Switch to compact fluorescents.

If all of us took a few minutes to consider how we can support our environment, Mother Earth and all who live upon her would be safer.

ACTION STEPS

➤ Form an environmental-awareness educational or action group at your place of worship or children's school. Support one another in changing your consumption habits for the good of all.

➤ Check out some Web sites: www.epa.gov has a wealth of information on recycling and composting. Calculate how much energy you use at www.energyguide.com.

Sit with Someone Who Is Dying

**When we are no longer able to change a situation,
we are challenged to change ourselves.**
—Victor Frankl, *Man's Search for Meaning*

Coming to terms with death means different things to each of us. Some individuals who are dying reach deep into their spiritual cores to find significance or hope.

If you are in touch with your own spiritual nature, you can create a lasting connection to these individuals on a deep and meaningful level that can also help reduce their stress and anxiety, promote a more positive outlook, or strengthen their will to live. Spirituality can be practiced in the form of prayer, meditation, silent observation, listening, or sharing ideas of gratitude. Sharing the rituals, symbolisms, and tenets of your faith can bring certain ease to the ideas of death for those who are dying, or their loved ones.

There are practical matters that need to be addressed as well, and your help can be invaluable. Sometimes, those who are dying are looking for a way to say good-bye. Recording last wishes, or even a life story, can be a wonderful experience in the final days of someone's life and provide inspiration to those left behind. And if you are fortunate to sit with someone while she makes this passage, know that your presence was known.

GETTING STARTED: Be prepared for each of your visits with someone at the end of life. Think of activities that promote the collection or revisiting of positive memories. Bring spiritual texts, books of poems, or readings that can engage conversation. Most of all, be yourself, and be grateful for what this shared experience can bring to both of you. One excellent resource is the book *The Needs of the Dying: A Guide for Bringing Hope, Comfort, and Love to Life's Final Chapter* by David Kessler.

Eldercare in the Gay Community

The longer I live the more beautiful life becomes.
—Frank Lloyd Wright

For twenty years, Tim and Charles shared a cozy flat with two cats, where their favorite hobby was tending to a small rooftop garden. But when Tim died unexpectedly, Charles received notice from the landlord that he was going to face eviction. Because Tim and Charles had never been married and Tim's name was on the lease, Charles had no right to stay. On top of the heartbreak of losing Tim, Charles now faced losing his home.

Getting old is never easy. But some gay and lesbian seniors face extra challenges because of discrimination. Since gay and lesbian elders are twice as likely to live alone than heterosexual seniors, and are more than four times as likely not to have children, the support of a family is often not available to them.

And despite the fact that social acceptance has changed since their youth, some GLBT seniors feel the need to go "back in the closet" when making important decisions such as choosing residential care. This in turn can contribute to the isolation and depression that can so easily darken the life of a senior. It can also make them much less likely to reach out for help when they need it.

SAGE (Services & Advocacy for GLBT Elders) is the world's oldest and largest nonprofit agency that addresses the needs of lesbian, gay, bisexual, and transgender seniors. SAGE advocates for the rights of gay and lesbian elders, works to combat discrimination, and helps create a network of caregiving support. They also raise awareness that some GLBT seniors are denied access to public services, even when that discrimination is illegal.

For hundreds of thousands of GLBT seniors who might otherwise feel isolated and alone, SAGE provides a safe and welcoming community. A donation helps SAGE to continue to reach out to people everywhere, especially people in rural areas who may not have ready access to a local GLBT community.

VISIT www.sageusa.org.

Happy Trails

**When one tugs at a single thing in nature, he
finds it attached to the rest of the world.**
—John Muir

If you love the outdoors, consider taking a volunteer vacation with the American Hiking Society. You'll spend a week building and maintaining trails at your choice of destinations on public lands across the country. All you have to bring is your camping gear and a willingness to get dirty. In return, you'll be fostering public-land stewardship and having a lot of fun.

A volunteer week on the trail can be on the rugged side. On most trips you'll be sleeping in tents, though cabins or dormitories are provided at some sites. Your trail hosts will most likely be rangers from a national or state park. They'll provide tools, food and water, and cooking gear, but you'll have to pitch in for cooking and clean-up.

Volunteer trail workers usually spend their time doing trail maintenance and repair; they also work on enhancements to existing trails, such as fixing up camping shelters and picnic areas and improving signage. The work is physically demanding, but it's also very rewarding, especially because it's done as part of a congenial work crew of fellow trail lovers. You'll be spending your week with six to fifteen volunteers, along with an experienced crew leader. Trips tend to cluster in the warmer weather, but volunteer vacations are available through most of the year.

To volunteer, you need to be physically fit, but there's no upper age limit. The program has accepted people in their eighties! You have to get yourself to your volunteer vacation destination, and there's generally a small fee of about $100 for the week to cover food. Aside from that, a volunteer vacation is a bargain—an enjoyable, constructive week in some of the country's most beautiful areas and a chance to give back to the trails you love.

FOR MORE information, contact:

American Hiking Society / 1422 Fenwick Lane / Silver Spring, MD 20910 / (800) 972–8608 / www.americanhiking.org

Fight Bullying in Your Community's Schools

No one has yet fully realized the wealth of sympathy, kindness and generosity hidden in the soul of a child.
—Emma Goldman

Studies show that 15 to 25 percent of students in the United States are bullied at some time. Most kids know who the bullies are in their schools. Often, though, kids don't discuss this with adults, for fear of being called "tattletales" or "rats."

Adults often believe that victims should "just get over it" or ignore the bullying. But being bullied can be a devastating experience for a child, and can lead to serious emotional problems. Bullied children often become depressed or anxious; have low self-esteem and/or physical ailments; and even contemplate suicide. The good news is, there are many things that parents, teachers, and kids can do to stop bullying.

ACTION STEPS

LOCAL: *Kids:* Find an adult who will listen, and tell them about the bullying. Support children who are being bullied; don't let them feel lonely. Confront bullies, if this feels safe for you. *Adults:* Stop, look, and listen! Don't brush off kids' complaints; intervene with bullies and make sure the bullying stops.

To get a dialogue started in your community, check out the Stop Bullying Now! Communications Kit at www.stopbullyingnow.hrsa.gov. It contains downloadable brochures and posters, as well as public service announcements for local print and broadcast media.

NATIONAL: Get your school to join Peaceful Schools International, www.peacefulschoolsinternational.org, which has anti-bullying help for kids, parents, and teachers.

Get involved in a national dialogue to help stop bullying at www.stopbullyingnow.hrsa.gov. There, you'll find bullying prevention resources from every area of the country. Share ideas and resources at www.bullyingresources.org.

Walking Among Friends

**If one comes across a person who has been shot
by an arrow, one does not spend time wondering
about where the arrow came from, or the caste of
the individual who shot it, or analyzing what type of
wood the shaft is made of, or the manner in which
the arrowhead was fashioned. Rather, one should
focus on immediately pulling out the arrow.**
—The Dalai Lama and Howard Cutler, *The Art of Happiness*

Sometimes the world is too much for us. We plug in the iPod and tune out the noise of the world. We know all the statistics about rising poverty, homelessness, hunger. We will donate when the next plea envelope with address labels arrives.

Yet if we take the time to literally walk among other people rather than closing ourselves off within our cars, within our own minds, if we take care to see individuals, not the statistic, we will experience how our very being, our presence, can influence the world. A smile—a "hey, good morning!" a presence of mind that we are not alone on this earth but walk among friends, unplugged, open to the world's joyful noise, ready to pull the arrows out if need be—may be the gentlest influence of our very being we can offer another and the greatest.

ACTION STEPS

➤ Go for a walk in an area where you are sure to encounter other people. Take in all that surrounds you. Notice what you usually ignore.

➤ Pull out an arrow. Suggest your local volunteer fire department organize a basic life-saving day. The American Red Cross First Aid, CPR and Automated External Defibrillator (AED) classes are designed to give the confidence to respond in an emergency situation. More at www.redcross.org. Add a walk-a-thon to the life-saving day to benefit the fire department. Walk with friends; your influence will impact many to do more if you are there, fully and joyfully there.

To Console the Inconsolable

Grief fills the room up of my absent child,
Lies in his bed, walks up and down with me,
Puts on his pretty looks, repeats his words,
Remembers me of all his gracious parts,
Stuffs out his vacant garments with his form:
Then have I reason to be fond of grief.
—William Shakespeare, *King John*

If there is a time when compassion is called for above all else, it is when you are faced with the overwhelming grief of people who have lost a loved one. Yet this is a terrifying prospect for most people, even the most compassionate. What can you say to those who are suffering the most unspeakable of losses? What can you do for people whose every word is lost in uncontrollable sobs?

Caring people often feel lost and useless in this situation. But your presence can be more powerful and healing than you realize, even if it's not apparent at the time.

ACTION STEPS

➤ When you are at a loss for words, stay that way. There is nothing you can say to take the hurt away. In fact, many people, rather than simply staying quiet, say things that are inadvertently hurtful. Your mere presence and caring touch are the most powerful balms you can offer at a time like this.

➤ Anticipate their needs and quietly make arrangements to meet them. If they have pets, assign someone to care for them. If they need transportation, arrange a pool of drivers. Bring in their newspapers, organize the meals that people send—always be on the watch for things that need tending to.

➤ Be there for the long haul. Many people are a fantastic help in the days following a tragedy. The grieving need that, but they also need those who will be there for them in the months, even years, ahead.

A Hand Up

**Until the great mass of the people shall be filled
with the sense of responsibility for each other's
welfare, social justice can never be attained.**
—Helen Keller

Third World poverty is crushing. No matter how difficult your circumstances, there are billions of destitute people much worse off than you. Yet, as with so many other important "causes," you may simply scratch your head and say, "What can I do? I'm just getting by myself."

There is a way to give the poor a hand up instead of a handout and line your own pocket at the same time—a win-win for everyone: microloans made to individuals struggling to start their own small enterprises. Given the scale of the Third World economies, these budding entrepreneurs need only a fraction of what we would need to develop a business—the average giver lends $300. One woman in Peru took out ten small loans totaling $10,000 to grow her pottery business from a struggling one-woman shop to a small studio with employees and several retail outlets. Not only did she lift herself out of poverty, but she was also supporting others in her community.

To date, $36 billion in microloans has been distributed to 99 million borrowers. Women comprise 85 percent of the borrowers, and the rate of repayment is 97 percent—an excellent investment. Interest rates range from 2 percent to 6 percent—what you would get from a bank. Making a microloan gives you a way to help yourself while supporting others in their quest for a better life.

ACTION STEPS

➤ To learn more and to get involved with microfinance, visit Unitus as www.unitus.com and Grameen Foundation at www.grammeenfoundation.org.

Build Someone a House:
Habitat for Humanity

Generosity gives assistance, rather than advice.
—Marquis de Vauvenargues

While Habitat for Humanity's most influential volunteer has been former president Jimmy Carter, it was actually founded in 1976 by Millard and Linda Fuller. Over the past thirty years, Habitat has built or rehabilitated more than 300,000 houses in more than 3,000 locations around the world. Through the work of Habitat, churches, community groups, and others have joined together in service allowing 1.5 million people to help themselves create a new life.

By volunteering with Habitat, you will be helping a family, or an individual, get through tough times, not with a handout but with a helping hand. What makes this organization unique is that it is not a giveaway program. Habitat requires the recipients of these homes to physically contribute between three hundred and five hundred hours to the building process and subsequently pay for their home. Habitat homes are sold to recipient families at no profit and financed with affordable loans. The mortgage payments are then used to build houses for others.

You can volunteer with Habitat for Humanity in many different ways, regardless of your age, race, or religion. Volunteer programs range from three-, six-, and twelve-month projects building affordable housing overseas to shorter stints here in the United States. You can also take a Habitat "vacation" and participate for one to three weeks. Volunteers physically build the homes, work in Habitat offices, or train new builders in construction skills. There are youth-oriented Habitat programs as well as Habitat chapters in high schools and colleges across the country.

GETTING STARTED: For more information, visit the Web site at www.habitat.org, or call (800) 422–4828 to find a program that suits your availability. You can also help the organization by donating or buying used and/or surplus building materials.

After the Race Is Over

Until one has loved an animal, a part of one's soul remains unawakened.
—Anatole France

The greyhound is a beautiful, sleek dog known for it speed, and greyhound racing is an exciting spectator sport that makes some people very rich. But after the racing dog has passed his prime, which happens at around age four, it is seen as expendable and, sadly, is often put down by its owner.

This is completely unnecessary—while the dog may no longer be winning races at the track, he or she can still make a wonderful pet. This is the message of the Greyhound Project, an all-volunteer organization that is committed to getting the word out about greyhound adoption and letting people know about these loyal and loving dogs.

"The forty-mile-an-hour couch potato," Michael McCann, president of the Greyhound Project, calls them affectionately. "They are large dogs, but they curl up into a small ball and sleep all day.

"I have had all kinds of dogs, but I never had a dog who was so sweet and gentle," he adds.

Greyhounds only need a couple of walks a day and will sleep most of the rest of the time. Because a racing dog has never been in a house before, it will need some time to adjust to being in the home and to things like mirrors, windows, and stairs, which it will have never seen before. The dogs are kennel trained and are very easy to house-train.

Along with letting the public know about greyhound adoption, the Greyhound Project helps to raise money for such organizations as the Morris Animal Foundation for their research efforts into canine cancer and the Ohio State University Greyhound Health and Wellness Program. They also publish a calendar that greyhound adoption agencies can use to fund-raise. A donation to the Greyhound Project will, among other things, help them pay for the airing of their new public-service TV announcements.

VISIT www.adopt-a-greyhound.org.

Clean Up Your Community

**What do you do then? Take a broom and clean
someone's house. That says enough.**
—Mother Teresa

Roadside litter, streams and ponds clogged with trash, graffiti and
peeling paint—your community almost certainly needs cleaning up.
Every year between March and May, thousands of communities around
the country do exactly that as part of the Great American Cleanup, sponsored by Keep America Beautiful.

If there's a cleanup happening near you, volunteering is very easy.
All you need to give is one Saturday morning to help with a scheduled
cleanup—even pitching in for an hour is useful. Cleanups are great
family projects because even little kids can feel they're helping; they are
also excellent volunteer opportunities for youth organizations, such as
Girl Scouts, 4-H, high-school service clubs, and church youth groups.

A Great American Cleanup usually focuses on eyesores such as roadside litter and trash-strewn vacant lots, but communities often do a little
bit more. They might plant trees and flowers or paint over a graffiti-
stained wall. Organizing a community cleanup takes a lot of volunteer
work for weeks in advance. Jobs include working with the local sanitation
department to arrange for trash bags and removing the trash you collect.
Volunteers are also needed to do media publicity and contact local organizations, schools, churches, and businesses to recruit help for cleanup
day. On the day itself, volunteers are needed to hand out supplies, direct
people to their cleanup area, and help with snacks and beverages.

One of the most encouraging aspects of a cleanup day is that your
volunteer efforts are clearly visible when it's over.

TO PARTICIPATE in a Great American Cleanup, contact:

Keep America Beautiful / 1010 Washington Boulevard / Stamford, CT
06901 / (203) 659–3000 / www.kab.org

Practice and Preach Nonviolence

An eye for eye only ends up making the whole world blind.
—Mohandas Gandhi

If you feel that there is too much violence in the world, consider that you can make a difference, for yourself and your community, through practicing and preaching nonviolence.

Dr. Martin Luther King Jr. defined nonviolence as "rejection of hatred, animosity, or violence of the spirit as well as refusal to commit physical violence." This method, proven effective in public struggles in many countries, is very useful in daily life. You can easily learn to practice nonviolence and spread knowledge of it to your community.

ACTION STEPS

➤ Nonviolence is active, not passive. It starts with the way you see yourself. Refrain from being angry with yourself, or judging yourself.

➤ Violence is not just physical; trying to control or punish someone verbally is also violence. Do not do this or allow it to be done to you.

➤ Teach kids that it can be courageous to walk away from an argument or fight.

➤ Think before you react to any provocative behavior. Anger is natural, but learn to express it in nonviolent ways, like gentle confrontation, writing down feelings, or talking to a friend. Remember that responding in anger only perpetuates violence.

NATIONAL/INTERNATIONAL: UNESCO nonviolence page for kids: www.portal.unesco.org/education/en/ev.php-URL_ID=2184&URL_DO=DO_TOPIC&URL_SECTION=201.html • Common Peace: www.nonviolenceworks.com • Fellowship of Reconciliation: www.forusa.org • Metta Center for Nonviolence Education: www.mettacenter.org

Under the Influence

**Oh, that it were my chief delight / To do
the things I ought! / Then let me try with all
my might / To mind what I am taught.**
—*Hymns for Infant Minds*, 1810

She was an honor student, a cheerleader, and a high-school senior in a middle-class suburb. Natalie Ciappa went to a party, snorted heroin, and didn't come home. The next morning, her parents found her unconscious, their daughter soon dead of a heroin overdose.

If once we thought, *not my kid, not hard drugs,* we need to cut out the willful naivete; our kids have. The National Drug Intelligence Center in 2007 noted that 30 percent of high-school seniors reported that they could obtain heroin "fairy easily."

Within a year, Doreen and Victor Ciappa turned their tragedy into an effort aimed at increasing awareness of teen heroin abuse. In late 2008, Nassau County on Long Island, New York, signed the first law of its kind in the country: the Natalie Ciappa Law. This law requires police to notify the school district about anyone arrested for heroin possession within that specific school district's boundaries or the arrest of a student from that district anywhere in the county. The police also established a Nassau Drug Mapping Index Web site available to the public, which will highlight arrests for possession and sale of heroin.

The crux of the Ciappas' influence, and their service to us all, is to insist on full public disclosure of an issue many would rather think doesn't exist. But it does.

ACTION STEPS

➤ Is there a community problem that needs public exposure? Speak to your local media about investigating and exposing the issue today.

➤ Get educated. Go to the "Web site of Parents. The Anti-Drug" at www .theantidrug.com or call the National Clearinghouse for Alcohol or Drug Information at (800) 788–2800.

Deserving Women

**Only the weak are cruel. Gentleness can
only be expected from the strong.**
—Leo Buscaglia

On a relatively regular basis, a female celebrity is abused by the man in her life, and the news of his arrest makes headlines for a while. Oftentimes, the woman goes back to her abuser, and the great public handwringing begins. *Why would she go back to him? Doesn't she know he'll do it again? What's wrong with her?*

And here's the thing that almost no one says but many think: Anyone who willingly goes back to someone like that deserves what she gets. The compassion we first felt for her withers quickly under what we perceive as her deliberate willingness to put herself in harm's way.

This usually happens in the headlines once or twice a year, but it happens in the towns and cities of this country many, many times a day. Every time a woman goes back to an abusive relationship, often with kids in tow, sympathy for her and other women like her, plummets.

You may not understand the psychology at play in situations such as this, but that shouldn't deter you from feeling compassion for those swept up in it. No one deserves to be abused. Period.

ACTION STEPS

➤ Women and children who arrive at shelters often do so in the middle of the night with nothing except the clothes they're wearing. Because of this, shelters are chronically low on certain items: bed sheets and pillows, toiletries, and new undergarments for both women and children. Make donations of these whenever you can.

➤ If you know someone in an abusive relationship, call a women's shelter for advice. You don't want to unwittingly exacerbate the situation.

➤ Most abused women desperately need someone who will simply listen to them, whether or not they're willing to admit to being abused. Be that person—nonjudgmental, supportive, concerned.

Some Kind of Help . . .

The fellow who isn't fired with enthusiasm is apt to be fired.
—B. C. Forbes, founder of *Forbes* magazine

You know the expression "Some kind of help is no kind of help at all"? Don't you hate it when people volunteer to sit on the PTA committee you're chairing and they don't pull their weight? They whine, they complain, they're perennially late, or they're just plain incompetent. Or, worse yet, they're obstructionists, blocking every forward movement your committee makes. "Just playing the devil's advocate," they say, but deep in your heart you know this is passive-aggressive behavior.

Of course, volunteers are not paid for their time, and it's hard to "fire" someone who wasn't "hired." But there's still a lesson to be gleaned from this behavior. If you're going to join an action group, one way of supporting it is to do your part. Don't tax the system by slowing it down with your own ambivalence. Step up when called upon, whether it's contacting ten members to remind them of your fund-raiser, making cold calls to retailers to solicit contributions for a silent auction, or hiring the caterer. If you're ill-suited or uncomfortable with the task assigned you, don't drag your heels and slow the operation. Ask to be reassigned. Maybe your talents are best used designing invitations or writing press releases. Maybe table decoration is your forte. Perhaps you'll serve as a greeter. There are so many ways to support a team effort. One of the easiest is to show up and do your part.

ACTION STEPS
➤ Be the oil that greases the wheel. Avoid gossip, fault finding, and criticizing. It is easy to see what doesn't work. Step up. Be the one to take on the challenge. Focus on actions that will keep everyone moving forward.

➤ If you find yourself shirking your responsibility, reevaluate your commitment. If it's not a good fit, perhaps both you and the organization would be best served if you move on.

Coaching Kids' Sports

**I've learned that people will forget what you
said, people will forget what you did, but people
will never forget how you made them feel.**
—Maya Angelou

Little League, Pee Wee football, town soccer, basketball, or lacrosse, all
need adult and/or parent volunteers. You might be thinking, *of course,
it's cheap labor,* and to some extent, you may be right. But a larger goal is
met as well: you can make a real difference in a kid's life, especially one
who isn't your own flesh and blood. Many people fondly remember their
coaches just because they were present at a critical time while they were
growing up. This could be especially rewarding if you volunteer outside
your comfort zone and in an disadvantaged neighborhood.

Great sports coaches are more than just adults who know the game
and can run the drills. They are first and foremost good listeners. They
are also cheerleaders for their teams, offering psychological advice, good
humor, and a dose of encouragement when needed. They can take a
benchwarmer and turn him or her into a star, or take a star down to size
so that the star can get along with the rest of the team. And they can
step in and help resolve family or school problems if a parent is too close
to the situation or too involved in other things.

If coaching isn't your thing, think about being a volunteer umpire or
referee. You'll still have the chance to get involved in the game but without the responsibility of overseeing the welfare of a group of children.

GETTING STARTED: If you have children, find out what sport they
are interested in; don't focus on which sport you excelled in or currently
enjoy. If you don't have kids, the volunteer sporting world is wide open.
Contact your local town's recreation department and see what programs
are offered and where you can help out. Then search the Web for sites
like www.littleleague.org that can provide free information on the basics
of coaching, including the rules for each particular game as well as information on how to handle the emotional angle of the job.

Rising from the Ashes

Once we accept our limits, we go beyond them.
—Albert Einstein

In 1967 six heroin addicts came together at a detox program and talked about how hard it was to stay clean. They decided to support one another, moved into a tenement apartment on Manhattan's West Side, and lived together as a community, encouraging and helping one another stay sober. When they did that, Phoenix House was born.

Since that time, Phoenix House has grown to become the nation's leading provider of alcohol and drug abuse treatment and prevention services. Currently, they serve more than seven thousand men, women (including women with children), and teens each day at more than 150 drug and alcohol treatment and prevention programs in ten states.

Phoenix House created one of the country's first correctional treatment units, a model now widely used in prisons throughout the nation. Phoenix House was also a pioneer in advocating treatment as an alternative to prison. And more than twenty years ago Phoenix House opened its first Phoenix Academy, a residential high school where teens can make up time in school they lost to drugs.

Phoenix House offers a variety of programs: long- and short-term residential drug-treatment centers for adults, intensive outpatient and day programs, after-school programs for teens, programs for mothers with small children, recovery residences, and programs for the mentally ill, for homeless persons, and for drug and alcohol abusers in prisons.

Studies have shown that three out of four Phoenix House program graduates of long-term residential treatment remained drug free, employed, and in no trouble with the law for at least three to five years. "But the measure of our success is not the number of lives we've changed, as much as the quality of those lives," says Karen Sodomick of Phoenix House.

Donations to Phoenix House are especially needed toward their programs for adolescents.

VISIT www.phoenixhouse.org.

Citizen Science: The Audubon Christmas Bird Count

The most significant thing a layperson can do to turn around the loss of biodiversity is to become part of the citizen scientist movement.
—Edward O. Wilson

Every year, between mid-December and early January, birders across the Western Hemisphere fan out for the National Audubon Society's annual Christmas Bird Count. On the day they select during this period, local volunteers count and identify all the birds they see within a fifteen-mile-diameter circle. Birds at feeders within the circle count, so it's possible to participate while sitting snugly indoors by a window. Most volunteers get out into the field, however, enjoying an invigorating day tallying bird species. The data they collect is combined with the data from the other 2,100 circles to help paint an accurate, ongoing picture of the bird population in the Western Hemisphere. The information is extremely valuable not just for ornithologists but for researchers in many other areas, such as conservation biology and climate change.

The first Christmas Bird Count was held in 1900 when Frank M. Chapman, an early member of what soon became the National Audubon Society, proposed an alternative to the traditional Christmas hunt. Chapman proposed counting instead of hunting the birds . Twenty-seven people participated in the first count. In 2008, nearly sixty thousand participated in this, one of the oldest and largest volunteer conservation projects.

Newcomers to birding are very welcome. There's no better way to learn identification skills than to spend time with experienced birders. And there's no better way to make new birding friends than to join the traditional potluck supper held at the end of the day.

TO LEARN more and find a count near you, contact:

National Audubon Society / 225 Varick Street, 7th Floor / New York, NY 10014 / (212) 979–3000 / www.audubon.org

Organize an Earth Day Celebration

In wilderness I sense the miracle of life, and behind it our scientific accomplishments fade to trivia.
—Charles A. Lindbergh

Earth Day, which was started in 1970 to raise environmental awareness, is now celebrated every April 22 by more than a billion people around the world. There are great ways for communities to observe Earth Day, such as tree planting, bike races, walk-a-thons, running events, beach or neighborhood cleanups, park maintenance, art, photography, poetry or essay contests, library exhibits, concerts, and film or lecture series.

ACTION STEPS

LOCAL: The idea behind Earth Day is that everyone can make a difference. Start a group in which each person can contribute, but strive to keep it focused. To begin, contact community-service organizations, environmental and nature groups, houses of worship, and schools to see if they have a plan for the next Earth Day. If so, volunteer; if not, request support to get your own event started. Ask if you can use their facilities for a meeting of all interested people in the area.

Write down a few possible projects to discuss at the first meeting. Make a list of all attendees, with their contact information and interests. Add their suggestions to your list. Ask for volunteers for the steering committee. From here on, you can use Earth Day Network's "Earth Day in a Box" (www.earthday.net/node/88), an extensive guide that will help you select and plan the event, step by step.

NATIONAL: To learn more about Earth Day visit:

www.earthday.net.

U.S. government Earth Day portal: www.earthday.gov.

U.S. Environmental Protection Agency: www.epa.gov/earthday/take homekit.htm.

The Wilderness Society: http://earthday.wilderness.org.

www.earthday.envirolink.org/history.html.

Giving Life

Remember that when you leave this earth, you can take with you nothing that you have received— only what you have given: a full heart, enriched by honest service, love, sacrifice and courage.
—St. Francis of Assisi

No other gift surpasses the gift of organ donation. It takes love, sacrifice, and courage to give this gift of life. Someone close, or even someone you don't know, may be facing kidney failure and is living on dialysis, hoping and praying for a new kidney. What would you do if you knew you were a match?

As of this writing, there are over one hundred thousand people in the United States on the waiting list for organ transplants according to the U.S. Informational Site on Organ and Tissue Donation and Transplantation. Each day approximately seventy people receive organ transplants, yet nineteen people die each day waiting for transplants that can't take place. No one is too old to donate. The condition of the organs is more important than age. There are few absolute exclusions (HIV positive, active cancer, systemic infection).

As influential people, we are asked to give much, but rarely do we face life and death decisions. Organ donation is one of those decisions.

ACTION STEPS

➤ Think seriously about your position on organ donation. Talk with your significant others about organ donation. Most religions support organ and tissue donation as a charitable act of love and giving. Speak with your clergyperson about your decision now. Every state has a donor registry. You can designate your decision on your driver's license. Or print out an organ donor card at www.organdonor.gov.

➤ Many people have questions about organ donation. If you support organ donation, help others understand the scope of this life-giving gift. At a local health fair, staff an organ-donation information booth.

Of These, Most of All

Keep your heart content and cherish compassion for all beings; this way alone can your holy vow be fulfilled.
—from *Shri Guru Granth Sahib*, the Sikh holy book

In the Sikh religion, compassion, or Daya, is considered the highest of the five holy virtues and is only approached in importance by truth, contentment, humility, and love. Sikhs meditate daily on Daya, along with the four other virtues, striving to infuse themselves with the essence of God.

Yet despite their focus on such noble goals, the 500,000 Sikhs in the United States are often the targets of racial slurs and attacks. This has increased substantially since the attacks on 9/11 because some of the ignorant among us feel threatened by anyone who looks different, despite the fact that no Sikhs were involved in the attacks.

The men, with their distinctive turbans covering long, well-groomed hair and with carefully combed beards, both of which have never been cut, are too easily singled out by the hateful. Their children often suffer discrimination in schools. They are refused entry into the military because their religion does not permit them to remove their turbans and cut their hair. They are singled out for screening at airport security at astronomical rates. They are not granted the very things they believe in most and which they freely grant to others.

ACTION STEPS

➤ To understand what it's like to be a Sikh in America, the land that guarantees religious freedom, go to www.sikhcoalition.org and learn more about the religion and the discrimination they face.

➤ Check out a copy of the *Shri Guru Granth Sahib* from the library, and read a few passages each day until you need to return it. If your library doesn't have a copy (and many don't), ask that they purchase one.

➤ If you see someone wearing traditional Sikh garb (you can see it at www.sikhcoalition.org), ask him to explain the concept of Daya to you and how you can put it into action.

Old Mother Hubbard

**A bone to the dog is not charity. Charity
is the bone shared with the dog, when
you are just as hungry as the dog.**
—Jack London

We as a nation love our pets. They provide unconditional love, companionship, and play. They mitigate loneliness and isolation. They even help the recovery of people who have physical ailments and provide some sense of balance to those who have a mental illness. They are a part of our support system, and more than half of American households now have a dog or cat.

But what happens when a family struggles financially? What if they are evicted from their home? Must they choose between feeding themselves and their beloved animals? Must they leave their pets behind? In Clackamas County, Oregon, one group of dog lovers tried to remedy this situation. Joni Taylor and some friends began rallying support for the local animal shelter, asking pet-shop owners and dog-food producers to contribute excess food and treats to abandoned animals. Tons of supplies were donated. Recently, Joni's efforts have expanded to include families who themselves are struggling to eat. Her organization, Friends Involved in Dog Outreach (FIDO), has created a dog food bank that now distributes a month's supply of pet food to anyone who shows up to their once-monthly giveaway. She has found a way to support the dogs as well as the people who love and need them.

ACTION STEPS

➤ Do you have or have you had a beloved pet? Imagine for a moment being faced with the agonizing decision about having to give up your pet because you can no longer afford to feed it. What might you do to support a family faced with this decision?

➤ Contact www.fido-clackamas.org to see how you can help their efforts or create a similar pet food bank in your community.

Become a Preceptor

The art of teaching is the art of assisting discovery.
—Mark van Doren, American poet

A preceptor is any individual responsible for upholding a certain law or tradition. Preceptors have historically maintained certain codes of ethics and group traditions and passed them on to others in an apprenticeship-like learning environment. Today preceptorships are common in colleges, universities, and social organizations like the Freemasons. In these roles a preceptor takes on a small group of students or members and teaches them the ways their organization works.

The term is now most commonly used within medical education: in this sense a preceptor is an established doctor, nurse, pharmacist, or faculty member who supervises students in clinical settings to allow them to receive practical experience rather than book-based knowledge.

As a preceptor, you will be responsible for teaching students the practical matters of being a physician or nurse within a community-based environment rather than the classroom. In short, you are providing more practical or hands-on training. Often preceptors take on one student at a time for the duration of a school year or a semester.

Preceptors provide students the opportunity to learn from a role model. They can also provide instant assessment and meaningful evaluation not only for medical decision making but also for their nonmedically related techniques, such as patient communication or "bedside manner."

Many physician or nursing preceptors find that the experience is highly rewarding and takes up less than half a day each week. Not only are they able to share their vast knowledge within their specialty, but they enjoy watching their students transform into able doctors. Some preceptors are able to recruit their former students directly into their practice.

GETTING STARTED: Contact your nearest medical, nursing, or pharmacy school and find out if they have a preceptor program. Many sub-specialties, such as gynecology, run their programs through national organizations rather than specific medical schools.

Dealing with Depression

There is no coming to consciousness without pain.
—Carl Jung

Several years ago, some young people gathered together to help a friend—nineteen-year-old Renee, who was struggling with depression, drugs, and self-harming. The night before, strung out on cocaine, she had locked herself in the bathroom and carved F**K UP into her arm with a razor blade. When Renee tried to enter rehab, the nurse saw the wound, discovered that she had drugs in her system, and refused her entry. Her friends gathered to support her while she sobered up enough to go back, and during those days one friend, Jamie, wrote a story called "To Write Love on Her Arms."

The friends printed up and started selling shirts with the saying "To Write Love on Her Arms" to help her pay for her treatment. At the same time, Jamie posted a MySpace page with Renee's story. The reaction to both was immediate: local musicians started wearing the shirts, sparking questions over its unusual message, and Jamie's MySpace entry began getting multiple hits from young people who identified with Renee's struggle with depression and cutting. (Teens are especially prone to depression, and untreated depression sometimes leads to self-harming behavior such as cutting, burning, punching, or hitting oneself.)

Young people began to contact the group that became TWLOHA (To Write Love on Her Arms). Some were sharing their own stories of pain; others had friends who had committed suicide. Since then, TWLOHA has responded to over ninety thousand messages from young people in forty countries. They have donated half a million dollars to organizations that provide treatment and assistance such as Teen Challenge and (800) SUICIDE (784–2433). Their T-shirts—their greatest source of revenue—are now available at the national stores Hot Topic and Zumiez.

The people of TWLOHA are not trained professionals, but rather people who act as a bridge between young people in pain and the organizations that can help them take the first steps toward wholeness.

VISIT www.twloha.com.

Read Aloud with a Kid

To learn to read is to light a fire; every syllable that is spelled out is a spark.
—Victor Hugo

Reading aloud with kids is the single most important activity for helping them to become successful readers. Sadly, many low-income kids don't get the chance to read aloud with an encouraging adult on a regular basis. When kids miss out on this crucial activity, the literacy gap widens.

By becoming a volunteer reading tutor, you can help bridge that gap. No special skills are required—all you need is an hour or two a week.

Finding kids to read with one-on-one is never a problem. Of all the activities schools and libraries need help with, reading tops the list. Contact your local elementary school or children's librarian and ask how you can help. Chances are very good that some sort of in-school or after-school program is already in place and you'll be welcome to sign on.

Your individual volunteer effort can become part of a larger national program called Everybody Wins! This program recruits reading volunteers from community organizations, government offices, and local companies. Participants spend their lunch hour or an hour after school once a week reading with their student partner. The volunteers help the kids learn to love reading. That's satisfying enough, but when a whole group of people helps a whole group of kids, both groups get stronger. Everybody Wins! provides training, coordination, supplies, and support, which makes it very easy for a community or work group to adopt a school and provide read-aloud partners on a regular basis. It's especially effective in low-income schools where even finding books to share can be a problem.

Locally managed affiliates of Everybody Wins! are active in over nine thousand public schools nationwide.

TO FIND the local program nearest you, contact:

Everybody Wins! / 71 Commercial Street / Boston, MA 02109–1320 / (617) 517-9747 / www.everybodywins.org

Bring Old-Time Skills Back
to Your Community

**To furnish the means of acquiring knowledge is . . . the
greatest benefit that can be conferred upon mankind.**
—John Quincy Adams

There is much to be learned from the past, and this is especially true
in lean times. Doing more with less, handmaking everyday items,
and repurposing worn things were standard operating procedure for our
grandparents. Kids are fascinated by such skills, and they are ideal ways
to introduce children to history. Every locality needs at least one place
where the old-fashioned ways are honored and kept alive. Volunteer to
help; this is an immensely enjoyable way to bring generations together.

ACTION STEPS

LOCAL: Bone up on local history. Visit a nearby historic house or
site and talk to the volunteer coordinator. Say you want to help develop
exhibits and demonstrations that show how our ancestors conserved resources, farmed, prepared and preserved food, and made clothes and im-
plements with what was on hand.

If no such venue exists, approach a community or senior center. Ask
if older people could demonstrate and/or teach almost-lost arts, such as
quilting and whittling. Start one Saturday a week; announcements at
schools and libraries will draw an audience.

NATIONAL: For ideas, visit local historic houses and sites wherever
you travel, and study their Web sites. For a list of historic house museums in the United States, go to www.oldhouses.com. Also visit:

Historic Williamsburg: www.history.org • Hancock Shaker Village:
www.hancockshakervillage.org • Historic crafts in Missouri: www
.mdc.mo.gov/teacher/highered/crafts • *Early American Life* magazine:
www.ealonline.com

Influential Upbringing

**Mama may have / Papa may have / But God
bless the child that's got his own.**
—Billy Holiday, "God Bless the Child"

S. Ann Soetoro, a girl named Stanley, a teen mother, a dreamer who
went on to a PhD in anthropology and a life serving others in the far
reaches of the world was a mother unlike many mothers—the mother of
a president of the United States, Barack Obama.

She was an early riser. While working in Indonesia, she woke her
son every day at 4 a.m. to give him lessons from a U.S. correspondence
course. She was concerned that the local schools were not challenging him
enough. One of her most lasting professional legacies was to help build a
microfinance program in Indonesia, before granting tiny loans was a clear
success story. Microfinancing is now a success across the world.

After two decades working on her anthropology doctoral thesis, she
finished in 1992. On November 7, 1995, she died of ovarian and uterine
cancer. As her son has said on the campaign trail and in the halls of
Congress, "My mother died of cancer at fifty-three. In those last painful
months, she was more worried about paying her medical bills than getting well. I hear stories like hers every day," and so he has vowed to make
healthcare reform one of the centerpieces of his administration.

Our parents' story influences our story, the way we give back, the way
we serve, and as the child, we bless our parents for that.

ACTION STEPS

➤ Make a donation in your mother's name to a cause or issue that she
was influenced by and that has since influenced you.

➤ Ask your mother—and any woman over forty close to you—if she has
had an annual mammogram and Pap test. If she has not, arrange for
one as her Mother's Day or birthday present today. Include a note telling her how much you love her and that you want her with you for as
much of your life as possible.

All-Weather Friends

To have a friend is to love the crows on his roof.
—Chinese proverb

In the 1970s a respected and well-liked young teacher was on his way home to his bachelor pad after a day of classes. Suddenly a dog ran in front of his car. In the way that time slows down at such moments, he saw the children who owned the dog weeping inconsolably at its death. It was unthinkable to him that he should cause such pain.

So on a narrow road with no shoulder, he swerved to the right and into the deep ditch. In those days before regular seat belt use, the teacher flew into the windshield and roof, breaking his back. He has not walked since.

During his recovery period, only two people visited regularly—his mother and a friend who was another teacher on staff. As he became accustomed to his new wheelchair-bound life, only two people continued visiting regularly—his mother and his friend. When he grew old and retired, only one person continued visiting—his friend. His mother had long since died.

In these days of vastly improving emergency medicine, most people—from ordinary citizens to soldiers on the battlefield—are surviving once-lethal injuries only to find themselves with lifelong disabilities. And, as with the teacher, most see the majority of their friends and even many family members simply drift away.

Which truly is the greater injury?

ACTION STEPS

➤ If you have a friend who is disabled, call this very day and make a date to see each other. Make sure there is no trace of pity or discomfort in your request, just a chance for friends to catch up.

➤ When you can, organize a larger group of friends to get together at his house, if he's housebound, or at a meeting place where you can all just hang out. The quicker you can get his other buddies past the whole disability discomfort, the faster you'll all regain a treasured friend.

Respect for Someone with a Mental Illness

Most people with mental illnesses can be diagnosed and treated and go on to live full and productive lives.
—Rosalynn Carter

The latest research shows that most serious mental illnesses—schizophrenia, depression, bipolar disorder, and anxiety disorders—are actually biologically based, developmental brain disorders. They begin in childhood or late adolescence and are triggered by the interplay of one's genetic heritage with environmental stressors. These disorders can disrupt education, career plans, intimate relationships, and financial stability. However, research shows that peer support groups can be effective in helping those with mental illness lead more normal lives.

NAMI, the National Alliance on Mental Illness, is the largest grassroots organization in the United States for people with mental illness and their families. With affiliates in every state and in more than 1,100 communities, NAMI advocates for people with these disorders and their families, acknowledging that resiliency and support coupled with the knowledge that recovery is possible can improve the quality of life of everyone affected. NAMI has established free weekly support groups open to adults with mental illnesses called NAMI Connection. In these peer-led groups, they share coping strategies, and offer encouragement, respect, understanding, and hope.

ACTION STEPS

➤ Only 30 percent of people who have a mental disorder seek treatment. One of the greatest barriers to care is the lack of knowledge that one's moodiness, impulsivity, or anxiety actually constitutes an illness. If you suspect that someone you love has a mental disorder, support him or her in seeking diagnosis and treatment.

➤ Seek the help of a support community like NAMI if mental illness is diagnosed: (800) 950–NAMI (6264) and www.nami.org. Support-group information: connection@nami.org.

Second Acts: Retired Attorneys Volunteer

You can only protect your liberties in this world
by protecting the other man's freedom.
—Clarence Darrow

We all know that lawyers, and their legal fees, are expensive. Our legal system demands that all citizens have the right to fair and equal representation in court. But for many, the cost of an attorney is prohibitive. To allow for balance and equal access to justice, the American Bar Association created a network of lawyers who are willing to represent clients for free. This is called pro-bono services, and they are offered in many different areas of the law.

However, there never seem to be enough pro-bono attorneys to cover all the legal needs of the poor and disadvantaged. According to an American Bar Association study, at least 40 percent of low- and moderate-income households experience a legal problem each year. Yet the same studies show that the existing civil legal-aid efforts are meeting only 20 percent of these legal needs.

A new initiative was started in 2004 by the Pro Bono Institute in Washington, DC, called Second Acts. This program supports transitioning and retired lawyers who are interested in a second, volunteer, career in public-interest law. Demographers forecast that if only 5 percent of currently retiring "baby boomer" attorneys volunteered their services, it would in effect double the number of hours available for pro-bono work.

By volunteering your services either in a Second Acts program, or any pro-bono situation, you can make an invaluable difference in someone's life during a very tough time.

GETTING STARTED: Contact your local bar association through the www.probono.net Web site for more information and existing opportunities for pro-bono legal work in your state. The Second Acts Web site, www.probonoinst.org, has information about the program and the pilot communities it is currently reaching.

Connecting the Body and Mind

**Yoga teaches us to cure what need not be
endured and endure what cannot be cured.**
—B. K. S. Iyengar

Matthew Sanford was only thirteen when a devastating car crash changed his life forever. In the accident, his father and sister were killed, and he was paralyzed from the waist down. He was told by doctors to forget his lower body and to only work on strengthening his upper body.

After twelve years as "a floating torso," Matthew decided to find a better way and began practicing yoga. When he did so, he realized he was experiencing a mind-body sensation that he had never been told to listen for. With the new understanding that there was more to mind-body communication than he ever thought possible, he decided to share what he was experiencing with others. He opened a yoga studio and started teaching yoga specially adapted for those with physical disabilities.

The results for his students have been remarkable. One man, a quadriplegic named Joe, had never been able to transfer himself in or out of his wheelchair. Now, after doing yoga and learning about balance and using his chest, Joe was able to get in and out of his chair by himself—a huge change that meant newfound independence and freedom.

Adaptive yoga has changed more than just the physical well-being of his students: one woman was finally willing to attend a family Thanksgiving because she had developed more confidence.

Today, Sanford's innovative work is gaining national attention and creating national demand. Mind Body Solutions is training yoga teachers from around the country and developing audio, video, print, and Web-based resources that are much needed by individuals who cannot get to a class.

For every five people who donate $100, Mind Body Solutions can produce a yoga video for their Web site. A gift of $250 buys a person two private yoga sessions. Three gifts of $500 pay for a six-week adaptive yoga class to disabled and veteran support groups.

VISIT www.mindbodysolutions.org.

Aiding Wounded Warriors

I may be compelled to face danger, but never fear it, and while our soldiers can stand and fight, I can stand and feed and nurse them.
—Clara Barton

When wounded warriors return to the United States, they often face months of hospitalization or intensive rehabilitation at medical centers that may be far from their homes and families.

Recognizing how difficult this time of great need can be, in 1991 philanthropist Zachary Fisher provided the funds and expertise to create a homelike temporary lodging facility at the National Naval Medical Center in Bethesda, Maryland. A second house, at Walter Reed Army Medical Center, was opened soon after. Today, more than forty Fisher Houses are located at military hospitals and Veteran Affairs (VA) medical centers across the country. The houses are part of a unique public/private partnership that allows the Fisher House Foundation to build or renovate the homes, furnish them, and transfer them to the U.S. government as gifts. The homes are then owned and maintained by the military or the VA.

Fisher Houses are designed to provide anywhere from 8 to 21 suites, along with communal kitchens and welcoming dining and living rooms. They're open to family members of wounded soldiers at no charge—the Fisher House Foundation underwrites the costs and pays for a manager for each home. This amazingly generous program so far has offered nearly 3 million days of lodging to more than 120,000 families.

The many families who stay at a Fisher House are grateful to local volunteers for transportation, child care, shopping, meal preparation, and other tasks that help lighten their load.

TO VOLUNTEER, contact:

Fisher House Foundation, Inc. / 111 Rockville Pike, Suite 420 / Rockville, MD 20850 / (888) 294–8560 / www.fisherhouse.org

Help Others Stop Smoking in Your Club or Place of Worship

There is no such thing in anyone's life as an unimportant day.
—Alexander Woollcott

If you have ever been a smoker, you know that it's tough to quit without support. Volunteer to be a friend to those who want to stop this unhealthy habit. According to the American Cancer Society (ACS), it may take five to seven attempts before a quitter succeeds, and this can be wearing on close friends and family. They may stop taking the person seriously or even ridicule her repeated attempts. Having a concerned but uninvolved third party to lean on can make a big difference to a quitter.

ACTION STEPS

LOCAL: Ask your club chairperson or religious counselor if you can volunteer to be a "quitter's friend." If you are a former smoker, so much the better. Tell the coordinator exactly what support you are willing to give. Make your boundaries clear: You may not want to accept phone calls from the quitter at all hours, for instance. Specify whether you want to be matched in gender, age, or interests with smokers.

Read up on the latest thinking about smoking cessation on the Internet, or ask your librarian to recommend up-to-date books or articles in health magazines.

NATIONAL: The ACS has plenty of support recommendations on their Web site, including:

www.cancer.org/docroot/PED/content/PED_10_13X_Guide_for_Quitting_Smoking.asp.

American Lung Association: www.lungusa.org.

www.smokefree.gov.

www.stopsmokingcenter.net.

Split-Finger Influence

Genius is 1 percent inspiration and 99 percent perspiration.
—Thomas Alva Edison

He never made a major league start. He was a relief pitcher, called in to save the game, and he led the National League five times in that role and in 2006 was elected to the Baseball Hall of Fame. Bruce Sutter's influence sparkled and is an example to us all in changing up the everyday. He revolutionized and popularized a new way to pitch the ball—the split-finger fastball—what he called "The Jewel."

Are there times when you are under pressure to use your best abilities to make things happen, to succeed at the task at hand when the stakes are high? With inspiration and perspiration, you can meet the challenge. Change the dynamics. Influence the outcome for all by taking it to another level. Save the game. In that moment, it's your job and you're there to do it better than anyone else.

Think of how your abilities are called upon, under pressure, to sparkle and influence outcome. Do you need to change it up? Is there a revolutionary way to approach your challenge?

ACTION STEPS

➤ Think of your influence like a pitch in the ninth inning. The pressure is on. Imagine the ball in your hand. It all starts with the right grip. Is there a way for you to release that ball and meet the challenge that will blaze a trail for others?

➤ Spark your influence. Revolutionize the way you do one extremely ordinary action in your work life. Demonstrate it to your colleagues. Show them your new pitch.

Compassion School

**Have you ever noticed that anybody driving
slower than you is an idiot, and anyone
going faster than you is a maniac?**
—George Carlin

Not many people know there is a school of compassion that is on par
with mankind's greatest institutes of higher learning. It's made of
asphalt and concrete, and it's called a public roadway.

The odds, unfortunately, are heavily stacked against you. Each time
you venture into this arena, you are faced with mankind at its most self-
ish, discourteous, and even downright dangerous. You need all your
skills, reflexes, knowledge, and middle digits just to survive in this madness, let alone practice concepts such as compassion that become strangely
abstract with the turn of a key.

But it is exactly this madness that makes our highways and byways
such an excellent place to learn compassion. If you can learn it here, you
are indeed worthy of the title "saint."

ACTION STEPS

➤ As you begin your next drive, start the engine, hold the steering wheel
lightly with both hands, take a deep breath, and exhale slowly. Before
you leave your driveway, ask yourself the question, "How would a
compassionate driver act?"

➤ Hold this thought firmly in mind during your entire drive. Assume
each driver you encounter is having the worst day of his life and that
you, as a compassionate person, don't want to add to that. Allow
people to merge in front of you. Don't tailgate slowpokes. Use your
turn signal faithfully. If it's dusk and someone hasn't turned on his
headlights, flick yours on and off to remind him.

➤ When you arrive at your destination, compare how you feel with how
you would normally feel after a hectic commute. If it's better, practice
compassionate driving until it becomes a habit.

Taking Care of Each Other and the World

**If I am not for myself, who will be for me? / If I am
not for others, what am I? And if not now, when?**
—Hillel, Jewish rabbi and teacher, 60 BC–AD 10

You may see inequities in the world and yearn to make a difference,
but as an individual, you may feel powerless to influence anything.
The voice of one is often drowned out on the world stage.

One organization has found a way to counter this impotence. Some
women wanted to mobilize people into long-term action without simply
creating more e-mail lists and Web sites. In studying how other organizations accomplished their goals, they discovered that megachurches had
small groups whose members took care of one another on a personal level
and then joined with other groups within the church to make national
and global social, environmental, and political change. From this and
other resources they learned that supporting people's personal needs can
lead to political and social commitment to cherished causes.

The Engage Network trains leaders to create self-replicating small
groups that simultaneously support people and change the world. Focus
is on three areas: (1) "What's Your Tree," which calls upon you to leave
your comfort zone to achieve a purpose larger than yourself; (2) "Off the
Mat into the World," which engages yoga teachers to inspire their students to take action beyond their classes; and (3) "Green for All," which
trains leaders to lift people out of poverty through environmentally
friendly business ventures. These community groups form an international network of people who have tapped into their purpose, passion,
and power to support environmental renewal and social change.

ACTION STEPS
➤ How might you support others while simultaneously taking care of
the world? Can you engage the leadership of your place of worship?
➤ Contact www.engagenet.org to add your voice to the small groups
dedicated to global change that are springing up around the country.

Adopt a Pet with a Long Lifespan

We can judge the heart of a man by his treatment of animals.
—Immanuel Kant

Most animal lovers have the best of intentions when they take on the responsibility of caring for a new pet. But often they really don't know what they are in for. Many people can manage through the lifespan of a dog or a cat but don't realize that a pet bird or lizard is a much greater commitment. Parrots of various breeds can live between twenty and sixty years, or longer. Even small lizards like the popular leopard gecko can live as long as twenty years.

For the furriest friends, there are animal shelters and adoption agencies in every state across the country. But how do you find a bird or other long-life creature that needs a loving home? One great resource is the Parrot Education & Adoption Center (PEAC). Begun in 1996, PEAC cares for unwanted parrots and other exotic birds until they are adopted by qualified applicants. By donating your own bird, or adopting another, you can provide it with a new home and the opportunity to flourish for years to come.

If you are interested in adopting a PEAC bird, you need to attend three seminars over the course of a year at any of the PEAC locations. An adoption application is then mailed to your home, and if the application is accepted, a home visit from a PEAC volunteer will be arranged. Once you are approved for adoption, you can choose from the available birds in your area.

GETTING STARTED: Visit www.peac.org for more information about adopting or donating a bird. Volunteers are also needed for their Foster Parent Program, which transports and reconditions the birds and their equipment and helps with fund-raising. Or you can simply donate your money instead of your time. By doing so, you will receive the satisfaction of knowing that you helped an exotic bird find a lifelong home.

Saving a Child

He who has health, has hope. And he who has hope, has everything.
—Arabian proverb

Unlike birth defects such as Down's syndrome and spina bifida—which receive a lot of attention—the most common birth defect of all, congenital heart disease, does not, even though one in a hundred babies is born with it. That is because in this country the surgery to correct it is a relatively routine procedure. However, in developing countries, this surgery is often not available. For example, in Ethiopia, which has over 78 million people, there are just two pediatric cardiologists.

Save a Child's Heart (SACH) is Israel's largest international humanitarian organization. At SACH, a medical team of seventy volunteers provides free pediatric cardiac care for children who cannot otherwise get the treatment they need. To date, SACH has saved more than 2,100 children who have come from more than thirty-five countries.

The doctors of SACH also offer a free weekly cardiology clinic for Palestinian children from the Gaza Strip and the West Bank. All children, regardless of race, religion, gender, or financial status receive the very best care that modern medicine has to offer.

In addition, SACH trains doctors from developing countries who come to Israel to learn the medical techniques. For those who cannot come to Israel, SACH has traveled to countries such as China, Nigeria, Russia, and Vietnam on medical missions and performed surgery side by side with hundreds of local doctors to train them in the procedures.

Unfortunately, more children need life-saving help than Save a Child's Heart can provide: There is a waiting list of one thousand children who need surgery. The medical personnel of SACH work for free, so the surgery only costs $10,000—a fraction of what it might cost otherwise.

A donation of $50 will pay for several days' recuperative care for a child in the SACH children's home following his or her surgery.

VISIT www.saveachildsheartus.org or call (301) 618–4588.

Conserve Fish and Wildlife

**Conservation is a state of harmony
between men and land.**
—Aldo Leopold

Being a good steward of the land is fundamental to the conservation ethic. Whenever you volunteer for any sort of environmental cause, you strengthen that ethic and contribute to conserving our natural heritage. One great way to be a good steward is to work as a volunteer for the nation's environmental steward, the U.S. Fish and Wildlife Service (FWS). This agency is in charge of 584 bird and wildlife refuges, covering 96 million acres, that preserve some of the most magnificent and untouched wild areas in the country. The FWS is also responsible for implementing and enforcing some of the nation's most important environmental laws, including the Endangered Species Act.

About 40 million people visit the public lands of the national refuge system each year. In addition, a great deal of scientific field research is conducted in the refuges. To help with all the work it takes to manage the land and support research, the FWS relies heavily on volunteers—some thirty-eight thousand of them every year. While some volunteer full-time, most contribute their time for just a few hours a week or a month, or during a particular season or special event.

If you're passionate about the outdoors, a national wildlife refuge is the ideal place for you to volunteer. Volunteers are needed to help conduct fish and wildlife population surveys, participate in bird-banding studies, stock streams with fish, lead nature walks and tours, and provide information and directions to visitors. A lot of help is needed for trail maintenance and habitat maintenance and restoration.

TO VOLUNTEER, contact the volunteer coordinator in the region where you'd like to work, and ask for an application and a list of field stations:

U.S. Fish and Wildlife Service / 1849 C Street NW / Washington, DC 20240 / (800) 344–WILD (9453) / www.fws.gov

Preserve Native American Culture

**When all the trees have been cut down, when all
the animals have been hunted, when all the waters
are polluted, when all the air is unsafe to breathe,
only then will you discover you cannot eat money.**
—Cree prophecy

Before the United States of America, the Great Plains tribes would freely follow the buffalo herds, finding new homes each season. And before lawnmowers, the aesthetic stomping dance called the Grass Dance was a ceremonial but practical way to flatten plains grass and clear an area to break camp! Sadly, this colorful culture and its deep connection with the land are struggling to survive as modern society and economic woe simultaneously strain the community.

ACTION STEPS:

LOCAL: Rediscover the historic indigenous civilizations of America at the online interactive museum, www.lostworlds.org. Take part in traditions and customs through www.snowwowl.com. Try their recipe for Meskwaki Indian Frybread or make one of the many handcrafts that characterize Native American art.

To truly see Native American peoples in their element, visit www.powwows.com to find a powwow in your area and learn about the many different styles of Native dance. Be sure to read the article on Powwow Etiquette so that you can respectfully participate in the ceremony!

NATIONAL: Many reservations are poverty-stricken and have high unemployment rates, poor education, and inadequate infrastructure. Two nonprofit organizations working to solve these problems are: Native American Heritage Association (www.naha-inc.org) and Pathways to Spirit (www.pathwaystospirit.org). Modern Native peoples are in a constant battle between supporting themselves economically and preserving their culture. The Adopt-an-Elder Program in Utah aims to ease the burden for traditional elders who live in the cultural tradition of the Dine' (Navajo) people. Visit www.anelder.org to contribute or learn more.

Influence Adds Up

There are parts of science, especially parts of math, that are just beautiful. And the reason to do them is . . . because you can figure out why things are true.
—Eric Larson, 17, winner of the 2009 Intel Talent Search, on being awarded a $100,000 scholarship

Half a dozen kids, the geeks, peer out from the math-team photo in the high-school yearbook. Who will lead us to the next technological breakthrough? (Where are their cheerleaders?) Your influence is needed now to make that math team as vital and central to the community spirit as any sports team.

But how do we know what will make all kids successful? We do know.

Due to advancements in technology, the major indicator of success—at any level in our society—regardless of income level, race, or ethnicity—is strong mathematics and problem-solving and reasoning skills, according to the U.S. Department of Education. We know what will make our kids the most successful at any career, but we need to first change our priorities in many communities, and that will take a lot of education. Your influence can add up now.

ACTION STEPS

➤ Review your school district's budget. Compare how much is spent on athletics vs. math and science clubs. Question the inequity at a school board meeting. Write a letter to your school board president and school superintendent. Publish that letter in your local newspaper.

➤ Research your state's academic standards and graduation requirements and its corresponding college and career readiness at the American Diploma Project at www.achieve.org. Thirty-four states are assessed. On their site, Math Works has an advocacy tool that will help you make the case for why all students—regardless of their plans after graduation—should engage in rigorous math courses. Use these tools to advocate for stronger math curriculums. Go math team!

Please Take Offense at That

If you're going to say something
filthy, please speak clearly.
—Recording on the answering machine of Vivian Stanshall,
British musician, wit, and writer

If you find yourself being offended on a regular basis, you really should seek it out more often. If that sounds completely nonsensical, consider this: Most matters of offense are a result of too little compassion for others, not the principled response that we often think it is.

The reason Stanshall asked people with filthy mouths to speak clearly is that he didn't want to miss any of what they said. For starters, he found it funny, and it gave him great material for his work. But more important, he had great affection and compassion for people whom others considered boorish, ignorant, ill-fitting, or just plain different. He himself had long been an outcast, even from his own family at times, and he felt deep empathy for others in the same situation.

What Stanshall, who died in 1995, understood was that the greatest lessons in life come from people whose opinions differ greatly from our own, not from those who agree with us on everything.

ACTION STEPS

➤ This is going to be painful, but do it anyway: Find a talk radio station or TV program that is in complete opposition to your political viewpoints. Suspend all judgments for a bit, and listen to it closely. The goal here is not to get you to necessarily agree, but to understand.

➤ Afterward, write down the things that offended you. Examine them closely. If they're based on things such as racism, sexism, and willful ignorance, maintain your opinion about them. But you may be surprised by how many things offend you simply because you consider them different from your particular standards. The compassionate thing to do in that case is to set aside your offense.

To Your Health

Health is worth more than learning.
—Thomas Jefferson

You probably want to lose weight, go to the gym, eat right, feel stronger and more energetic, and stop smoking and drinking (if you indulge) . . . yet probably you find it hard to reach those goals. You may start and stop, start and stop, swearing that you'll do better this time but never actually shedding those pounds or those bad habits. Support from an outside source may be just the ticket though.

And that's what's happening more and more frequently in corporate America. Many companies and insurers are offering employees incentives to change their ways. These inducements can take the form of outright cash payments, gift cards for healthful snacks, discounts on gym equipment, coupons for memberships to Weight Watchers, prizes such as Wii games, and lowered prices for fitness centers, acupuncturists, and chiropractors.

Of course, this kind of support is not entirely magnanimous. Employers know that a healthier and leaner workforce will reduce healthcare expenses down the road—that's just smart business. But that doesn't mean you can't take advantage of their strategy and feel better in the bargain. If a little bribe supports you in changing unhealthful habits, then so be it.

ACTION STEPS

➤ If you work for a large organization, reread your insurance policy to see if healthy lifestyle incentives have been built into your benefits. If you don't have the patience to wade through all the legalese, speak to your HR advisor or benefits counselor.

➤ If you're in a position to institute a rewards program for health-enhancing behaviors for your employees, research what large companies like ExxonMobil, JC Penney, and American Express are doing. It can be as simple as offering employees a $5 reward every time they go to the gym or walk or bike to work.

Doctors Without Borders

Be the change you want to see in the world.
—Mahatma Gandhi

Doctors Without Borders (known in France as Médecins Sans Frontières) is an international, impartial, medical humanitarian organization created in France by doctors and journalists in 1971. Today they provide medical aid in nearly sixty countries to people whose survival is threatened by armed conflict, epidemics, malnutrition, exclusion from healthcare, or natural disasters. The success of the organization is due to its neutrality: the organization does not take sides in armed conflicts and provides care on the basis of need alone.

As an international movement, this organization is made up of nineteen associate organizations, each based in a different country. The U.S. branch was founded in 1990. This means that you would be working with an international team of volunteers. During the mission, all of the participants are taught to put aside their personal politics so that they can work together toward common goals.

More than twenty-seven thousand committed individuals representing dozens of countries provide assistance to people caught in crises around the world. They are doctors, nurses, logistics experts, administrators, epidemiologists, laboratory technicians, mental-health professionals, and other essential nonmedical personnel. Volunteers are required to have at least two years of relevant professional experience. The time commitment is nine to twelve months with the exception of surgeons and anesthesiologists, who may be accepted for shorter assignments. Currently, the organization is urgently looking for administrators and financial controllers. As a Doctors Without Borders volunteer, you will be bringing medical care to those who most desperately need it.

GETTING STARTED: The Doctors Without Borders Web site, www .doctorswithoutborders.org, is packed with information, including application forms and audio/video recollections from previous volunteers. For more information, call (212) 679–6800.

Feeding the Children

The belly rules the mind.
—Spanish proverb

Nine-year-old Cindy is sitting in the front row of her English class, but she can't focus. She didn't have breakfast this morning, and that's making it hard for her to concentrate. By noon she's irritable and picks a fight with another child. Cindy's teacher decides she's showing behavioral problems.

Because Cindy is overweight, no one would suspect that she's hungry. But the surprising fact is that many children in this country are simultaneously undernourished and overweight, and this makes their real issues hard to identify.

The reality is that more than 12 million children in America—that's one in six—are at risk of hunger. And not getting the proper nutrition means that they will have weaker immune systems, more headaches, fatigue, behavioral issues, more difficulty in school and in athletics, and a host of other challenges that can last a lifetime.

Share Our Strength wants to put an end to this problem. They sponsor:

➤ The Great American Bake Sale: People all over the country hold bake sales and donate the proceeds to Share Our Strength.

➤ The Great American Dine Out: Thousands of restaurants across America help raise funds—you simply dine out at participating restaurants.

➤ Taste of the Nation: The finest drinks and wine from the nation's hottest mixologists and chefs, where 100 percent of proceeds go to fighting childhood hunger.

If you would prefer to give directly, $35 helps feed a child three meals a day for more than a month, $50 helps provide preschool children with lunch for a day, and $100 provides twenty-five bags of nutritious food.

VISIT www.shareourstrength.org.

Adult Literacy

**It is not true that we have only one life to live;
if we can read, we can live as many more lives
and as many kinds of lives as we wish.**
—S. I. Hayakawa

In our complex society, any adult who can't read and write easily is very seriously handicapped. Many adults with low literacy are immigrants who didn't have the opportunity for much education in their home countries. Others are people who struggled in school, never really achieved full literacy, and dropped out of the education system. As adults, they realize how much their lack of literacy holds them back. They can't read to their kids, and their job prospects are very limited.

You can give the gift of reading by being a tutor in an adult literacy program. An extensive nationwide network of these programs is already in place. Even so, demand is so high that there simply aren't enough volunteers to keep up. Indeed, literacy programs and programs that help people get their GED top the list of areas that urgently need volunteers.

You don't have to have a background in education to volunteer as a tutor. Most programs will send you for a short training course and provide you with appropriate books and materials to use with your student. You provide only commitment and enthusiasm. In larger programs that offer group classes, volunteers are needed as teachers' aides.

Finding a nearby literacy program should be easy. Check with your community library first; also check with local social- or human-services agencies. Most adult literacy programs meet in the evening for just two hours or less once a week. So a couple of hours a week of your time is all it takes to help a willing adult make progress toward better reading skills and a better life.

FOR HELP in finding or expanding a nearby literacy program for people of any age, or for ideas for starting one, contact:

National Institute for Literacy / 1775 I Street NW, Suite 730 / Washington, DC 20006 / (202) 233–2025 / www.nifl.gov

Open a Free Store

I resolve to stop accumulating and begin the infinitely more serious and difficult task of wise distribution.
—Andrew Carnegie

A free store is a store where nothing is sold; everything is free for the taking. Creating such a store in your community will encourage people to recycle clothes, books, and household goods. A free store can also become a place where likeminded people can meet and enjoy free entertainment and food while committing to the idea of reducing waste and sharing with others.

ACTION STEPS

LOCAL: First, you will need a space. Approach local business owners to see if they might donate one. You'll need a lease so that you don't have to give up your space unexpectedly. Shelves, garment racks, and a try-on room will be necessities. Someone will need to schedule volunteers so the store is covered during specified hours, at least a few hours on a few days per week. Create a flyer asking for donations and pass it out at schools, community centers, and places of worship; list hours when the store will be open for drop-offs. Volunteers might also offer to take donations from their friends, relatives, and colleagues, and bring them to the store. Some stores clean and mend items; others take them only "as is." In any case, make arrangements to recycle any items that are not usable.

When you have a sufficient number of donations, schedule an opening a few weeks in advance; write a press release and send it to local media. Try to make this day a big event that the whole community will enjoy. Have flyers available for guests to take home. Remember that publicity must be ongoing in order to have a steady stream of donations.

NATIONAL: Check out these Web sites to see how some communities are creating free stores: www.freestorebaltimore.org. • www.thefreestore .org.

Speak Up

**As long as there are human rights to be defended;
as long as there are great interests to be guarded;
as long as the welfare of nations is a matter for
discussion, so long will public speaking have its place.**
—William Jennings Bryan

You run the homeless shelter, the suicide hotline; you have organized your company's walkathon, marathon, bikeathon; you have used every aspect of your being as a person who serves others. Now you have been asked to share your thoughts, to give a speech before the local Rotary Club with many of the leading businesspeople and local government officials in attendance. Or your company has asked you to outline your division's cause-related efforts at a companywide meeting. And you freak out. You can't give a speech! Yes, you can. Your role now is to speak up for those who cannot, so that through your ability to influence, persuade, and convince, others will be better served.

ACTION STEPS

➤ Practice your public speaking. Consider joining or starting a local club of Toastmasters International, a nonprofit organization dedicated to helping people become more competent and comfortable in front of an audience. It's a safe place to practice and hone communication and leadership skills. Most Toastmasters meetings are composed of about twenty people who meet weekly for an hour or two, where members critique one another in a positive manner.

➤ One specific bit of speech-making advice is to use humor, a funny line, a joke, or a personal anecdote in any speech to help you bond with your audience. Be sure to not tell a joke at someone else's expense. Practice with family or friends telling a joke. Repeating jokes out loud gets you in the habit of telling them and gauging the pace and rhythm that works best. More at www.toastmasters.org.

(Not) Born in the USA

**Call it a clan, call it a network, call it a
tribe, call it a family. Whatever you call it,
whoever you are, you need one.**
—Jane Howard

A little store you used to frequent now houses a bodega, and it makes
you shake your head a little each time you pass. You get copied on a
chain e-mail that says, in part, "I shouldn't have to press 1 for English,"
and you secretly agree. You find the rapid-fire chatter of another language
hard on your ears.

You don't consider yourself a racist and, truthfully, you're probably
not one. But there is something deeply ingrained in human nature that
makes it easy to make the distinction between "us" and "them." And
lately, it seems that there's a lot more of "them" around.

The first thing you need to know is that this reaction once was a
useful defense mechanism. You needed to immediately know who was a
stranger in order to defend your clan from danger.

The second thing you need to know is that this mechanism is mostly
obsolete and that compassion can help you overcome it.

ACTION STEPS

➤ Most local newspapers publish the upcoming dates of American citi-
zenship ceremonies, or you can find out from your county courthouse.
If you've never been to one, take an hour or two out of your day to go
to the next one. Your heart will be gladdened to see the joy on the
faces of this country's newest citizens.

➤ There's usually a meet-and-greet afterward, often sponsored by various community organizations. Stay for a while and ask people about
their stories; what made them leave their birth country, whether they
miss it? You will hear stories of heroism and heartache you never
imagined.

The Wisdom of Children

**Listen to the desires of your children.
Encourage them and then give them the
autonomy to make their own decisions.**
—Denis Waitley, motivational speaker

We all have expectations for our children. Our culture is rife with expressions that tell us so, like, "He's just like you!" But what if your child wants to paint, though you feel he should play football. If she wants to play dress-up but you're pushing math, a subject you excelled in? How do you keep from crushing a child's spirit by your own needs for success?

Too much involvement can impede your child's development. She may end up working at a task to fulfill your needs, not hers. This can interfere with the development of her own thinking style. She may perceive your suggestions as criticism.

To be supportive, really listen to your child's concerns with empathy. Tell her how hard learning French was for you. Validate and support her feelings by saying, "I understand this is difficult. What can we do together to make it easier?" In one family a girl struggled on the soccer team. She was small, and the opposing team pushed her down and ran over her. After struggling with this for two years, her parents finally heard she was unhappy even though "everybody plays." Together they decided she might be happier in a sport where there was less body contact. She enrolled in swimming and gymnastics and excelled in both.

ACTION STEPS

➤ To be supportive, be receptive to who your child really is, not who you want him to be. Be curious. Ask, "Why do you think you did poorly on this test?" "What scares you about playing baseball?" Then really listen to the answers nonjudgmentally. How better to learn about his inner world?

➤ Apply the good listening skills of mirroring and validation to your interactions at home. Those around you will feel supported and heard.

Get Involved at a Boys & Girls Club

These days, the streets are 100 times more dangerous than they were when I was growing up. Now it's more important than ever for adults to provide safe havens for kids.
—Denzel Washington

In our increasingly hectic world, many boys and girls are left to their own devices after school and on weekends. Boys & Girls Clubs offer one of the safest environments for kids to play and learn, keeping them off the streets and out of trouble.

More than ever before, our youth is facing a crisis. High-school dropout rates are soaring, and so are obesity levels. Boys & Girls Clubs provide a myriad of activities to address these issues, including sports and athletics, homework help, and nutritional guidance. They offer a safe, dedicated space that is just for kids, so that kids know there is somewhere they can always turn to for help. Their doors are open seven days a week, and the dues are affordable for everyone: usually the annual fee is less than $10. Their programs are consistent from one neighborhood to the next and cover important topics like the environment, the arts, careers, alcohol/drug and pregnancy prevention, gang prevention, and leadership development.

The Clubs work with children of every socioeconomic level. Their programs and services promote and enhance development by instilling a sense of competence, usefulness, belonging, and influence. The Clubs rely on volunteers in many areas, including sports coaching, teaching, and general mentoring. If you would like to make a difference in the lives and well-being of our youth, you can do so by volunteering your time as a mentor and role model.

GETTING STARTED: Visit www.bgca.org and type in your zip code to find the Boys & Girls Club closest to you. Then go to that Web site and see what volunteer opportunities are available. Usually there will be choices for adults, college-age internships, and high-school programs.

Too Young for This

**I could be a bit of a pain in the arse. Since I've
come out of my cancer, I must say I intend
to be even more of a pain in the arse.**
—Harold Pinter

Matthew Zachary was only twenty-one when he was diagnosed with brain cancer. The diagnosis was shocking—and he was further shocked to learn that people between the ages of fifteen and forty who are diagnosed with cancer have a higher fatality rate than other age groups due to late detection.

Matthew started a Web site to draw together all the resources available to young people with cancer, and the site was soon named one of the fifty best by *Time* magazine and became the most trafficked of its kind. His organization, i[2]y (I'm too young for this), now has social clubs in forty U.S. cities, leads conferences and training seminars, and records and produces *The Stupid Cancer Show*, an internationally syndicated talk radio show.

The i[2]y Web site is geared toward a generation that is comfortable with Facebooking, Twittering, and blogging. It has an edgy voice, calling cancer "crapness" and marketing T-shirts with mottos like "Bald Is the New Black" and "Mmmm . . . chemo!"

"My generation responds to an irreverent indifference," says Matthew. "We don't ask, 'Why me?' but, 'Are you kidding me?'"

Dating is hard for all young people but especially so if you have only one breast or one testicle. i[2]y provides resources on dating, as well as fertility, employment, and college scholarships.

"A donation to i[2]y permanently transforms the life of a young adult with cancer," says Matthew. "You are offering a much better quality of life, which has been clinically proven to increase longevity."

Twenty-five dollars pays for two young adults to attend an i[2]y community support event, $50 helps produce and donate twenty-five CD/Toolkits, and $500 produces one episode of *The Stupid Cancer Show*.

VISIT www.stupidcancer.com.

Therapy Dogs

The dog is the god of frolic.
—Henry Ward Beecher

Your dog is wonderful, of course, because he's your dog. He can also be wonderful to other people by becoming a therapy dog.

Volunteering for therapy-dog work is a serious commitment. As a team, you and your dog will need at least ten hours of formal training, and a lot of practice at home, before you can start going on therapy visits. Once your training is complete, you and your dog will go on regular visits to hospitals, nursing homes, mental hospitals, hospices, and group homes—all places where a personal visit from a happy dog can really brighten the day and raise the spirits of the people there, staff included.

The first step to becoming a therapy-dog team is to assess your dog. The crucial trait is an even temperament. A good therapy dog is outgoing and friendly to everyone, including fearful people and active kids. The dog also needs to be tolerant of other dogs and not aggressive toward other pets, such as cats. An obedient nature and a basically calm temperament are also important—therapy dogs should be lively but not exuberant. Small dogs, big dogs, purebreds, and mutts can all be therapy dogs if they have the right personality.

To find out if your dog has the right temperament to be a therapy dog—and if you have the time for this big volunteer commitment—arrange for an assessment by a local therapy-dog group. A professional trainer will evaluate your dog. If he's suitable for therapy work, you can enroll in a training class that teaches you how to work as a team in a healthcare environment. On graduation, your dog is certified as an official therapy dog and you're ready to start bringing some doggy joy into the lives of others.

A GOOD starting point for learning more is:

Therapy Dogs International / 88 Bartley Road / Flanders, NJ 07836 / (973) 252–9800 / www.tdi-dog.org

Support Dozens of Worthy Causes Without Spending a Penny

Action indeed is the sole medium of expression for ethics.
—Jane Addams

Did you know that donations to many excellent charities can be given absolutely free over the Internet? It won't cost you a cent or more than a few minutes of your time. All you have to do is log on to a free donation Web site and click the "donate now" button. Donations are paid for by advertisers on these sites; they hope that users will patronize their businesses in return for the businesses' contributions to these causes. Most sites have a wide selection of charities to choose from. Participating funds include environmental groups, wildlife preservation, world hunger, cancer research, animal rights, and just about any other cause you may have heard of. If everyone made a pledge to click just once daily, millions of dollars would be given to these causes every year.

ACTION STEPS

LOCAL: Get everyone you know to give donations on these sites daily or weekly. This is also a great way to get kids interested in good causes and in donating regularly. Kids might even compete to see who can make the most clicks in a given time period. It's easiest to set up a "click donation" site as your home page and to make it a habit to donate as soon as you turn on your computer daily. You can change to another site weekly or monthly to spread donations around, or stick with one. If you are interested in a particular cause, do a Web search to see if a click charity is associated with it.

NATIONAL: These are just a few of the sites: www.care2.com/click2 donate • www.thenonprofits.com • www.thehungersite.com • www.oneclickatatime.org • www.freedonation.com

Kids to Kids, Connecting the World

So I put out my prayer, "What else can I do?" I have devoted much of my personal and professional life to helping children but it was no longer enough, I needed to do something more.
—Susan Randlett

Luis's village had one community pump. His family was better off than some; his father worked as a street vendor and they lived in a home protected by a corrugated metal roof. His family was sponsored via an international charity—and an American social worker, Susan Randlett, wrote out a check every month.

But Susan Randlett wanted to do more.

In the summer of 2000, Ms. Randlett participated in a silent retreat. In her prayers, she thought of Luis and all the other children like him. Maintaining her vow of silence, she walked through a local park.

During that week, through a series of dreams, meditations, and a revelation in the chapel, the idea of Children Helping Children (CHC) was born. Her inspiration was to connect children with children around the world.

Put out a prayer, envision a connection you can make with your influence to help those better equipped connect with the many who are not.

ACTION STEPS

➤ Ask your children to bring something they value to the dinner table and ask if they would consider donating it to help another child in need. Discuss what the idea of charity means to them, and to you.

➤ Children Helping Children seeks to help children throughout the United States and other established countries show their generosity to less fortunate children of the world. Link your child with others around the world. Go to www.children-helping-children.com.

How Hospitals Really Heal

**I think the biggest disease this world suffers
from is people feeling unloved.**
—Diana, Princess of Wales

Princess Diana visited hospitals all over the world. She would have comforted many people such as fourteen-year-old Jacob Samuel, who developed the flu a week before Christmas one year. He got weaker and weaker until, barely conscious, he was admitted to the hospital on Christmas Eve.

The next day Jacob was tethered to emergency oxygen and having a powerful cocktail of antibiotics pumped into him intravenously. He was too sick to notice that he was missing Christmas.

Later in the day, there was a knock at the door. A family of four asked if they could come in. They said they simply wanted to let children in the hospital know they weren't forgotten at Christmastime. The parents gave Jacob a small gift. The children gave him pictures they had drawn. They wished him a Merry Christmas and left within moments of their arrival.

Jacob lay staring at the door, then smiled and said his first full sentences in days. "They didn't have to do that. But I'm really glad they did." Two years later, he still has the drawings the kids made for him.

ACTION STEPS

➤ It's almost instinctive to avoid hospitals. Many people are uncomfortable around the sick and the hurting. But these are the people who need your compassion the most. Remember this.

➤ Nurses and doctors can be wonderful with patients. But nothing beats the unprompted, unpaid presence of someone who just wants to do what he or she can to alleviate the suffering. Choose a couple of occasions a year to visit a hospital. The hardest times for people to be there are holidays, birthdays, and anniversaries. Check with the nursing staff to see who needs a visit most.

➤ Don't stay long. Sick people aren't usually in the mood to socialize. Leave a small gift or note to let them know they're in your thoughts.

Research Benefits All of Us

Medical science has proven time and again that when the resources are provided, great progress in the treatment, cure, and prevention of disease can occur.
—Michael J. Fox

All the support systems in the world don't measure up to one cure, be it for Parkinson's, cancer, diabetes, cardiovascular disease, stroke, Alzheimer's, or MS. All of us are eventually touched by illnesses; we need to support scientific efforts to find cures for them. We can show our support in many ways: contributing time and/or money to disease-specific organizations and advocacy groups, contacting legislators regarding important bills, buying products that support research, participating in walk/run fund-raisers or other events, and becoming involved in clinical trials.

Before any treatment can be put into practice, it must be shown to be both effective and safe in people. This is established during clinical trials, which are conducted with medications already approved to treat other conditions and new or experimental medications or behavioral procedures. This last stage of research involves the cooperation of individuals with the illness. It can require the involvement of thousands of people, including those who are healthy to act as a "control" group.

Participation in a clinical trial is a concrete step many of us can take to help ensure that cures are found for the most common diseases that beset humankind. It is a brave and noble thing to do.

ACTION STEPS

➤ Drug development can cost hundreds of millions of dollars. Funding for this research comes from government agencies, advocacy groups, and pharmaceutical companies. Do your part to support this effort by becoming involved in advocacy group fund-raisers.

➤ Talk to your physician about how to join a clinical trial. Information is also available at www.clinicaltrials.gov, a registry of federally and privately supported research.

Teach for America

**The mediocre teacher tells. The good
teacher explains. The superior teacher
demonstrates. The great teacher inspires.**
—William Arthur Ward

Educational inequity continues in our country, most notably along socioeconomic and racial lines. Even with governmental acts like No Child Left Behind, the public schools system unfairly impacts more than 13 million American children growing up in poverty today. Yet when these same children are given the opportunity, they can, and will, achieve at high levels.

Since 1990, Teach for America exists solely to eradicate this inequity by recruiting recent college graduates of all majors and career interests. More than 20,000 past and current participants have been trained as teachers. Known as corps members, they commit to the program for at least two years. They are in effect trading other, more lucrative, career opportunities or "cushier" teaching positions to work in urban and rural public schools, in any of twenty-nine different locations throughout the country. The program consists of an intense five weeks of training, followed by university course work and professional coaching post placement. Corps members teach in all grade levels, including two new initiatives: one that focuses on prekindergarten, and a second on math.

Unlike in the Peace Corps, Teach for America corps members are paid. They receive a salary directly from the school districts in which they work. However, the time they give is just as important, helping to close the achievement gap between the poorest students and the rest of the country.

GETTING STARTED: To apply, visit www.teachforamerica.org or call (800) 832–1230. Http://TeachFor.Us is an independent blog created by a 2006 corps member. Read their blogs and find out what it's truly like to be a corps member.

Caring for Cats

As every cat owner knows, nobody owns a cat.
—Ellen Perry Berkeley

We all love cats—or we at least admire their grace, beauty, and ability to turn humans into servants who tend to their every whim. But feral cats must fend for themselves and can never be taken into a home. Unfortunately, feral cats are not classified as wildlife, so they do not have the protections that wildlife does. (For example, you cannot just catch a raccoon and kill it, but this is not true of a feral cat.) Trapping and killing feral cats does not work to reduce their population, because the other feral cats just keep reproducing. A much more effective way to deal with the problem of feral cats is through a trap/neuter/return program, where the feral-cat community population levels out.

Alley Cat Rescue (ACR) is an organization that is dedicated to the health, well-being, and welfare of all cats. ARC works to help contain feral-cat populations on both local and international levels (with a trap/neuter/return program in Mexico and one in the works in South Africa). ARC also provides information to the public on cat health, cat behavior, and special needs.

ARC particularly wants to educate people about the benefits of spaying and neutering: A single unsterilized female cat can produce hundreds of kittens in her lifetime. In contrast, sterilized cats live longer, healthier lives and will ultimately save the community money by reducing the burden on local shelters.

"County shelters spend millions of our tax dollars putting feral cats to sleep, but it is actually cheaper to trap, neuter, and return them," says Kylie Riser of ACR. "You don't have to keep doing it in a never-ending cycle."

ACR believes that all so-called "pest" and "nuisance" animals such as feral cats should be treated with kindness and compassion, and it promotes humane care for *all* cats.

VISIT www.saveacat.org.

I Hate My Volunteer Job!

Our own share of miseries is sufficient: why enter then as volunteers into those of another?
—Thomas Jefferson

You volunteered to help an organization you believe in, and now you realize you made a big mistake. The work you're doing for the organization simply isn't a good fit for you. Maybe it's not making the best use of your skills. Perhaps you've been asked to do work that's boring or mindless, or that you find too difficult. Or maybe the hours you're being asked to give don't mesh well with your schedule. Perhaps the skills you hoped to learn from volunteering aren't being taught to you. You made a commitment, but it's just not working out. What now?

A bad fit in volunteering isn't uncommon. The problem may lie with the volunteer organization itself. Poor management of volunteers is a chronic problem in the charitable world. All too often, these operations run on tight budgets with small staffs. They may not have someone acting as volunteer director to help attract and keep volunteers by finding them meaningful work. As a volunteer, you may be assigned to help someone who doesn't really have much experience with volunteers and who may just dump a bunch of routine work on you instead. The work needs to be done, of course, but you signed up with the organization to help save the world, or at least to do something directly involved with the group's mission. That's hard to remember when you're stuck in an office stuffing envelopes.

IF YOU'RE truly unhappy with your volunteer work, don't just disappear. Speak up instead. Talk to the volunteer director if there is one, or to the head of the organization. Suggest some ways you could do volunteer work that's more in tune with your skills or fits better into your schedule. If you still can't work out a volunteer assignment that's appropriate, it may be time to move on. Your options are many—keep searching until you find the volunteer job you love. VolunteerMatch offers myriad possibilities and guidance on finding your perfect match at www.volunteermatch.org.

Start a "Local Food" Movement

The goal of life is living in agreement with nature.
—Zeno (335 BC–264 BC)

The local food movement—also called Community Supported Agriculture (CSA)—supports local farmers, improves food quality and safety, and saves the fuel used to transport food for long distances. Farmers can give better prices to restaurants, shops, and consumers when they are guaranteed a steady market for their produce. Members of the community benefit from better food and a more intimate connection with what they eat.

Community Supported Farms (CSFs) are farms that offer shares to members of their community. Individuals and families can join and receive a specified amount of food weekly, in exchange for their membership fee. In some CSFs, members have the option of visiting and perhaps doing some work on the farm; they may also help bag and distribute the food.

ACTION STEPS

LOCAL: Contact nearby farmers through your Department of Agriculture or county extension service; learn as much as you can about them, sample their food, and decide which are worthy of your support (not all will be—some, for instance, may be polluting water sources or using inhumane livestock practices).

Approach your local government's Department of the Environment about sponsoring a farmers' market once or twice a week, and supply information about the farms to them. Ask restaurant owners where they buy their food, pass on the information you have gained, and tell them you intend to patronize places that buy local.

To learn how to get fresh food by starting your own CSF group, go to www.thekitchn.com/thekitchn/green-ideas/how-to-start-a-new-csa-interview-with-paula-lukats-of-just-food-043227.

NATIONAL/INTERNATIONAL: Learn more about the U.S. local food movement at www.localharvest.org. For worldwide news and information, go to the American Farmland Trust Web site: www.farmland.org.

The Power of One

We would not have war at all if everyone could learn how to live with true love, hope and forgiveness. If that little girl in the picture can do it, ask yourself: Can you?
—Kim Phuc as recounted in "This I Believe"

He killed and starved millions. And Joseph Stalin, leader of the Soviet Union, knew this: "a single death is a tragedy, a million deaths a statistic." These words speak a truth, that an influential person can use to put a face on a cause.

One story, one photo, can change everything.

On June 8, 1972, Kim Phuc was nine-years-old when she was pictured running naked and screaming on a road near Saigon, her skin on fire from an American bombing. Her photo, taken by Huynh Cong "Nick" Ut, an Associated Press photographer, ran around the world, and many consider it highly influential in turning American public opinion against the Vietnam War.

Shape public opinion in your own community. Know that in focusing on one person's story, you tell the story of many. People connect to one family who lost all in a flood, one starving boy, one girl scarred in war. You can show, through the story of one, how an issue or event affects all.

ACTION STEPS

➤ Break through the statistics. Identify someone who has been dramatically affected by the issue at hand. Encourage that spokesperson to speak out. Start in a small venue, your living room, among friends. Stand by that person and let her know you will be there if she becomes the face of the cause.

➤ Identifying this one story is a major responsibility for you. You need to be mindful of not exploiting another's tragedy. Yet if you both understand the importance of making the unimaginable personal, your influence together will change a statistic into a tragedy that encourages us all to act now.

A Dog's Life

**I wonder what goes through his mind when
he sees us peeing in his water bowl.**
—Penny Ward Moser

We feed them, we walk them, we pet them, we love them, but we often forget to feel compassion toward the pets in our homes. You may ask, what exactly does that mean? If we do all those caring things, isn't that compassion?

No, it isn't, because compassion is all about understanding the plight of others and being moved enough to act on that plight—whether the others are human or not. With that in mind, when was the last time you considered things from your pet's point of view?

This isn't just a hippy-dippy, loopy-doopy thing to do. It's a legitimate exercise in understanding how our pets see the world. People have a tendency to treat animals as furry little people, and this they are most assuredly not.

Once you understand their viewpoint, you can provide them with outlets for their natural tendencies. And once you do that, fewer shoes get chewed, people don't get bitten, carpets stay unsoiled, and pets don't get abandoned at shelters because their owners can't take it anymore. This is truly compassion at work.

ACTION STEPS

➤ Your dog needs exercise. Inactive dogs are destructive and unhappy dogs. Find a dog park or other place where he can run, and take him there daily. Always leave him with company. Dogs are social animals and hate being alone. Another pet in the house will make him much more content and better behaved, even if it's a cat. At the very least, tune in a broadcast such as the one at www.dogcatradio.com, which sends out tunes and voices to soothe lonely pets. Seek out advice and information locally in the Pets forum on www.craigslist.org. You'll also find opportunities to help and support local animal shelters there.

Feeding America

Hunger is the best sauce in the world.
—Miguel de Cervantes

In February 2009, just when the need was the greatest, President Obama declared, "The food banks in America don't have enough to meet the demand." Hunger is the worst of pains, and it is rising at astonishing rates in America—35 million of us don't have enough to eat. Food banks once serving mostly the homeless and dispossessed now take care of thousands of middle-class people who suddenly find themselves out of work and out of luck.

All of us who can must do more to support our neighbors in need. Of course, we can work at a food bank to distribute needed supplies, but we can also support Feeding America, the nation's leading domestic hunger-relief charity. The Feeding America network provides food assistance to more than 25 million people facing hunger each year, including more than 9 million children and 3 million seniors.

Their network distributes 2 billion pounds of donated food and grocery products annually and supports 63,000 local charitable organizations that operate 70,000 programs including food pantries, soup kitchens, emergency shelters, and after-school programs. And they do it in a unique, efficient, and cost-effective way. Each year, supermarkets dump billions of pounds of food and grocery products. Feeding America intervenes in this terribly wasteful practice by receiving healthy and safe items as donations. It then redistributes the food to people who need it.

ACTION STEPS

➤ Pledge to host a dinner with family and friends to talk about childhood hunger, and Stouffer's will donate $5 to provide meals for children and their families. You'll find details at www.feedingamerica.org.

➤ Join the Hunger Action Center at Feeding America to start solving the problem of hunger in your community. Faith-based responses are also supported.

Experience Corps

**We make a living by what we get, we
make a life by what we give.**
—Winston Churchill

Experience Corps is a national program that engages older, retired
Americans (those over fifty-five) in helping struggling elementary-
school students. The organization was founded in 1995 and now boasts
more than two thousand Experience Corps volunteer tutors and mentors
who work directly with students, help teachers in their classrooms, or
lead after-school activities. Independent research shows that Experience
Corps not only boosts student academic performance, but also improves
the lives of the older adults in the process.

As an Experience Corps member, you can volunteer at a school in
one of twenty-three cities across the country. Each volunteer is asked to
commit approximately fifteen hours a week. The response to the project
has been overwhelmingly positive. Schools report increases in test scores
as well as decreases in classroom misbehavior. A Washington University
study found that students with Experience Corps tutors make 60 percent
more progress in critical reading skills than students without tutors. On
every imaginable scale, you will be enhancing the lives of students and
those who teach them.

Best of all, as you help children either individually or in small groups,
you are also taking better care of yourself. Numerous studies have shown
that Experience Corps members feel better about themselves, expand
their circle of friends, and become healthier and more active once they
begin the program. This is truly an opportunity to give and receive.

GETTING STARTED: For more information, call (202) 478–6190 or
visit the Web site: www.experiencecorps.org. Their free newsletter, *The
Voice of Experience,* provides details on what you can expect to encounter
as a volunteer and best practices other Experience Corps members have
used. If Experience Corps is not currently operating in your city, consider
starting an Experience Corps project in your area.

Love for Living Beings

**The greatness of a nation and its moral progress
can be judged by the way its animals are treated.**
—Mahatma Ghandi

Most of us have the uncomfortable knowledge that millions of animals each year in this country experience pain, suffering, and death in the name of research and testing. But we have been told that this is necessary to make progress in medicine, so we turn a blind eye and try not to think about it too much. However, the truth is that with today's advanced technology, there are many humane alternatives to animal testing.

"It's a very exciting time to be in this field," says Sue Leary of the American Anti-Vivisection Society (AAVS), the oldest nonprofit animal advocacy and educational organization in the United States dedicated to ending experimentation on animals. "There is a fabulous opportunity with the new technology to use human cell cultures and human tissues to explore what is happening in human diseases. Science supports moving away from using animal models because they are flawed, anyway," she adds. "Mice are not just small people."

She points out that when AAVS was started 125 years ago, the big issue was the treatment of horses (the major mode of transportation of the time), which were being driven to death in the streets. But once the Ford motorcar came along, that automatically changed.

So why are people still using animals for testing? Change comes slowly, she says. But it does come eventually. In Europe there is now a complete ban on the sale of cosmetic products where animals are used for testing. (You can go to www.leapingbunny.org to get a list of products that have not been tested on animals in this country.)

AAVS advocates against the use of animal testing and educates teachers, scientists, and the general public about humane alternatives to animal testing. Membership in AAVS, which helps the organization continue its advocacy for animals, is as little as $15.

VISIT www.aavs.org or call (800) 729–2287.

Global Youth Service Day

In a lot of areas of my life, particularly in my teenage years, I began to think about the world, and to think about the universe as being a part of my conscious everyday life.
—Julius Erving

Once a year, millions of youth get the chance to change the world. Global Youth Service Day, actually a three-day event held annually in late April, engages young people in community-service projects in more than one hundred countries. Founded in 1988, Global Youth Service Day has grown to become the largest service event in the world. It's dedicated to creating a global culture of engaged youth committed to a lifetime of service, learning, leadership, and achievement.

Global Youth Service Day has three main goals: (1) to mobilize youth to identify and address the needs of their communities through service; (2) to support programs that put youth on a lifelong path of service, learning, and civic engagement; and (3) to honor the many young people who contribute to their communities year-round.

The projects that take place on Global Youth Service Day are all designed and led by the youth themselves—even elementary-school kids can get involved. In 2009 in the United States, nearly 1,700 different projects took place over that weekend in almost every state. They ranged from community cleanups to fund-raising relay races to health fairs and community gardening. Some projects were simple, some were complicated, but all showed that young people can make a difference.

Global Youth Service Day in the United States is organized by the nonprofit organization Youth Service America in coordination with the National Youth Leadership Council, the Global Youth Action Network, and with thousands of partners in the United Stated and across the world.

LEARN MORE at:

Youth Service America / 1101 15th Street, Suite 200 / Washington, DC 20005 / (202) 296–2992 / www.ysa.org

Knit for a Good Cause with a Group
of Knitters in Your Community

**Life's most urgent question is: what
are you doing for others?**
—Dr. Martin Luther King Jr.

Knitting is not just an enjoyable hobby; it is a valuable tool that can
help people in need, in your own community and around the world.
Knitting-for-charity groups are a relatively new twist on an old practice,
since knitters have been getting together to talk while they work for
centuries. The entire group can contribute to the same charity, or each
knitter can choose his or her own.

ACTION STEPS

LOCAL: First, get connected with other knitters. Log on to the Web site
of Stitch 'n Bitch to help you start or join a group: www.knithappens.com.

Set a time and place for your first meeting. Talk to knitters you know,
and post notices about the group at knitting shops, craft shops, cafés,
community centers, and bookstores. When you see someone knitting
around town, invite the person to the meeting.

At the initial get-together, agree on regular times, places, and ground
rules for your meetings. Discuss the sorts of charities you want to donate
to, and assign members to check out each and report back.

NATIONAL: All about knitting: www.knitting.about.com. All about
knitting for charity: www.knittingforcharity.org • Searchable knitting
charity registry: www.lionbrand.com/charityconnection.html • List of
charities that take knitted goods by state: www.woolworks.org/charity
.html • Knitting for Native American and Central Asian children: www
.warmwoolies.org • Caps for chemotherapy patients: www.chemocaps
.com • Afghans for Afghans: www.afghansforafghans.org • Blankets for
shelter animals: www.snugglesproject.org

Speaking Truth to Power

**The only thing necessary for the triumph of
evil is for good men to do nothing.**
—Edmund Burke

They face imprisonment, torture, even death. They are journalists, teachers, priests and nuns. Some are Nobel prize winners like Mrs. Daw Aung San Suu Kyi, leader of the Myanmar opposition party, the National League for Democracy, who has been under house arrest since 1995. Others are mothers or fathers of the missing or the dead. They will not be silenced.

They risk all to speak truth to power. Their voices are a call to humanity—often from the darkest places on Earth, and sometimes closer to home than we realize. We must listen, stand with them, and raise our voices in unison, for that is our great power.

And sometimes we must speak truth directly to power ourselves.

ACTION STEPS

➤ Speak Truth to Power is a division of the Robert F. Kennedy Memorial. Their interactive map spotlights "The Defenders," human rights defenders, by country and cause. An exhibition of powerful portraits of these defenders is also online at www.speaktruth.org.

➤ PEN American Center supports writers here and abroad. PEN also leads campaigns to end attacks on freedom of expression. The PEN Action Center (www.pen.org) lists five things you can do to strengthen freedom of expression today.

➤ View and share the July 2009 short video from Amnesty International (www.amnesty.org) featuring U2's lead singer, Bono, announcing that Daw Aung San Suu Kyi was honored with the 2009 Amnesty International Ambassador of Conscience Award. U2 also performs the song "Walk On," which they have dedicated to her.

Clouded Compassion

**Smoking kills. If you're killed you've lost
a very important part of your life.**
—Brooke Shields

Smokers are quickly becoming today's lepers. Like lepers, they're forced away from the rest of society because of the health danger their habit poses to others. They're looked at with disgust and contempt. They're treated as if they have a defect of biblical proportions.

In other words, many nonsmokers are as sanctimonious and judgmental as you can get to another human being. This is a huge disservice to people on both ends of the cigarette. To begin with, when people feel under attack by others, their first instinct is to defend themselves. For smokers, this means firing one up. That doesn't serve anyone's best interest.

Surveys consistently show that the majority of smokers want to quit. A little bit of compassion could have a far more beneficial impact on the issue of tobacco use. Smokers would feel supported in their attempts to give it up, but not while under siege in those moments when they're unable to quit.

ACTION STEPS

➤ The next time you catch a whiff of a cigarette, don't immediately huff loudly and look upon the smoker with scorn. If you're honest with yourself, you'll admit that your reaction is more about what smoking represents than the smell itself. If you hear that someone has quit or is trying to quit, let the person know how great that is. If you've never smoked, say, "I hear it's brutally hard to quit. Good for you." If you're a former smoker yourself, say something like, "It took me six tries, but I finally got there. Keep it up."

➤ If you want to understand how incredibly difficult it is to quit, go without your favorite food for a few days. Take that intense craving, multiply it by a factor of ten, and extend it out over many weeks, even months. Now you know what a quitting smoker is going through. That deserves your respect and your compassion.

Love and Loss

If, as I can't help suspecting, the dead also feel the pains of separation (and this may be one of their purgatorial sufferings), then for both lovers, and for all pairs of lovers without exception, bereavement is a universal and integral part of our experience of love.

—C. S. Lewis

The English novelist Iris Murdoch said, "Bereavement is a darkness impenetrable to the imagination of the unbereaved." Yet who among us is "unbereaved"? Profound loss is part of the human condition.

Grief is a natural reaction after the death of a loved one. Yet few of us are prepared for its intensity and scope. In Judaism, one is in mourning for a year following the death of a spouse, sibling, parent, or child. During the week immediately following the burial, the family "sits shiva." Friends and family stop in to pray, share a meal and a sweet memory, and be supportive. This brings immediate comfort, but neither time nor the well-wishes of others may heal the wounds. People in mourning also need long-term understanding, support, and connection.

If grief is complicated, intense, and long-lived, it's important to seek the help of a bereavement support group. Many are held in places of worship, counseling centers, or hospitals. In Los Angeles, Our House has helped thousands of children, teens, and adults find grief-support services, education, resources, healing, and hope.

ACTION STEPS

➤ If somebody you love is in mourning, support that person's joining a bereavement support group in your community. It helps to talk with others who have experienced the death of someone close.

➤ If no bereavement group exists in your community, consider starting one. Contact your clergy, hospital, or local counseling center. Or reach out to Our House: www.ourhouse-grief.org, (310) 475–0299.

Providing Financial Relief

**If we act virtuously, the seed we
plant will result in happiness.**
—Sakyong Mipham

There are so many ways that we can spend our money in an effort to help others make a passage to a better circumstance. In these troubling economic times, we don't have to look to faraway countries or the poverty in our own to lend a hand. It seems that we all know someone who is facing a change to the way they lived, either because of a job loss or a depleted savings or retirement fund. Living with financial uncertainty might be a completely new experience for them, or it might be a way of life. Now is the time for you to do something meaningful for someone you know.

Give generously according to what you can afford. Your gift may be as simple as taking over the heating bill for the upcoming year, or paying for school supplies. You may be putting a down payment on a better car, or even help with the mortgage or rent. Whatever you can give will be helping to ease their burden, letting them sleep through the night so they can conquer the next day.

While this type of giving isn't glamorous (they'll be no benefit party to attend) or financially lucrative (forget the tax write-off), it's necessary. This is the mettle of friendship; it's how true communities are made and how we all survive together.

GETTING STARTED: This unique opportunity takes both money and tact on your part. If you are uncomfortable making the offer, read *Difficult Conversations: How to Discuss What Matters Most* by Douglas Stone, Bruce Patton, Sheila Heen, and Roger Fisher, or another excellent book, *Crucial Conversations: Tools for Talking When Stakes Are High,* by Kerry Patterson, Joseph Grenny, Ron McMillan, Al Switzler, and Stephen Covey.

Fighting for the Rights of All

In the confrontation between the stream and the rock, the stream always wins, not through strength but by perseverance.
—H. Jackson Brown

War is hell. But most people agree that when war is unavoidable, certain cruel practices should not be permitted, such as the torture of prisoners of war. Unfortunately, despite the Geneva Convention, the torture of prisoners still takes place every day. So do other global tragedies, such as genocide, forced prostitution, and the spread of AIDS.

In 1986, a small group of doctors from Cambridge, Massachusetts, heard about a fellow doctor in Chile who had been kidnapped by the Pinochet regime. (Under a dictatorship, doctors are sometimes punished for giving medical care to people who do not agree with the government's ideology.) The American doctors traveled to Chile, campaigned for their colleague's release, and—when they were successful—realized they could use their professional clout to make a real difference in the world. Thus, Physicians for Human Rights was born, and today the organization has a network of more than 20,000 people (of whom the vast majority are doctors and medical students) actively working to protect the human rights of people around the world. Their tireless efforts for health, dignity, and justice resulted in their being co-awarded the Nobel Peace Prize in 1997.

"We are voices in the vanguard to restore the rule of law," says John Hutson of Physicians for Human Rights. "We documented the collapse of Zimbabwe's health system and traced that collapse to human rights abuses, and we were the first organization to use the word 'genocide' concerning the calamity in Darfur."

A donation to Physicians for Human Rights helps end human rights abuses, supplies funding for physicians to travel to where they can document what is taking place, and provides advocates for victims of abuse everywhere who have no one else to speak for them.

VISIT www.phrusa.org.

337

Help at the Library

**What is more important in a library than anything
else—than everything else—is the fact that it exists.**
—Archibald MacLeish

Your local public library is one of your community's greatest assets,
yet when budget time rolls around, its funding is the first to be cut.
Ironically, budget cuts generally come during hard economic times, when
people need their libraries more than ever.

By volunteering at your local library, you help stretch the budget dollars
and keep the library open for as many hours a week as possible. When you
take over the routine work of checking books in and out and reshelving
them, you free up the trained librarians to help patrons with more complex
issues, like using the computer to look for a job or preparing a résumé.

Library volunteering goes beyond the routine, however. Libraries often
function as community learning centers, sponsoring after-school homework help, adult literacy programs, and English-language tutoring. Libraries also sponsor programs for senior citizens, have game nights for
kids, and even offer tax seminars. Volunteers are also often badly needed
in special areas of the library, such as the young-adult section or the local
history and genealogy rooms. Your help in any of these areas, especially
if you have some expertise, is always welcome.

One of the most enjoyable library jobs is being a story-hour volunteer. This could be as simple as picking a few favorite kids' books from
the shelves and reading them aloud to the group. Story hour is often
more complex than just reading, however. Often the children's librarian
chooses not just the book but also creates a project or special program
related to the book—and volunteers are needed for things like setting up
the arts-and-crafts materials and preparing the snacks.

OTHER WAYS to volunteer at the library include serving on the library board, helping with a book sale, and tidying up the magazine reading room. Community libraries have always counted on and been grateful
for volunteer help, and today they need you more than ever.

Start a Book Club on an Important Topic

There is more treasure in books than in all the pirates' loot on Treasure Island and best of all, you can enjoy these riches every day of your life.
—Walt Disney

Many of us are interested in learning more about a "serious" subject but either can't find the time or are intimidated by all the books available. We don't know where to start, so we do nothing. A dedicated group, meeting regularly, can help us focus our attention, narrow down book choices, and process what we learn. It can also make a serious subject a lot more fun.

ACTION STEPS

LOCAL: Make a list of a few possible subjects for your book group. Then talk to people you know. Find at least two who share one of your interests and would like to start a group on that subject.

Discuss how many should join. An ideal number is eight to eleven people, but it's okay to start small; the group can grow as word gets around. Post notices at libraries and bookstores, cafés, health-food stores, and community centers. Advertise with such online sources as www.craigslist.com or www.meetup.com.

At the first get-together, establish guidelines. How often will you meet? Set a regular time, once or twice a month. Where will your meetings be held? Often they are rotated at members' homes, but you might use a library, restaurant, or community center. How will you choose books? Who will lead discussions? Will food be served?

NATIONAL: How to start a book club: www.bestsellers.about.com/od/bookclubresources/ht/startbookclub.htm • Running a book club: www.book-clubs-resource.com • How to lead a book club discussion: www.bestsellers.about.com/od/bookclubresources/ht/howleadtalk.htm

Star Influence

Peace is not just a colored ribbon . . . it's not just a donation or a 5k race . . . peace is certainly more than a celebrity endorsement . . . peace like war must be waged.
—George Clooney, public service announcement in support of
www.betterworldcampaign.org

George Clooney. Do we have your interest now? This famous actor's interest in the Darfur region of Sudan has kept the spotlight on that African genocide.

If you communicate with passion, precision, and urgency to people of influence, you can garner celebrity support and widen your impact to serve others. You may have to be realistic, but you can aim high. Celebrity-charity relationships can generate greater recognition and media coverage for your cause—and for the celebrity.

But you still want George Clooney. Become involved in a nonprofit organization he founded along with Don Cheadle, Matt Damon, Brad Pitt, producer Jerry Weintraub, and human-rights lawyer David Pressman: Not On Our Watch (www.notonourwatchproject.org), which helps victims of humanitarian crises and disasters.

ACTION STEPS

➤ Use your influence to approach local celebrities first. Local media personalities, popular politicians, and collegiate sports stars are often eager to give back to their communities. Or plan a hometown celebration tied into your cause and invite a celebrity from your home state.

➤ Celebrity Service provides the largest database of celebrity contacts in the world—for a fee. This is what the pros use to track celebrities (www.celebrityservice.com). If you are involved in a local chapter of a national cause, a celebrity may be attached to the larger effort. Signed memorabilia to auction for fund-raising purposes is often a more realistic request than an appearance. Several Web sites monitor celebrities and their causes—among them www.looktothestars.org.

The Value of Nothing

**Few things are so deadly as a misguided
sense of compassion.**
—Charles Colson

Compassion, for good reason, is considered one of the greatest virtues by all major religions and most forms of philosophy. How then could it be deadly?

Consider, for example, the American Indian boarding schools that once dotted the country and enrolled hundreds of thousands of Native American children. Reformers and missionaries at the time thought they were doing right by helping the children assimilate into the new order of things. They were acting compassionately, they thought, by teaching these children English (and forbidding the use of their native language), converting them to Christianity, and schooling them in the manner of whites.

Many of these children grew up to be lost in both the American Indian and the white worlds. They were subject to higher rates of suicide, alcohol abuse, and violent crime, both as perpetrator and victim. For many of them, compassion was indeed deadly.

On a smaller scale, someone might see a parent smack her child at a playground and say something to the parent. What that person didn't know is that the parent will often take out her anger on the child later in the privacy of their home. Well-intended actions cause the child to suffer more.

ACTION STEPS

➤ Take some advice from doctors, who swear to "First, do no harm." Compassion rarely requires an immediate response. Before you decide on any course of compassionate action, spend the necessary time to consider all angles of your action. That may take five minutes or five weeks, depending on the circumstance.

➤ Consult with others whose opinion you respect. Find out what they have done in similar circumstances.

Get Involved

**Take the first step in faith. You don't have to take
the whole staircase, just take the first step.**
—Martin Luther King Jr.

How many times have you sat idly by, fuming about an injustice or a deficit in your community? You feel powerless to make a change, yet you're so dissatisfied with the current reality.

There is an antidote to this situation—your involvement. You're unhappy with the state of your children's school? Join the PTA and work toward changing the status quo. Perhaps you will organize a fund-raiser to buy new books for the library or hire more teachers' aides. You're frustrated with the way city government is handling recycling? Attend city council meetings and speak up when the mike is open to community comment. You object to the landing path at your local airstrip? Volunteer to lead the citizen's committee that may redirect the planes away from residential areas.

In fact, it might be interesting to volunteer for a committee that no one wants to chair. There are many unrecognized benefits to putting yourself in a leadership position. You may come into contact with other civic leaders with whom you might never have spoken. You may let your many talents shine. You may find yourself taking on responsibility for more issues that affect you and your family's lives. You may even consider running for public office. Supporting your community by becoming involved has the benefit of helping you feel more empowered. And this is a wonderful example to impart to your children.

ACTION STEPS

➤ Define for yourself what areas of your life are calling out for remediation. Rank them in order of importance for you. Now commit yourself to becoming involved in the first two on your list.

➤ When you feel you've accomplished what you want in these areas, move on to the next two.

Mentoring Pregnant Teens and Young Mothers

The art of mothering is to teach the art of living to children.
—Elain Heffner

Motherhood is something that no woman is completely prepared for. For those lucky women in stable, loving relationships, or who have parents or close friends who live nearby, they can create their own network of resources they can call on. But what about the youngest mothers, or single mothers who are living alone, without the necessary resources, role models, or guidance?

Mother-mentoring programs across the country help to ease the burden for these women and provide information and resources to them. One national organization, the Gentle Art of Mother Mentoring, pairs experienced mothers with these young mothers. Local organizations abound as well. By becoming a mother mentor, you will be passing on the womanly arts of mothering to the women who need it most.

As a mother mentor, you will be providing friendship, support, and education on important issues like breast-feeding, postpartum emotional adjustments, infant attachment, and parenting skills. You also need to be available to these women, helping them to counteract the isolation that many new mothers face and helping to link them more effectively to community resources. By giving of your time and providing them with a positive role model for good parenting, you are ensuring the best life possible for these women, and their children.

Many of these independent organizations match mentors with new mothers by identifying common interests, along with your availability. Often, mentors receive some training and are asked to commit to a young mother for a period of three months to one year.

GETTING STARTED: Contact the Gentle Art of Mother Mentoring program at www.americanmothers.org/?q-node/25.

La Educación Es Oro

No hay mal que por bien no venga. (There is no bad that comes without good.)
—Mexican saying

Manuel is an intelligent and hard-working sixteen-year-old who loves Twittering, playing Wii, and listening to Kanye West. He also loves mathematics and has dreams of one day becoming an architect. Unfortunately, his parents, natives of Chihuahua, Mexico, who have worked hard to raise their five children in this country, do not have the money to send him to college.

And Manuel is not alone. Hispanic youth make up only 17 percent of the total youth population, yet they account for 40 percent of high-school dropouts. Just 10 percent of Hispanic adults have bachelor degrees, compared to the national average of 20 percent. And 90 percent of the fastest-growing jobs in America require postsecondary education, but only 6 percent of students enrolled in four-year institutions are Hispanic.

Luckily for Manuel and other young people, there is the Hispanic Scholarship Fund (HSF). HSF is the nation's leading organization supporting Hispanic higher education and has a mission of doubling the rate of Hispanics earning college degrees. To try to reach this goal, HSF provides the Hispanic community with more college scholarships and educational outreach support than any other organization in the country. In 2008 HSF awarded almost 4,100 scholarships totaling more than $26.6 million.

With the goal of helping young Hispanics to achieve the very best possible futures, HSF has created several different scholarship programs to help high-school students get into college and to help college students stay in college and get their degrees. They also offer a scholarship to help students in community colleges transition into four-year colleges.

Every young person deserves the best education possible. The Hispanic Scholarship Fund relies on donations to provide educational opportunities for this underserved population.

VISIT www.hsf.net or call (877) 473–4636.

Nursing-Home Pen Pals

Letters are expectation packaged in an envelope.
—Shana Alexander

In the age of e-mail and Twitter, getting an actual letter in the mail from a friend is always a pleasant surprise. Mail makes you feel connected to the larger world. Sadly, many nursing-home residents don't ever get much in the way of mail. Their lives can be very restricted and lonesome.

By volunteering to be a nursing-home pen pal, you form a supportive connection with a nursing-home resident eager for contact. This is a great way for people with busy schedules to still volunteer. All you have to do is find the fifteen or twenty minutes it takes once a week or so to drop your nursing-home pen pal a short note. What do you say? Anything, really. The important thing is to connect—after that, the correspondence can be about whatever interests you both. Not all seniors can respond to your letters, but even when they can't, the bond that grows between pen pals can be very strong, even when they live many miles apart and never meet.

Nursing-home pen pals are also a great way to get the family involved in volunteering. Get out the construction paper, stickers, rubber stamps, and glitter, and let the kids make cards for their senior pen pal. If you're on a family trip, have them send postcards. The kids get to practice handwriting and composition skills while cheering someone's day at the same time. Extend the service circle and ask your family and friends to add your pen pal to their holiday card list and to send a card on his or her birthday. The time and cost are minimal; the pleasure you give is priceless.

TO FIND a nursing-home pen pal, just look around you—chances are you or someone in your network of friends and family knows someone who'd be happy to get mail from you. If not, check with the volunteer directors of local nursing homes.

Help to Start a Low- or No-Cost Spaying/ Neutering Program for Pets

**An animal's eyes have the power to
speak a great language.**
—Martin Buber

It's a tragedy that millions of healthy cats and dogs are put to death each year in the United States because there aren't enough homes for them. Coping with unwanted pets drains resources too: it costs American taxpayers and private humane agencies over a billion dollars each year. Spaying/neutering is the answer.

A number of organizations provide these services affordably. But if they are not available in your area, you can help to establish them with the assistance of SPAY/USA.

ACTION STEPS

LOCAL: First, determine the need for a low-cost spay/neuter clinic. Ask the local animal-control office if your target area has a pet overpopulation problem; get an estimate of how many unspayed pets live within its borders. Ask local veterinarians and animal shelters if low-cost spaying is available. If it is, ask if they are able to meet the demand.

Once you have determined that there is a need, make use of guidance offered by SPAY/USA at www.spayusa.org in setting up spay/neuter clinics.

NATIONAL: Information on spaying/neutering:

The American Veterinary Medical Association: www.avma.org/ animal_health/brochures/spay_neuter/spay_neuter_brochure.pdf.

The ASPCA: www.aspca.org/site/DocServer/Why_spayneuter-English .pdf?docID=188.

The Humane Society of the United States: www.hsus.org/pets/pet _care/why_you_should_spay_or_neuter_your_pet.html.

Directories of spaying/neutering services: www.aspca.org/pet-care/ spayneuter • www.pets911.com/services/spayneuter/locations.php

Green Fields Forever

It breaks your heart. It is designed to break your heart.
—A. Bartlett Giamatti, "The Green Fields of the Mind"

There's the moment your stomach gallops before the first pitch is thrown, and then the wood hits the ball. You're racing around the bases. You smell the green grass. You hear the cheer of the crowd, but the real spark is embedded in you: the speed of your arms and legs, the thrill of the game, the idea that you will be young forever. This feeling brings you back to the game, as a player, as a fan, and it will sustain you, revive you, mark the seasons of your life, and you will find in it a passion to bring to all you serve, even as it breaks your heart.

"It," for A. Bartlett Giamatti, is baseball and its lasting influence. "Of course, there are those who learn after the first few times. They grow out of sports. And there are others who were born with the wisdom to know that nothing lasts. . . . I need to think something lasts forever, and it might as well be that state of being that is a game; it might as well be that, in a green field, in the sun." The influence of this former commissioner of baseball soars. Play ball!

ACTION STEPS

➤ Close your eyes for ten seconds. It's the first day of the season. You've hit the ball, or kicked it, or run with it, depending on your sport. Now detail your love of the game in an essay for your local paper or blog or social-networking page.

➤ Share the joy! Approach the local sports facility; for example, a minor league baseball park. As a promotion, teams often have kids race the bases. Propose a different spin: adults' day. Grown-ups trot the bases and relive being in the game. Feel the roar of the crowd!

Once a Friend

**The ones who are bound to be your best
friends must lose your trust just once to
prove that they can win it back.**
—Author unknown

It is a difficult thing to watch someone you once considered a friend turn his or her back on you and walk in a different direction. The loss of a good friend can be bewildering, maddening, and heartbreaking, no matter whose fault it was or whose actions led to the rift.

What is a more difficult thing, yet infinitely more important, is to maintain compassion for the friend you lost. You may not understand why the parting of ways occurred, and you may not find yourself able to immediately forgive a terrible wrong done to you. But what you must maintain is an openness to the possibility of reuniting with your friend, because friendship, like marriage, is one of those relationships where the sum is greater than the total of its parts.

ACTION STEPS

➤ If you feel betrayed, recognize first that your friendship was given conditionally. Unconditional friendship, by its very nature, cannot be betrayed. It's normal to feel hurt, but set aside any feeling of betrayal.

➤ Practice these words: "I don't understand why you've chosen this path, but I guarantee you that I will always be here if you ever need me." Say them or write them to your friend and mean them with all your heart.

➤ Make brief contact from time to time. Writing a note or an e-mail is best because it doesn't require a response. Don't have any motive except a genuine wish for the person's well-being. You could write something like, "I saw something today that reminded me of you."

➤ If this person does come back into your life, accept him or her wholeheartedly and joyfully as a gift that has returned. If he or she doesn't return, let nothing diminish the memories of the time you shared.

Save the Wolves

Killing a wolf is [. . .] a way of participating in the myth of the West. That myth nearly drove the species to extinction.
—Verlyn Klinkenborg, *New York Times* columnist

For years we've been hearing about the extinction and near-extinction of species on our planet. The climate changes we face may speed this sad march toward oblivion. We want our children to inherit as diverse a biosphere as we've enjoyed. Life would be emptier for all of us without spouting whales to watch, intelligent elephants to marvel over, and the haunting howl of wolves to fear.

Gray wolves in particular have been getting a bum rap. Aerial wolf hunting in Alaska struck many as inhumane and unfair, though some state officials claim it's needed to reduce the number of wolves that attack caribou and moose—competing with humans for food resources. In Idaho and Montana, wolves are being removed from the endangered species list. They have repopulated well, but without curbs on hunting, it's feared sportsmen will once again decimate their ranks. We're in the grip of mythology when we think of wolves (*Little Red Riding Hood* and *Peter and the Wolf*), but these animals don't kill people. They're responsible for fewer livestock deaths than domestic dogs, and federal and state programs pay ranchers who lose cattle to them. Wolves are at the top of the food chain, as are we humans, and so a rivalry may be natural. But they deserve our support. Ecosystems need their predators in order to maintain balance. And our world would be a much poorer place without them.

ACTION STEPS

➤ Write to the secretary of the interior to voice your concerns about wolf hunting in the West: www.doi.gov.

➤ Are there any other endangered species you want to support? The World Wildlife Fund (www.worldwildlife.org) let's you adopt a species. Or you can take action through WWF's Conservation Action Network.

Art from the Heart

A room hung with pictures is a room hung with thoughts.
—Sir Joshua Reynolds

Sometimes, just a simple change of scenery is all it takes to bring some-one you love out of a funk. And what could be easier than changing their view right in their own home?

Artist Karen Morganbesser understands the power of art and how it helps people cope with transition, illness, or even life changes. She cre-ated the Art from the Heart organization in 2004 with her seventeen-year-old daughter, Kimberly, as a way to improve the lives of others with their own set of creative skills. Their idea was simple but effective: transform children's bedrooms into a personal wonderland. Today, as part of the Circle of Care organization of Fairfield County, Connecticut, they hold a lottery and commit to redecorating and painting four children's bedrooms each year.

You can easily incorporate this idea to help anyone you know that is going through a difficult life passage. You might know a recent empty nester, or someone who has just gone through a divorce or lost a close family member. They might need a room in their house repurposed to help them through their trauma. Or, they might appreciate a new bed-room for themselves to brighten their spirits. By volunteering to paint, wallpaper, or even pick out (or purchase) new furniture, you are helping someone take the first steps out of a crisis and back into their lives.

GETTING STARTED: Every professional decorator will tell you that there's no cheaper, more effective design tool then a fresh coat of paint. Talk with the person you are helping to pick a color that is both soothing and uplifting, as well as a color that resonates with them. If you've got good design sense, then you are off and running. If you need help, there are a myriad of free services available, including in-store design consul-tants at shops like Crate and Barrel (www.crateandbarrel.com) and Ethan Allan (www.ethanallen.com), which even has tools to play with right on their Web site.

The Gift of Sight

Let your heart feel for the afflictions and distress of everyone, and let your hand give in proportion to your purse.
—George Washington

It is hard to imagine anything more terrifying than going blind. Yet every year in this country, as many as 12,000 people lose their sight because of glaucoma—and 90 percent of that blindness that could have been prevented with early detection and treatment.

Glaucoma is a sneaky and insidious disease because in its early stages—when it can be treated—the disease usually has no symptoms. For this reason, half of the 3 million people in this country who have it—and 90 percent of all people in developing countries who have it—do not know it. If undetected and untreated, glaucoma will gradually claim all peripheral vision and go on to cause total blindness. By the time vision is lost, the disease is already in its advanced stages. Glaucoma is the leading cause of blindness in African Americans in this country. Other people at risk include those with a family history of glaucoma, people who are very nearsighted or farsighted, and anyone over the age of sixty. With early detection, glaucoma can be treated with eye drops, lasers, and surgery. (Treatment can usually halt the disease, but it cannot reverse the damage that has been done.)

The Glaucoma Foundation is one of the premier not-for-profit organizations dedicated to wiping out blindness from glaucoma. The Glaucoma Foundation funds research, educates the public about the importance of early detection and treatment, and offers a number of online support groups for people with glaucoma. The organization's "Eye to Eye" newsletter keeps more than 30,000 households informed about research news and other developments.

The Glaucoma Foundation relies on the generous support of the public—it does not receive government funding.

VISIT www.glaucomafoundation.org or call (212) 285–0080.

ReServe

People who refuse to rest honorably on their laurels when they reach retirement age seem very admirable to me.
—Helen Hayes

After a lifetime of working, you've acquired some pretty useful business skills. Now as you approach retirement (or maybe you're already retired and bored), you have the chance to put your years of professional experience to work again, this time as a volunteer in your community.

Many excellent programs connect retired executives with small businesses that need help. Perhaps the best known is SCORE (Service Corps of Retired Executives), a long-standing nonprofit dedicated to the formation, growth, and success of small businesses. With 370 chapters nationwide and more than 11,000 active volunteers, SCORE has helped over 8 million small businesses succeed.

As valuable as SCORE and similar organizations are, they're oriented toward helping businesses. But what if you want to volunteer for the public good? ReServe, based in New York City, connects retired professionals with part-time service opportunities for nonprofit and civic groups. The retired executives use their lifetime experience to help in areas that need professional skills, such as accounting, financial services, graphic design, information technology, and legal advice. What really sets ReServe apart, however, is that volunteers receive a small stipend of $10 an hour for their time, up to nineteen hours a week; the organization they work with provides the payment. This philosophy helps the volunteers and the organizations take their commitment seriously, but the stipend is so small that the volunteers still feel like volunteers, not employees. ReServe now offers opportunities at over 150 nonprofit organizations and city agencies throughout New York City.

TO FIND out how it works—and how you could start something similar—contact:

ReServe Elder Services, Inc. / 6 East 39 Street, 10th Floor / New York, NY 10016 / (212) 792–6205 / www.reserveinc.org

Set Up a Birdcam for Nature Lovers in Your Area

See into life—don't just look at it.
—Anne Baxter

A birdcam is a video camera permanently mounted in a place where birds gather. It sends a live feed to a Web site, so people from anywhere in the world can watch your local birds in real time. This is a fun, easy, and inexpensive way to promote the beauty of nature in your area.

ACTION STEPS

LOCAL: First, talk to local birders, naturalists, and environmental groups. They will know where to find the most unusual and colorful birds and/or places that have the most bird traffic. Ask if bird feeders or houses might be a good idea. Consider approaching the group about cosponsoring your birdcam. Their participation would start you off with valuable expertise, help with publicity, and a built-in group of immediate fans.

If your locality has a Web site, look at it to find the administrator (perhaps the chamber of commerce). Call that office and say you would like to set up a birdcam on the site as a service to nature lovers, kids, and tourists. If not, it's easy to set up a Web site using one of many inexpensive design and hosting services (such as www.godaddy.com).

Then simply purchase a birdcam and set it up in a practice location. It may take time and patience to find just the right spot. Have a place for feedback on the Web site. You may be surprised how popular it will become!

NATIONAL: Any birdcam needs to avoid disturbing the birds' normal activities, especially breeding, in any way. When in doubt, consult with an expert from your state's regional office of the U.S. Fish and Wildlife Service (check www.fws.gov for details).

One manufacturer of birdcams: www.wingscapes.com • Links to birdcams around the world: www.beakspeak.com/index.php/birdcams • The National Audubon Society: www.audubon.org

Enthusiasm Leads the Way

Can Wisdom be out in a silver rod?
Or Love in a golden bowl?
—William Blake

Local artists are crafting over one thousand ceramics bowls. One college student says he's dreaming about making bowls after making many.

"Our Empty Bowl event raises funds for the Huntington Area Food Bank to fight hunger in our area," says an enthusiastic Meagan Sellards, the local Empty Bowls campaign director and infectious can-do spirit. With Marshall University students volunteering, the Keramos Art Guild producing the beautiful hand-crafted bowls, and local businesses involved, her hopes are high because, "the need is so much higher."

The enthusiasm for an Empty Bowls event brims over with Sellards as she adapts this national initiative to fight hunger locally. Guests will purchase a handmade ceramic bowl, which they can keep as a reminder of the hunger problems in the world and will be served a simple meal of good bread and hearty soup.

All monies raised will go to the Huntington Food Bank, which services 290 nonprofit member agencies in seventeen counties in West Virginia, Ohio, and Kentucky and helps feed about eighty-five thousand people each month. Many of the families served by the food bank are the working poor—people who work hard and have to choose between eating and other basic necessitates such as medicine and housing.

ACTION STEPS

➤ Is there an enthusiastic, influential young person in your community? Offer to help him or her, with you as a second or third in command. Let him or her lead the fight, and allow your self to follow and learn.

➤ Learn about more innovative ways you can serve your community. Find a special toolkit for supporting your local food bank at www .serve.gov.

➤ To learn more about the Huntington Area Food Bank, visit www .hafb.org.

The Toughest Decisions to Make

**In a world where death is the hunter, my friend,
there is no time for regrets or
doubts. There is only time for decisions.**
—Don Juan, the main character in the Carlos Castaneda book
Journey to Ixtlan

The place where it's perhaps easiest to lose any sense of compassion, both for ourselves and for others, is in the decisions we make. The thoughts run too easily through our heads: *How could she have done that? What on God's green earth was he thinking? How could I have been so stupid?* Second-guessing ourselves, usually in the harshest terms, is an almost obsessive part of our nature. Why we're so hard on ourselves and others over so-called poor life decisions we make is the debate of many psychologists, philosophers, and theologians.

But the truth is this—none of us truly knows what we are doing, and all of us have made some decisions on the fly. If anyone tells you he has this life thing figured out, he's a compulsive liar or delusional (both good reasons to feel compassion for him, of course).

ACTION STEPS

➤ Recognize that every decision of yours, and every decision of any other person, was made in the belief that it was the best choice available. No one deliberately chooses wrongly. This is a hard thing to contemplate, so take your time with it.

➤ In hindsight, it's easier to see that bad decisions were made. This is called learning. If someone can come to the conclusion that they chose poorly, that person is worthy of respect, because self-honesty is a hard-won ability.

➤ Regardless of what anyone else thinks of the outcome, compassion is an appropriate response to anyone who has a tough choice to make. Life isn't easy and the path isn't always clear. We all need to be more cognizant of that fact, both in regard to ourselves and others.

355

Taking Charge

In politics, nothing happens by accident. If it happens, you can bet it was planned that way.
—Franklin D. Roosevelt

Your life is filled with concerns—about the environment, the economy, education, healthcare, taxes, energy, agriculture, the arts, human rights, our cities, wars . . . Our elected officials evaluate solutions and act upon them. Bills are passed and written into law. Changes are made that affect all of us. How do you as a citizen in a democracy make your voice heard? How do you support an issue that's dear to your heart?

If you're uncomfortable in the limelight, slap a bumper sticker on your car and a placard in your front window to raise awareness. Call a radio talk show. Write a letter to the editor or your senator. Create a blog that supports your cause. Join online social-networking groups. Post a You-Tube video. Join organizations that have like-minded people or support their activities with financial contributions. If you enjoy being a mover and shaker, take your ideas to a civic group. Give a speech. Organize a rally. Get out there and do what you can!

How can you follow what's going on in Congress? *Roll Call,* the newspaper of Capitol Hill, will keep you up-to-date on the latest legislative activities including ongoing investigations. It's available online at www.rollcall.com. Try www.congress.org to track bills before Congress. Log in your zip code to get the names of your representatives. There is so much you can do to support your cause. It's just a matter of political will.

ACTION STEPS

➤ Center for Responsive Politics is a research group that tracks money in U.S. politics and its effect on elections and public policy. Their Web site, www.opensecrets.org, is a comprehensive resource for campaign contributions, lobbying data, and analysis.

➤ Check www.maplight.org to help you track bills currently before Congress.

Improving the Lives of Women in Guatemala

**When women thrive, all of society benefits, and
succeeding generations are given a better start in life.**
—Kofi Annan

Indigenous women in Guatemala lead hard and dangerous lives. Colonization, civil war, and new governments have destroyed the Mayan tradition of equality between men and women and replaced it with a more European, patriarchal society. The erosion of their native cultures, along with rampant racial discrimination and limited educational opportunities, has led to an increased number of indigenous families living with alcoholism, poverty, and depression. These conditions take a particular toll on the women, who often live with domestic violence and a lack of political clout.

Several social organizations within Guatemala, including the UN, have been working to provide literacy training along with basic economic, family, and health education to these women to improve their quality of life. These initiatives give women the tools they need to improve their own lives as well as their family's economic and social conditions. The underlying belief is that if the women understand that they are entitled to be treated more fairly, their entire community will be able to flourish.

As a volunteer working with these women, you can make a difference by participating in these types of social initiatives. Several organizations sponsor volunteer vacations where you can stay with host families and assist social workers in providing workshops on human rights, women's rights, reproductive health, cooking, handicrafts, and economic development. By working with these women, you will be able to help them make an incredible passage out of poverty toward a brighter future.

GETTING STARTED: Volunteers with specialized skills are needed, along with individuals simply looking to make a difference. World Endeavors is one organization providing the opportunity for a volunteer vacation. For more information, visit their Web site at www.world endeavors.com/Guatemala/_country/indigenous-women%27s-assistance-in-guatemala.html.

Respecting Our Youth

**We cannot always build the future for our youth,
but we can build our youth for the future.**
—Franklin D. Roosevelt

It's not easy being a kid today, and it's especially not easy being a kid who is African American and male. African American boys are at higher risk of suspension, expulsion, and dropping out of school than boys of other racial groups. To address the issues of this vulnerable population, the African American Male Initiative serves second-, third-, and fourth-grade African American boys of Harlem with the following services:

➤ Life Coaches to inspire boys to have dreams and to help them develop ways to reach those dreams.

➤ A Saturday Academy, which provides cultural-enrichment activities highlighting African American history in Harlem.

➤ Academic support and twice weekly one-on-one tutoring.

➤ Positive black male volunteers, who serve as role models to the boys.

Both Life Coaches and male volunteers provide stability for boys who may not have fathers or whose fathers may be present but not a positive influence. For example, Jason was a bright and sensitive fifth-grader who was close to his grandmother. When she died, Jason felt like his life had fallen apart.

After keeping his pain bottled up, Jason called his Life Coach, broke down crying, and talked to him for an hour. With a trusted male adult whom he could confide in, Jason was finally able to process the experience and move forward in a healthy way.

The African American Male Initiative tries to catch kids at a very young age, before they are most at risk of incarceration, drugs, or gangs. The Initiative also helps families to meet the challenges of raising an African American male in today's society.

VISIT www.stepstosuccess.org or call (212) 949–4969.

Volunteer Wisely

**One is not born into the world to do
everything but to do something.**
—Henry David Thoreau

Recent surveys show that about a quarter of all Americans—over 61 million people—volunteer at least once each year. That adds up to a huge amount of volunteer time. According to the Bureau of Labor Statistics, the average volunteer donates fifty-two hours a year. Using an industry standard that values a volunteer hour at $18.77, the average American volunteer gives the equivalent of nearly a thousand dollars a year in time and energy.

If you've decided to join your fellow citizens as a volunteer in your community, think carefully about what you'd like to do. For some, the decision is easy—they want to volunteer for their church, at their child's school, or somewhere else that's already familiar to them. For others, the volunteer opportunity that suits them best may take some research to find. It's time worth spending. Wouldn't you look carefully into a charity before writing a check for a thousand dollars? Likewise, look carefully into any volunteer organization, and ask yourself:

➤ What do I want to accomplish with my volunteer time? Look for a charity that matches your interests and is convenient to your home.

➤ Is this organization financially strong? It doesn't have to be. In fact, your volunteer work could be aimed at making it stronger, but at the same time, an organization tottering on the brink isn't usually carrying out its mission very well.

➤ Are the programs effective? Look at what the charity has accomplished over the past few years. Did it meet its goals? Are the programs growing better over time? Are the volunteers sticking with the organization or drifting away quickly?

IF YOU'RE satisfied that the organization is in good shape and is achieving its goals, and if you think you can contribute something valuable with your volunteer time, go for it!

Start a Community Food Garden, and Share the Harvest with Those Less Fortunate

We are indeed much more than what we eat, but what we eat can nevertheless help us to be much more than what we are.
—Adelle Davis

Community food gardens have been around for years, but hard economic times are making them more popular than ever. Fresh produce is healthier; gardens improve neighborhoods and create a sense of community. Gardeners can donate vegetables to local charities or allow those in need to pick their own. Gardening is easy, but it's not just scattering seeds in an empty lot.

ACTION STEPS

LOCAL: Who will the garden serve? Organize a meeting of interested people. Form a planning committee, including some experienced gardeners. Look for a sponsor to contribute supplies and/or funds. Ask the Community Development Office about Community Development Block Grants. Find a garden site near the people it will serve. Make sure it has six to eight hours per day of sunlight and access to water. Learn who owns the land. Look in public records if necessary. Test soil for dangerous substances before making a commitment. Ask your department of the environment for help. Arrange for transfer of ownership, or get a lease for the land. Decide how the space will be divided: will it contain individual plots, be communal, or a combination? Decide if gardeners should pay dues. Make a budget. Establish rules. Consult books, Web sites, and your Cooperative Extension Office for planting advice.

NATIONAL: Learn about the White House vegetable garden: www .whitehousefarmer.com.

For more information: www.communitygarden.org • www.organic gardening.com • www.organicgardeninfo.com • www.organicgardening guru.com

Influencing America's Progress

**The test of our progress is not whether we add more to
the abundance of those who have much; it is whether
we provide enough for those who have too little.**
—Franklin D. Roosevelt

The United States has a higher rate of this than twenty-eight countries,
including Cuba, Hungary, Russia, Bulgaria, and Romania. Over the
past forty years our ranking has become worse, not better.

What are we being ranked on?

Infant mortality.

Twenty-eight thousand children under the age of one die in the
United States each year, ranking us near the bottom of the developed
world in infant mortality. Our influence as a nation to act individually
and collectively has yet to succeed to help the youngest and weakest
among us. Our government tracks infant mortality worldwide precisely
because it's seen as a barometer of a country's health. What does this rate
of infant mortality say about us?

ACTION STEPS

➤ Speak with the director of a local hospital about infant mortality rates in
your community. Offer to help target the area most in need, and bring
an established health professional into that neighborhood, to a church
or community center, for a special free prenatal program. Arrange for
baby-related donations for the mothers-to-be to entice attendance.

➤ Celebrate by giving. Honor your child's birthday or other milestone
event (a baby shower!) by donating to another child in need. One innovative nonprofit based in New York and Boston, Room to Grow
(www.roomtogrow.org), enriches the lives of babies born into poverty
with a program that requires participation throughout the critical first
three years of the child's development. Room to Grow accepts gently
used and new items and donates all directly to their needy families.

The True Meaning of Compassion

**I would rather feel compassion than
know the meaning of it.**
—Thomas Aquinas

In formal debating, one of the first things you are taught is to define
your terms. What's the point of debating the merits of compassion,
for example, if all six people in the room hold different meanings of the
word?

But compassion is a funny thing. It has a dictionary meaning, of
course, and it brings up fairly similar images in most people's minds.
But it is one of those mysterious structures of the universe that, like its
close relative love, is instead truly defined by its practice, not its meaning. To feel compassion, you must show compassion. It must be created
from within.

ACTION STEPS

➤ A crash course in showing compassion would look something like
this: Be a good listener, even to those considered dim and dull.

➤ Look people in the eye when you're with them. This is the most effective way of showing you're genuinely interested.

➤ Be an advocate for people who can't advocate for themselves. Always
stick up for the bullied and the underdogs.

➤ Befriend people you consider compassionate. Watch how they conduct
themselves and what they say and do. Your life will be immensely
richer because of it.

➤ Spend a few minutes before you fall asleep each night reviewing your
day. Look for places where you could have shown more compassion.
Don't feel bad if you missed an opportunity. Simply vow to do better
next time.

➤ Practice, practice, practice.

Acts of Loving-Kindness

**The happiness of life is made up of minute fractions—
the little soon forgotten charities of a kiss, a smile, a
kind look, a heartfelt compliment, and the countless
infinitesimals of pleasurable, genial feeling.**
—Samuel Taylor Coleridge

The Golden Rule is about engaging in acts of loving-kindness—treating someone as you would want to be treated yourself. Every day there are "countless infinitesimals"—opportunities to share kindnesses and spread love. Help an elderly person at the market grab that can of soup and smile while you thank her for the opportunity to be of assistance. Spare some change for the homeless person. Anticipate your wife's need for quiet and take the children to the park. Cook soup and bring it to a sick friend. Babysit so your sister and her husband can finally have a "date." Compliment your daughter on her excellent grades; compliment your son on his fine physique; compliment your husband on his successes; let them know you see them in ways they value. Turn the other cheek, forgive, and let go. Open your home for a political meeting. Open your heart to someone in need.

Kiss your child on the forehead for no reason at all. Kiss your husband on the lips for no reason at all. Kiss your parents and siblings for no reason at all . . . no reason except with your kindnesses you express love. And that's the deepest form of support of all.

ACTION STEPS

➤ Spend some time thinking about what would make you happy. What could others do that would make you feel loved, supported, enveloped in grace? Write down these actions. Now turn around and do unto others. Share yourself in ways that make others feel supported.

➤ How can you translate "kindness" into the larger world? Does it mean supporting a favorite cause? Speaking out when you see injustice? Being kind to the environment? What does kindness mean to you?

Clean Up a River

**You can never step into the same river; for
new waters are always flowing on to you.**
—Heraclitus of Ephesus

With all the talk of global warming and the impact of our carbon footprint, many people are focusing on melting polar ice caps and dwindling rain forests. Yet the fact is that global warming is already affecting our rivers in the form of increased droughts, floods, and water-borne diseases. If we want to pass on a cleaner, greener planet to our children, we need to start protecting and supporting our rivers—and river wildlife—now.

Rivers are literally the backbone of America. They provide our drinking water, flood protection, fish and wildlife habitats, as well as scenes of immense beauty. That's why it's our responsibility to keep them clean and trash free. One national organization is dedicated to keeping millions of tons of trash out of our rivers and streams and returning them to their original pristine condition for future generations to enjoy.

American Rivers sponsors the National River Cleanup, the most popular and successful stream-cleanup program in the country. Since 1991, more than 600,000 volunteers have participated in thousands of cleanups, covering more than 100,000 miles of waterways nationwide. They have already removed more than a thousand tons of litter, and their efforts increase every year.

As a volunteer, you would be doing a huge service to the entire country by cleaning up just one mile of a local river. You can join an existing effort or organize a project of your own. Through the organization's Web site, you can recruit other volunteers, or create a project just for your friends and family. It's a great opportunity to create community and set a precedent for the continuous care of our rivers.

GETTING STARTED: Visit their Web site at www.americanrivers.org. Not only will they provide you with cleaning supplies, like trash bags, their interactive site lets you find or list a cleanup on a Google map.

Ken Berger
President & Chief Executive Officer, Charity Navigator

Ken Berger joined Charity Navigator in 2008 after almost thirty years' experience working in the charitable nonprofit sector. He has held leadership positions at a variety of human service and healthcare agencies, both large and small, and has operated programs serving the homeless, the developmentally disabled, the mentally ill, substance abusers, the medically underserved, and persons with HIV/AIDS, among many others.

Most recently, Ken was a chief operating officer (COO) of Jawonio and earlier in his career director of operations at Professional Service Centers for the Handicapped. In both positions he oversaw residential, educational, employment, clinical, and healthcare service to individuals with disabilities and special needs. Prior to Jawonio, Ken was the executive vice president and COO and then the president and chief executive officer (CEO) of The Floating Hospital, an agency that provided healthcare, social services, and education to disadvantaged lower-income or at-risk adults, children, and families across New York City. Ken also held several leadership positions at Volunteers of America–Greater New York and the Morris Shelter, managing a wide array of services to thousands of homeless families and individuals.

Ken has a deep passion for helping donors become wise givers by learning to make intelligent social investments in high-impact nonprofits. He also has a deep interest in encouraging charitable nonprofits to excel and thrive even in challenging times. He is a regular presenter at conferences on both the domestic and international stage, is frequently interviewed by both regional and national media on nonprofit issues, and has published a number of papers on issues affecting the sector's effectiveness. He is also the author of Ken's Commentary, a blog about the nonprofit sector. Ken earned his bachelor's degree at the University of Buffalo. He went on to obtain a master's degree in psychology from Antioch University and a master's degree in business administration from Rutgers University.

About Charity Navigator

Charity Navigator (www.charitynavigator.org) was founded in 2001 on the premise that people are amazingly generous and derive great satisfaction from helping others, but are not always sure how to help.

Its founders envisioned an unbiased source of information that would assist givers from every state, and with every type of charitable interest, in finding a charity to support.

Today, Charity Navigator is the nation's largest and most-utilized independent evaluator of charities. Using our objective, numbers-based rating system we have assessed the financial health of over 5,000 of America's charities. Millions of people visit our Web site annually, resulting in our ratings influencing an estimated $10 billion of charitable giving in 2008.

Charity Navigator's rating system examines two broad areas of a charity's financial health—how it functions day to day and how well positioned it is to sustain its programs over time. Each charity is then awarded an overall rating, ranging from zero to four stars. To help donors avoid becoming victims of mailing-list appeals, each charity's commitment to keeping donors' personal information confidential is assessed. Among the site's many additional features are listings of the CEO's salaries, opinion pieces by Charity Navigator experts, and donation tips.

Time magazine called Charity Navigator "One of America's 50 Coolest Websites." The site is a two-time Forbes award winner for "Best of the Web," was selected by *Reader's Digest* as one of the "100 Best Things about America," and was singled out by *Kiplinger's Personal Finance* as "One of the Best Services to Make Life Easier."

Charity Navigator accepts no funding from the charities we evaluate, ensuring that our ratings remain objective. In our commitment to help philanthropists of all levels make informed giving decisions, we do not charge our users for this data. As a result, Charity Navigator, a 501(c)(3) public charity, depends on support from those who believe we provide a much-needed service to charitable givers.

Greg Baldwin
President, VolunteerMatch

Greg Baldwin joined what is now VolunteerMatch in the spring of 1998 as its chief imagination officer to finish hotwiring the Internet to help everybody find a great place to volunteer. Today, VolunteerMatch is a leader in the nonprofit world. Its popular Web service is strengthening communities and organizations across the country by making it easier for good people and good causes to connect. Greg believes in the power of a big idea. He began his career at the Leo Burnett advertising agency, where many big ideas were born, and later tested his own as a cofounder of 2d Interactive, Inc.—a Boston-based technology start-up. Greg completed his undergraduate studies at Brown University in 1990 with a degree in public policy. He is a lifelong volunteer and regularly speaks at nonprofit events and conferences on the subjects of volunteering, communication, and the Internet.

About VolunteerMatch

By making it easier for good people and good causes to connect, VolunteerMatch is helping Americans turn the spirit of service into action.

Since 1998, the organization's popular Web service, www.volunteer match.org, has been synonymous with discovering great volunteer opportunities on the Internet. Originally founded by a group of Silicon Valley entrepreneurs, the organization pioneered many of the features of online volunteer engagement that have become standard in the Web era. Today more than 10 million yearly visitors who are committed to civic engagement come to VolunteerMatch for a variety of online services and to search for volunteer opportunities from a diverse network of 68,000 participating organizations large and small.

VolunteerMatch is also a leader in the movement to put employee volunteering at the center of corporate social responsibility. Through tools and services that connect employee volunteers with active volunteer opportunities, VolunteerMatch is making it easy for corporations of all sizes to join with nonprofit organizations to solve local problems.

The organization is committed to building world-class Internet applications that bring our communities closer together, expand the capacity of civil society, and encourage a culture of individual empowerment and participation.

➤ To search for volunteer opportunities, visit: www.volunteermatch.org.

➤ To register an organization at VolunteerMatch, visit: www.volunteer match.org/post/register/np/overview.jsp.

➤ To learn about using VolunteerMatch for your employee volunteer program, visit: www.volunteermatch.org/corporations.

Kriss Deiglmeier

Executive Director, Center for Social Innovation

Upon coming to CSI, Kriss Deiglmeier embarked on a strategic planning process that set forth a new mission and strategy focused on breaking down sector boundaries.

Kriss has more than twenty years of management experience spanning the business, social enterprise, nonprofit, and philanthropic sectors. Prior to Stanford, Kriss worked as a management consultant to foundation, business, and nonprofit enterprises. She served as chief operating officer for Juma Ventures. Before joining Juma, Kriss worked with the United Way of King County, Larkin Street Youth Center, and Nordstrom. Kriss has presented nationally and internationally on topics including social entrepreneurship and public-private partnerships. Kriss has guest-lectured at the University of California Berkeley, Stanford Graduate School of Business, Hitotsubashi University, Kyoto University, Kyushu University, and Nagoya University. She coauthored the articles "Leading the Social Purpose Business: An Examination of Organizational Culture" and "Managing the Social Enterprise." Her most recent article is "Rediscovering Social Innovation." Kriss received her BA from the University of Washington and her MBA from the University of California, Berkeley.

About the Center for Social Innovation

The Center for Social Innovation at the Stanford Graduate School of Business cultivates leaders to solve the world's toughest social and environmental problems. With innovative and cross-sector research, education, and experiential programs, the Center helps participants lead corporate efforts to improve sustainable practices, manage nonprofits through strategic growth, and launch social enterprises that bring life-changing solutions such as loans to small businesses and safe lighting to the world's poorest places.

Our Programs

Over forty faculty affiliates from the GSB and across Stanford contribute to the Center's programs and initiatives that build the awareness, skills, and actions of social innovators. Moreover, the Center's location, in the heart of Silicon Valley, imbues it with the risk-taking, paradigm-shifting spirit of the Internet Revolution.

The Center offers programs for MBA students, alumni, faculty, and field practitioners, including:

Research—Academic research and ongoing evaluation are essential to understanding what works and what does not in this new era of social innovation. Through the discovery of new ideas via research, cases, and publications such as the *Stanford Social Innovation Review,* the Center contributes new thinking on ways to achieve social impact.

Education—The Center's education activities disseminate important ideas to a global community of scholars, field practitioners, and students, providing social innovators with a toolbox to increase their effectiveness. Education vehicles include the *Stanford Social Innovation Review,* the Social Innovation Conversations podcasts, speakers and conferences, and Executive Education courses. Additional programs specifically for MBA students include elective courses, the Public Management Certificate, and joint degrees.

Action—The Center provides a bridge between academia and practice. Our offerings have a direct social impact in the world and provide hands-on experience and inspiration that transform ordinary leaders into mission-driven leaders. MBA students learn, alumni engage, and nonprofits benefit through programs such as service learning trips, nonprofit board matching, summer internships, and Alumni Consulting Teams.

Joseph Grenny
Co-Chairman, VitalSmarts
Chairman & Cofounder, Unitus

Joseph's enduring interest is *influence*. He believes fundamentally that the capacity to help people learn to influence profound and sustainable behavior change is key to not only solving the most pressing of human problems, but is also essential to creating the world we all want.

In 1990 Joseph and his colleagues founded VitalSmarts, a world leader in the study and practice of human change. Joseph's corporate clients include 300 of the Fortune 500 companies. His research into what helps and hinders people's ability to achieve valued results has resulted in three *New York Times* bestselling books—*Crucial Conversations: Tools for Talking When Stakes are High, Crucial Confrontations: Tools for Resolving Broken Promises, Violated Expectations and Bad Behaviors,* and, most recently, *Influencer: The Power to Change Anything.* Joseph's work has been taught and used by over 2 million people worldwide and has been translated into over two dozen languages.

For many years Joseph has studied efforts to influence positive change among the poorest of the poor. He was disappointed to see so many well-intended government and nongovernment efforts focus exclusively on technology, infrastructure or relief efforts with little consideration for the influence these efforts would have on the behavior of the intended beneficiaries. In the early 80s he began following the work of Muhammad Yunus, as it appeared to be one of the most sound approaches to helping others in a way that honored the agency, intelligence, and independence of the poor. Finally, convinced of the robust power of microcredit, Joseph and a small group of successful businesspeople founded Unitus, a Seattle-based nonprofit focused on influencing dramatic acceleration of access to microfinance services to the poor worldwide. By 2009 Unitus's efforts had contributed to the extension of these empowering services to over 7 million clients in Asia, Africa, and Latin America.

About Unitus
Unitus, an international nonprofit organization, fights global poverty by accelerating the growth of microfinance—small loans and other financial tools for self-empowerment—where it is needed most.

Close to half the world's population survives on less than $2 a day. In places such as sub-Saharan Africa, the total living below this line approaches 75 percent. For millions of families in need, microfinance offers the hope for a successful small business and more: increased economic stability, better healthcare and housing, the opportunity for education, and, ultimately, the real possibility of self-sufficiency.

Unitus is not your traditional nonprofit. In addition to on-the-ground microfinance expertise, we bring executive experience from banking, technology, and corporate consulting backgrounds to employ market-driven solutions to age-old problems of financial exclusion and poverty. Our model focuses on seeking out and partnering with young, high-potential microfinance institutions (small banking organizations that serve the poor, often called MFIs), helping them build capacity, attract capital, and unite with our network to achieve rapid, sustainable growth.

Microfinance is most effective when a microcredit loan is supported by a range of client-supporting products and services such as business skills training, savings programs, and basic insurance plans. In support of these innovations, Unitus encourages the development of "high-impact" microfinance: a combination of increased access to these tools with an emphasis on sustainability, client protection, and social impact.

We target our efforts in high-need regions of the developing world, where microfinance has promise but is struggling to grow. Once MFIs and/or regions reach critical milestones and demonstrate sustainability, we shift our resources to where they can be used most effectively.

The devastating downward cycle of extreme poverty is not inevitable. Microfinance can help reverse a family's fortunes in a single generation. The greatest challenge is extending microfinance fast enough—and far enough—to make it available to the hundreds of millions still waiting.

Unitus works with 24 microfinance partners in India, Southeast Asia, East Africa, South America, and Mexico. These MFIs are growing 7 times faster than their peers, demonstrating the strength of their leadership and the promise of our approach. In just 7 years, we've helped our partners serve more than 8 million families. Our goal is to serve 15 million families by 2015.

To learn more about microfinance or how you can get involved, visit us at www.unitus.com today!

Sister Mary Scullion
Cofounder, Project H.O.M.E.

Sister Mary Scullion has been involved in service work and advocacy for homeless and mentally ill persons since 1978. In 1985, she cofounded Woman of Hope, which provides supportive housing for homeless mentally ill women. In 1988, she helped establish the Outreach Coordination Center, a nationally recognized model, which coordinates street outreach to chronically homeless persons in Philadelphia. In 1989, Sister Mary and Joan Dawson McConnon cofounded Project H.O.M.E.

Sister Mary is also a powerful voice on political issues affecting homeless and mentally ill persons. Her advocacy efforts resulted in the right of homeless persons to vote as well as a landmark federal court decision that affects the fair-housing rights of persons with disabilities.

Sister Mary has received numerous awards, including the Ford Foundation's prestigious Leadership for a Changing World Award, which she was awarded with cofounder Joan McConnon; an Eisenhower Fellowship; and the Philadelphia Award. Under Sister Mary and Joan's leadership, Project H.O.M.E. has also won many awards. Most recently, the National Alliance to End Homelessness awarded Project H.O.M.E. the Nonprofit Sector Achievement Award and the National Law Center on Homelessness & Poverty awarded Project H.O.M.E. a STAR Award. In addition, the U.S. Department of Housing and Urban Development (HUD) selected Project H.O.M.E. as one of the "100 Best Practices" nationwide out of 3,000 nominees, and the *Philanthropy Roundtable* selected Project H.O.M.E. as one of the "16 Most Efficient and Innovative Charities We Know of Anywhere." In May 2009, Sister Mary was honored as one of *Time* magazine's "100's Most Influential People."

About Project H.O.M.E.

Rooted in the strong spiritual conviction of the dignity of every person, Project H.O.M.E. seeks to use affordable housing, education, advocacy, and community to combat homelessness and poverty. Since its founding in 1989 by Sister Mary Scullion and Joan Dawson McConnon, Project H.O.M.E. has grown tremendously; it now offers 459 units of housing in Philadelphia, including 272 units of supportive housing. Project H.O.M.E. provides many affordable options, ranging from Kate's Place

(144 apartments for low- to moderate-income individuals in the heart of Rittenhouse Square) to Women of Change, a permanent residence for mentally ill women from the streets. Most recently the organization renovated St. Elizabeth's Recovery Residence, providing 24 units to two special-needs populations: homeless veterans and homeless men with physical disabilities.

Project H.O.M.E. has also increased its efforts to address the structural causes of homelessness and poverty through neighborhood revitalization in North Central Philadelphia. As part of the effort, Project H.O.M.E. has rehabbed and sold 43 houses to first-time homebuyers, started a homeownership program and is developing a community-based health center. Their catalyst for revitalization is the Honickman Learning Center and Comcast Technology Labs, a state-of-the-art technology center. With programs for children, youth, adults, and families, the center provides educational and workforce development opportunities for the community. In addition, there are three job-training/employment initiatives, the Back H.O.M.E. Cafe, Our Daily Threads thrift store, and the HOME Page Cafe located in the Free Library of Philadelphia.

Project H.O.M.E.'s vision: None of us are home until all of us are home.

www.projecthome.org

Peter Samuelson

Peter Samuelson has three decades of experience running large media organizations across the media landscape and has produced and managed content teams in every major vertical: film, television, Web, mobile, videogames, and print. He has produced two dozen motion pictures over 25 years, including *Revenge of the Nerds, Arlington Road,* and the Academy Award–nominated *Tom & Viv.* Peter served as chairman of the executive committee of Panavision Inc. and was executive chairman of the North American division as well as a main board director of Samuelson Group PLC and its wholly owned operating subsidiaries AVHQ, VDI, and SCPI. Peter is a graduate of the Anderson School of Business at UCLA and also has a master's degree from Cambridge University, England.

In 1982, Peter founded the Starlight Children's Foundation, an international charity that provides psychosocial services to 2.4 million seriously ill children annually in five countries on a $65 million budget. Peter also founded, with Steven Spielberg and General Norman Schwarzkopf, the Starbright Foundation, a charity dedicated to developing media- and technology-based programs to educate and empower ill children. On June 5, 1995, Peter Samuelson and Steven Spielberg launched the world's first fully-interactive social network, Starbright World, delivering video-, sound-, text-, and avatar-based communication to hospitalized children. Starbright World still serves children 24 hours per day. In 1999, Peter founded First Star, a separate national 501(c)(3) charity headquartered in Washington, DC, that works to improve the public health, safety, and family life of America's abused and neglected children.

In 2006, Peter founded EDAR, "Everyone Deserves A Roof" Inc. to widely distribute the mobile single-user shelter he invented for our urban homeless. At a sponsorship price point of $500, 170 EDARs are now deployed in a beta test under an efficacy study by the Rand Institute. In December 2008, Peter was named "An Inspiring Mind" by the CNN Television Network.

Peter has been awarded many honors, including a Caring Award from the U.S. Senate. He has lectured on media, entrepreneurship and pro-social subjects at USC, UCLA, and Oxford Universities and delivered the Plenary lecture at the 2009 World Conference on Child and Family Maltreatment in San Diego. Peter served on the three-person founding advisory board of Participant Media, producer of such films as *An Inconvenient Truth, Syriana,* and *The Soloist.* He is bilingual in French and English and the fourth of five family generations to work in filmed entertainment. He lives in Holmby Hills, California, with his wife, Saryl, and four children.

www.samuelson.la

About Starlight Children's Foundation

For more than twenty-five years, Starlight Children's Foundation has been dedicated to improving the quality of life for children with chronic and life-threatening illnesses and life-altering injuries by providing entertainment, education, and family activities that help them cope with pain, fear, and isolation.

We understand what families go through when a child is sick, and how important it is to find relief from worry and isolation. Our programs distract children from their pain, help them better manage their illnesses, and connect families facing similar challenges so that no one feels alone.

Unlike any other charity, Starlight offers outpatient, hospital-based, and Web offerings that provide ongoing support for children and families—from diagnosis through the entire course of medical treatment. Programs include:

➤ **Family activities and outings** that give families a chance to have fun together away from the hospital so they can relax and return home with a renewed sense of strength and hope. The events also forge connections between families struggling with similar issues to combat feelings of isolation.

➤ **In-hospital entertainment technology** that helps kids fill hours in hospitals or treatment centers with therapeutic fun; find distraction during long or painful medical procedures; and stay connected with school and the outside world during extended hospitalizations.

➤ **Online communities and interactive Web sites** that help seriously ill teens connect with each other and learn how to cope with their medical conditions.

➤ **In-hospital playrooms, kid-friendly treatment rooms, and special events** that help ease the loneliness, fear, and boredom that accompany hospital stays.

➤ **Educational programming**—delivered via online interactive games, ezines, and webisodes—to help sick children dealing with cancer, sickle cell, cystic fibrosis, asthma, Crohn's and colitis, severe burns, and kidney disease.

Visit www.starlight.org to learn how you can help us brighten their world a little each day!

About First Star

Established in 1999, First Star's mission is to improve the lives of America's abused and neglected children by strengthening their rights, illuminating systemic failures, and igniting reform to correct them. We pursue our mission through research, public engagement, policy advocacy, and litigation.

Our nonpartisan, multidisciplinary approach fosters collaborative action among organizations, advocates, practitioners, and policymakers working to benefit children.

First Star's Vision is a future in which America's abused and neglected children have won their right to be heard and protected within the systems legally entrusted with their care, and a future in which those systems are fully resourced, transparent, and accountable to the public.

Through our Campaign for a Child's Right to Counsel program, First Star is working to ensure that all abused and neglected children in America have competent legal representation and a voice in the most critical decisions of their young lives. Our Campaign for a Child's Right to Counsel takes a four-pronged approach to reform: research, federal and state legislation, litigation, and advocacy.

First Star is also working to increase the transparency and accountability of child welfare systems when reporting child fatalities and near fatalities. The goal of our State Secrecy and Child Deaths program is to ensure that all fifty states fulfill their duty under the Child Abuse and Prevention Act (CAPTA) to report child fatalities and near fatalities. CAPTA aims to protect the confidentiality of child victims; however, more often than not, it is state agencies that are protected by shielding child fatality information from public scrutiny. Increased transparency will lead to greater accountability and consistency and, ultimately, fewer child deaths.

For more information about First Star, please visit www.firststar.org or call (202) 293–3703.

About EDAR

EDAR (Everyone Deserves A Roof) is a 501(c)(3) nonprofit organization that provides unique mobile shelters to the homeless. EDAR works with homeless agency and government partnerships, offering a safe environment for the homeless population to begin a new life of dignity.

What Is an EDAR?

An EDAR is a four-wheeled unit, based on a mobile cart design, that provides security for belongings, privacy, and protection from the elements. During the day, the EDAR is a compact portable unit with sturdy wheels and waterproof protection. The steering is maneuverable and there is a brake and locking mechanism that ensures the unit will not move on its own.

At night, the EDAR opens up easily into "nighttime mode" and provides a comfortable sleeping unit. Unfolding the unit allows it to lock in place as the flat metal base extends. The metal base has a removable mattress and fire-resistant cover, providing tentlike shelter. The unit is waterproof, windproof, and helps protect from the elements. There is a window that provides light, ventilation, and a view of the surrounding area. By refolding the unit into "day mode," the EDAR quickly returns to its compact design and can be pushed around as a cart for use during the day.

EDAR units have been in use since the summer of 2008 in Southern California. With the help of our generous supporters, we continue to place additional units in California and cities nationwide.

For more information about EDAR, please visit www.edar.org or contact us at (310) 208–1000, ext.

YOU'VE READ THE BOOK, NOW GET INVOLVED!

Great online resources and community add to the SPIRIT OF SERVICE experience.

VISIT
www.thespiritofservice365.com
to get started today.

The Web site has ...

◊ A list of every organization mentioned in the book with a link to the organization's homepage
◊ A special search tool for finding local service opportunities
◊ Inspirational essays from the book's contributors
◊ An e-card to send to your friends and family inspiring them to serve

Get into the Spirit of Service today—join the Facebook community at www.tinyurl.com/SOSonFB.

VISIT HARPERONE ONLINE

HOMEPAGE: www.harperone.com
FACEBOOK: www.tinyurl.com/h1onfb
BLOG: www.goodbooksinbadtimes.com
TWITTER: www.twitter.com/harperone

HarperOne
An Imprint of HarperCollins*Publishers*